CW00495270

The Heart To Car
A Biography Of Canadian Poe

Anthony L Frost

Copyright Anthony L Frost 2024

ISBN: 978-1-3999-7958-0

Dedication

To my wife Tracy and my daughter Esmeralda without whose help, love and support on a daily basis, during a difficult time this book would not have been possible and to my daughter Rhiannah for her continued love and support.

Acknowledgements

Harriet Fisher whose efforts as proofreader and editor and overall support were invaluable
David Lang for his continued support and encouragement, editorial advice and his valuable information about the Warr family
James Frost for script and historical advice and support
Alan Peat for editorial advice and overall support

Contents

Introduction

On the night of April third 1943 the seven men of the bomber crew of Halifax F for Freddie of RAF's 158 squadron climbed aboard their aircraft for the last time. Wearing their bulky flying suites and carrying their parachute packs the men would have made their way along the narrow passageway to their crew positions. Part of the crew that night was a young Canadian, Bertram Warr. Bert was the crew's bomb aimer. Lying prone in his position in the nose it was the bomb aimer who directed the aircraft once it was over the target and it was the bomb aimer who released the bombs which would rain down on the city below.

Their target on this night was Essen in the heart of Germany's industrial Ruhr Valley. It was an area bristling with ack-ack anti aircraft batteries and Luftwaffe night fighters. This was the 14th sortie for Bert and his crew and it would be their last. They would be shot down and killed by a Luftwaffe fighter ace on the return leg of their flight.

Bertram Warr, a socialist and pacifist was one of the most promising poets of his generation. A man of whom Canadian poet Earle Birney would say "had he lived could have been one of the leading poets of his generation." How did a man of Bert's convictions and beliefs end up in the belly of an RAF bomber raining destruction down on the cities of Nazi Germany?

This is his story. It is the story of how this young man with plenty of enthusiasm and a budding talent for writing made his way from provincial Toronto Canada to the heart of the British literary world of London, to study and learn his art. It is also the story of how just as he was beginning to mature as a man and a poet he became caught up in the great events of his time and was killed and his voice was lost to us. Bert was only 25 when he was killed. His few dozen pieces of published work serve mainly to show us the potential, largely unrealised that he had.

1

Bertram Warr was my uncle. He was one of my mother's two older brothers, Frank being the other one. Both brothers were in the Airforce, Bert was in the RAF and Frank the RCAF. Both were killed within 6 months of each other in 1943. The family trauma of losing both brothers was so intense that even some 25 years plus after they were killed the subject of the brothers was almost taboo in my mother's family. Growing up in the 1960s and 70s we were never encouraged to talk or ask questions about Bert or Frank. I grew up knowing only the bare minimum about "the boys" as they were always called the few times they did come up in conversation. These conversations were always short and the subject would invariably be quickly changed especially if my grandparents were within ear shot.

My grandfather Bertram Howard Warr once said that a man dies twice when he loses a son and he lost three. For her part my grandmother took the loss of the boys perhaps the heaviest of all of the family. Years later when the organisers of the Remembrance Day parade in Toronto approached her to participate in this annual event which marched down Toronto's main north-south thoroughfare, Younge Street to the war memorial she flat out refused, coldly telling them "You killed my boys."

All this is a roundabout way of saying that while I was growing up I didn't know much about my two uncles who had died in the war. Reaching adulthood I didn't take much interest in them either. I was living very much in the now and they were very much of the then. That itself is a bit strange because I always did have a keen interest in history. Be that as it may by the time I took an interest in learning more about my two Airforce uncles it was almost too late. I say that because not only were Bert and Frank themselves dead but nearly everyone who had known them when they were alive was also dead. My research for this book had to rely almost exclusively on the letters that Bert and Frank sent home during their time in the Airforce. Luckily many, if not most of these were saved by my Aunt Mary.

Mary was devoted to the memories of her two brothers and although she didn't like to speak about the boys much to us she guarded their memories diligently. Mary kept all their letters and all of Bert's work published and unpublished that she could get hold of. It is primarily from these letters, notes and essays along with some articles published by poetry magazine editors and writers who admired Bert that I have drawn the material for this book.

Bert was strongly socialist and very much against being part of the military. This remained true even after he volunteered for duty in Bomber Command. I do not believe that Bert would have wanted to be remembered as a member of the military. He served and did his duty to help end the Nazi tyranny but he did so because it had to be done not because he wanted to. Bert wanted to be a poet and it is as a poet that he would have wished to be remembered. However, a great many, in fact most of Bert's letters that remain are from his time in the Airforce. He spent over 4 years away from home living in England, the last 20 months of that time in the RAF so that a large part of this book by necessity focuses on Bert's time in the RAF.

Of course a lot of my research led me through RAF material and to Bert's squadron, RAF 158. The members of RAF 158 Squadron Association's archive team proved an invaluable source for material. This was true not only for information about Bert but for information about his squadron and the RAF in general. They were so helpful that to give something back I ended up volunteering to be on their archive team and now I also run their website. In fact it is safe to say that if I had not become involved with Bert's RAF Squadron Association that I would not have written this book. That is a story for another time however.

While pouring over the letters sent by Bert to the family along with his notes, essays and poems I feel that I have in a small way gotten to know Bert as a person, at least as much as is possible by only reading letters and other material.

3

Bert lived in an era before social media of course so we don't have any tweets, blogs, snapchat postings etc and have to rely solely on hard copies of letters that have survived down through these last 80 years since his death in 1943. I have tried to present Bert as fully rounded human being and not as some idealised version of himself. This proved more challenging than may at first be apparent because to do that I had to rely almost exclusively on things that Bert himself wrote in his letters and notes. Most if not all of the letters written by other people to the family and of course all of the obituary material focuses on the positive aspects of Bert's personality and his immense potential as a writer. The one or two reviews of Bert's poetry that survive focus on his writing and how he was still maturing and learning as a poet but do not explore Bert's character. We learn very little about Bert the man from these articles. As for Bert's letters home they present us with the version of his life that he wanted to show his family. While they are a rich source of material they are perhaps not always as candid as letters to friends may have been. Things people tell their families are often quite different to what they would tell a best friend. None of Bert's letters to friends have survived but luckily we do have another very rich source of Bert's letters, those that he wrote to Mrs Nora Senjem. She seems to have saved all of Bert's letters and after his death she sent them to the family. Nora Senjem was a Hungarian refugee whom Bert had met shortly after he arrived in London. She was very involved in the world of the refugee artists and intellectuals whom had fled Austria and Hungary in an effort to escape the Nazis. Mrs Senjem had also taken Bert under her wing and over the years became very close to him. It seems that she was almost like a second mother to Bert. Bert's letters to Mrs Senjem are full of things that he did not write to the family about and even things that he did write to both are often written to Mrs Senjem with a very different slant to them. After Bert was killed, Frank met with Nora Senjem, and he sent word of these meetings home in letters. I have also drawn much material from Frank's letters home.

It was a great delight to have access to all the surviving letters that Frank wrote to the family. These cover the time from when he left home to head overseas with the RCAF in September of 1942 until his untimely and unlucky death in October 1943 six months after Bert died. Many thanks to Dave and Claire Lang for these letters. Frank and Bert, although both very close to the family and both exhibiting that fierce family loyalty that was a Warr family trait were very different at least judging them on the contents of their letters home. Bert was very reserved and very aloof from those around him. With very few exceptions he tells us nothing or next to nothing about the people in his life. This is true from his very first letter home, written from Bigwin Resort in May 1938 to the very last letter he ever wrote home from RAF Lissett with 158 shortly before his last flight.

Frank on the other hand, was very open in his letters and very informative about all his friends and acquaintances. Frank comes across as much more open and friendly than Bert. However this is misleading. Bert was indeed aloof and was often to be found sitting quietly in a corner smoking his pipe and sipping on his whiskey at social gatherings but he always was ready to lend a helping hand to anyone and everyone whom he felt needed it. Bert often even went to the extreme lengths of getting himself into debt so that he could offer money to someone who he thought was in more need than he was.

I hope that I have managed in this book to convey these traits of both the brothers. I have given Frank two whole chapters of his own as I believe that his story deserves to be told along with Bert's and not only that, Frank's story interweaves with Bert's. I feel that you cannot tell Bert's story without including Frank and of course, Bert's sister Mary as well. I have written about Mary in this book because not only were Bert and Mary very close but the publication of Bert's book "Acknowledge to Life" would not have happened without Mary's perseverance. Also We would not know what happened to Frank's aircraft with out

5

the dogged determination and some incredible detective work by Mary, but more about that in the chapters about Frank.

I hope that this book entertains and informs but most of all I hope that it is in some small way a worthy attempt to keep alive the memory of Bertram War and perhaps will introduce new readers to his poetry. I have deliberately not tried to analyse any of Bert's poems as I am in no way qualified to even attempt such a thing. I will leave that to the likes of people like Alan Gardener, John Gawsworth and Earle Birney who are eminently more qualified than me for such a task. My intention was to give the reader an insight into Bert the man and the events of his life while introducing the reader to Bert's poetry along the way. Above all though, I wanted to try to leave a fitting memorial to Bert, and Frank too. I believe that these two brave brothers deserve at least that much and more. I hope that the reader may think so too and that I have at least succeeded in some small way of keeping the memories of Bert and Frank alive in a way worthy of them.

Chapter 1: A Little Family History

Bertram James Warr was my mother's brother. Uncle Bert was born in Toronto Canada on December 7th 1917. His father, my grandfather, Bertram Howard Warr had come to Canada from Bristol England in 1903 and his mother, who was my grandmother, Mary Teresa Henneberry had come from Waterford Ireland in 1913.

My grandfather was born in 1883 in the Clifton suburb of Bristol known as Pill and his parents were Edward Warr and Myra Cook. They had 6 children of which Bertram Howard was the youngest. His father was a partner in the local firm of Withers and Warr: Farmers and Foragers and they seem to have been a comfortably well off late Victorian British middle class family. The 1891 census reveals that they had at least one servant the curiously named Minnie Cowmeadow. There were close ties between the Withers and Warr clans with at least one marriage between the two families. Bertram Howard's sister Emily married Richard Beard Withers. Emily and Richard had 8 children one of whom Joan, would later lodge at the same rooms as Bertram James in pre war London. Because Bertram Howard was the youngest son there was presumably no prospect of him going into the family business and without a university education or any formal training in a profession, his prospects in England were limited. He decided to take a gamble and roll the dice on a future in Canada. He had heard that there were great opportunities in Canada for hard working men. In 1903, aged 20, Bertram Howard set sail from Liverpool for Canada with his 24 year old brother George. He had to work hard all his life though to provide a home for his family. Money was never plentiful in the Warr household in Toronto, especially during the depression. My grandfather had various jobs throughout the depression years. At times he delivered ice to the neighbourhood families using a horse drawn wagon. He shovelled snow off neighbourhood driveways in winter and in the spring and summer offered his services as a gardener. He also worked as a caretaker in a local school.

Bertram Warr's mother, Mary Teresa Henneberry was born in Kilkenny Ireland on 26 September 1891 and grew up in the outskirts of nearby Waterford. Mary's parents were Walter Henneberry and Bridget Murphy. Mary Teresa was the third child born into a family of 8, 4 boys and 4 girls. At age 15 her mother sent Mary and her 20 year old sister Kate to work in a Quaker school in Waterford. The job was a live in position. The girls worked from 7 in the morning until 10 at night with only one or two afternoons off a week.

They began their day by going around the school and lighting all the fires in order to make sure the place was nice and warm for when the staff and students arrived. After that Mary would spend the greater part of her day in the kitchen washing dirty dishes from all the school meals. And this little person, she stood only 5ft 1in, spent most of the day standing in front of a sink full of water, soaking wet from the dish water running down the front of her apron.

Because Mary was only 15 she wasn't permitted to go out of the school grounds. On her afternoons off the only thing she could do to relax was lay down on her bed and rest. That was in between beatings she got from sister Kate. Kate being older was allowed off school grounds during the afternoons off and it seems that she expected Mary to clean her shoes for her so she could be ready for the off. If Mary was too tired or didn't get tKate's shoes cleaned fast enough in her own free time Kate, annoyed at having her free time delayed, would beat her little sister.

Mary and Kate's mother, Bridget would come to the school to collect the girl's wages which she then used to look after the other children of the family and run the house. The girls saw very little if any of their wages. Years later when questioned about how she felt about having all her money taken by her mother, Mary just shrugged her shoulders and said "Well, she needed it for the family."

8

It seems that Kate's belligerence was not restricted to her sister, she was always getting in to quarrels with the other staff. This got so bad that she had to leave the school. Although the school was happy with Mary and wanted her to stay she went back home with Kate.

Nell, one of their relatives in Wales, wrote that she was getting married and wanted Mary to take over her position in the house of a Mrs Lewis. Nell looked after the Lewis's child and was a sort of companion for Mrs Lewis. Mary agreed and at age 17 she crossed the Irish sea by boat and went to work in Wales. Nell and her husband met the boat at the dock and took her to the Lewises. Mary worked hard for Mr Lewis, who was a manager of a mine. He and his wife grew very fond of her and she them. But that life was far from ideal The only recreation that Mary had while with the Lewis's was taking their young son out to parks and for walks and her health was poor in Wales. Mary longed for a way out of the place. Reading in the local papers of the money to be made in Canada, Mary wrote to the British government in London and got permission to emigrate. She went home to Waterford to say goodbye to her family, they slipped two or three pounds into her hands for the trip and off she went to Dublin to board ship bound for Liverpool. Her mother went with her to see her off on the boat to Liverpool. From Liverpool she boarded a ship for Canada. Mary Henneberry was 22 years old in 1913 when she crossed the Atlantic on her own to start a new life in Canada. Mary set off on this new life into the unknown completely on her own, having no relatives nor any friends in Toronto. Some years later her brother Jim would emigrate to Toronto but by then Mary was married and had a family. Those first years in Toronto she was all on her own. Mary spent the rest of her life in Toronto, returning to her homeland only once or twice for short visits over the next 60+ years of her life.

Bertram Howard and Mary Teresa met in 1913 and married in 1915 and would have 7 children. Bertram James born

December 7 1917 was the second child the family had.
Bert's older brother Frank, destined to meet his end as a
navigator in an RCAF 424 Squadron Wellington bomber,
had been born the year before in 1916. The boys had four
younger sisters, Mary born 1919, Marjorie born 1920,
Emily born 1924, and my mother, little Cecelia born 1931.
There was a third boy, Richard. There is no record of when
Richard was born. He was either born between Marjorie and
Emily or Emily and Cecilia. Richard had serious health
problems and died as a toddler. The only word Richard ever
uttered was "mama" shortly before he died in his mother's
arms.

The six Warr children grew up in a rented house in the St
Claire area of Toronto. In the early 1940s they moved to
another rented house in the area at 84 Cloverlawn Avenue
just east of Dufferin Street. Bertram and Mary would live
there until the 1970s when the landlord sold the house.
Then, together with their daughter Mary, they bought a
house in the Toronto suburb of Etobicoke. There they would
end their days. Mary lived with them and looked after them
and the house as they grew older. My grandad continued to
work in his garden, which he took a lot of pride in. He hated
winter because it meant that he couldn't work in his garden
and would count the days until the spring thaw would again
allow him to get out and get cracking in his flower beds.

In the early 1950s Mary had met Patrick Connolly and they
had gone out for several years but Pat felt unable to commit
to a relationship at the time because he had to care for his
sick mother.. In the mid 1950s Mary broke off the
relationship and moved to New York, where she worked for
a time as a secretary at the United Nations. After Pat's
mother passed, away Mary moved back to Toronto and
resumed the relationship with Pat. Patrick James Connolly
and Mary Myra Warr were married in 1958. They had plans
to build a house and bought some vacant land with this in
mind. There were no water or sewage services to this land,
so they spent a great deal of time digging to look for water
in order to sink a well. They never did find any, and the

house was never built. Shortly after this Pat got sick with cancer.

For Mary a lifetime of caregiving was about to begin. Mary cared for Pat until he died in 1962. It was after this that Mary began caring for her parents full time. The owner of the house on Cloverlawn Avenue sold up, and the new owners were not interested in renting. 1964 Mary and her parents bought a house together on Prince Edward Drive in the Toronto suburb of Etobicoke in the west of the city.

That house was less than 2 Km from where her sister Emily and her family lived. Emily had married Victor Lang in 1951 and they moved in to a house on Lilibet Avenue which is south of Bloor Street and east of Islington Avenue in Etobicoke. Emily and Victor had three sons, Michael, Richard and David. In the house on Prince Edward Drive Mary cared for her ageing parents until their deaths. Grandpa, Bertram Howard Warr, died at the grand old age of 92 in 1976 and my grandma, Mary Warr died at the equally grand age of 89 on 14 July 1980. Mary then sold that house and moved to a house even closer to Emily and her family on Coney Avenue just east of Islington Avenue and south of Dundas Street.

In 1982 my mother, Cecelia had a massive stroke and underwent emergency surgery which saved her life. However she never fully recovered from her stroke and was severely disabled for the rest of her life. Mary again stepped in and brought her ailing sister home to live with her. Cecelia's two youngest children my sister Maureen Anne aged 18 and brother James Patrick aged 17 at the time also moved in with Mary. Jim was named for both his uncle Bertram James Warr and Mary's husband Pat. Mary cared for her sister until in 1986 when she finally succumbed to her illnesses and passed away. Maureen and Jim continued to live with Mary until she died from cancer aged 80 in the year 2000. On top of the stroke, Cecelia had been living with the lifetime effects of polio which she had contracted in the 1950s. After a long battle with that she recovered, married and had four children of which I am the eldest. After me was born Mary Catherine and then Maureen and Jim. At the time of her stroke she and her husband, Harry had been divorced for over two years.

The three Warr sisters were very close their whole lives. Mary, Emily and Cecelia would gather with their children and later with their grandchildren and great grandchildren in either one of the two houses for get togethers for every birthday, anniversary, Christmas and Easter. Like her mother Emily was a devoted mother and her home was always full of love. Emily was not as strict with her three boys as her mother had been with her children. But, she must have found a pretty good balance because her boys between them produced two PhDs and a Masters degree and have lovely children and grandchildren of their own. Family get togethers were at Aunt Em's or at Aunt Mary's and were always occasions that we looked forward to weeks in advance. They were filled with great food, lively conversation, and always plenty of laughter. Mary and Emily loved to have the family over and Christmas was especially a time that everyone looked forward to. In later years we would usually spend Christmas day at Aunt Mary's. Dinner was of course the traditional turkey cooked to perfection with all the trimmings and plenty of veg. Boxing Day we spent at Aunt Em's and that day we usually had a glorious ham, again cooked to perfection with plenty of fresh veg to go along with it.

The fourth sister Marjory, married Ed Van Vlyman in 1948. Marjory was 28 when she married Ed. They had 8 children. They were not as close as the rest of the family simply because they lived thousands of miles away in Southern California. Ed was an aircraft engineer and worked for Avro Canada near Malton Airport (Now Toronto's Pearson International). When Prime Minister Diefenbaker cancelled the Arrow project and Avro closed its doors Ed was thrown out of work along with 50,000 others that the company had employed. Ed was offered a great opportunity working for a company involved in the design and manufacturing of the tyres and wheels for the Lunar Rover used on the Apollo moon landing program. This was at their plant in California. So Ed and Marjory sold their house in Toronto, bought a motor home and set off with their brood of 8 for California. Where they lived for the rest of their lives, heading north to visit the family in Toronto when they could.

Chapter 2: A Poet Growing Up

All six of the Warr children went to St Clare elementary school and all of the children were good academically. After school when homework was finished they were allowed to play with the neighbourhood kids. During the cold Toronto winters Bert and Frank played hockey in the streets near their home with the other boys of the neighbourhood who called the pair the Battling Warrs.

In the 1920s that part of Toronto was still fairly rural and there was a big field at the end of the Warr's street with an orchard in it. In the summer all the children would spend hours playing in the field and the orchard. No doubt the Warr's and their dog, would have spent many happy hours playing in those fields. There was always a family dog in the Warr household. Even years later when my grandparents were living with Aunt Mary they always had a dog and it was usually a springer Spaniel. Looking at family photos from the early 1940s the family dog, Skippy is often there front and centre. In what would become one of Aunt Mary's favourite photos, a uniformed Frank can be seen kneeling down tightly holding onto the beloved Skippy.

They were a very close knit family who looked out for each other. If trouble with neighbouring kids was brewing a favourite family saying was "My name is Warr and if you want to start one just keep it up." It was very much a case of if you took on one of the Warr children you took on the whole clan.

Granddad Warr worked during the day and relaxed in the evenings sitting in a big armchair in the living room smoking one of his pipes. I remember years later there was still a rack full of pipes beside that chair. Granddad would pick the pipe he wanted to smoke that evening from that rack. He was a devoted father, but left the day to day running of the house and the raising of the children to his wife, Mary. Mary was a caring and loving mother but she

14

brooked no nonsense and was strict with the kids. That was probably true of most working class families of the time.

Mary was a devout Roman Catholic who went to mass as many as 3 times a week. The 6 children were often involved with all kinds of church activities. All the children were brought up as Catholic and all the sisters remained devoted to the faith their whole lives. Young Bert's declaration of agnosticism, at age 20, caused a lot of friction between Bert and his parents and was one of the factors in his decision to leave home. Granddad Warr was Church of England but he was not religious. He did support his wife in her beliefs and was happy to have the children raised as Catholics.

Although they were a loving family, at times there were fireworks. Emily Warr said that "My mother was Irish and my father was English, let the fight begin." I remember that whenever we visited my grandparents and Aunt Mary and there was an argument, usually between me and my sister Cathy, Aunt Mary would at some point interrupt with "Fight ya divils, I hate peace."

My earliest memories of my grandparent's house were of their house on Cloverlawn Avenue. That house had a big wooden front veranda that was covered by an overhang that was the floor of one of the second floor bedrooms, and which allowed you to sit out in all sorts of weather. Inside the front door was an umbrella stand which in true British fashion was always full of a variety of brollies. That hallway had a wooden floor which led back to the kitchen at the rear of the house. A door to the right just past the entrance led to a big front room in the corner of which stood my grandfather's big comfy chair and his pipe rack.

Bert loved smoking pipes too. In one of his letters home he speaks about finding a lovely old pipe in a second hand shop which after a thorough cleaning became one of his favourite smokes. After Bert joined the RAF he would often receive packages from home or from department stores back in Toronto. The most common items in these were cakes, chocolates and cigarettes but sometimes they would also include pipe tobacco. Bert would share out the cakes,

15

chocolates and cigarettes with his mates but he never shared his pipe tobacco. That he kept to himself. After Frank arrived in the UK Bert would quite often save the cigarettes from these packages or at least some of them for him because Frank hadn't yet developed a taste for British cigarettes. Neither Frank nor Bert liked British coffee which they said was made with chicory and had a very bitter taste. So if any of these packages ever contained coffee it was shared between the two of them. Frank never mentions smoking a pipe in any of his letters so I'm guessing he was not a pipe smoker, that would seem to have been Bert and Grandad Warr's vice exclusively.

After watching grandad Warr clean his pipes I would often go back out into the hallway and head to the kitchen which was at the back of the house. A door at the back of the kitchen led to a back porch and my grandfather's beloved garden. In one corner of the kitchen were grandma's birds. Grandma Warr always kept one or two budgies in a bird cage in the corner. One of the birds was always named Petie. I have no idea how many Peties there were down through the years, but there must have been a few. Back in the hallway, once you passed the door to the front room, but before reaching the kitchen was another door on the right which led to the dining room. We had many happy meals seated around the big dining room table. Before reaching that door however were the stairs which led up to the bedrooms and the bathroom. These memories of this house must have been very early because I remember always having to go for an afternoon nap and being made to lie down on grandma's huge bed which was covered by a very puffy down blanket that puffed up and surrounded you when you lay on it. Tired or not I never got any sleep and during these nap times and had to pretend to go to sleep for an hour so before being allowed to come back down stairs and join the rest of the family. I must have been very young at this time but Cathy must have also been there and equally she must have had to go for a nap in another one of the bedrooms. This would have been several years before Maureen or Jim were born.

Grandma was always knitting us woollen socks. we got knitted woollen socks from grandma Warr for every birthday and every Christmas from my earliest memories until she passed away in 1980. Knitting socks must have been a lifetime habit because in a letter home in the summer of 1943 Frank wrote "By the way mom I think I have enough woollen socks to last me a long time thanks to you."

In his delivery days and afterwards when he shovelled snow and worked in the springs and summers as a gardener to support the family my grandfather Bertram would write poems which from time to time were printed in the Toronto Star Daily newspaper. In some of his letters home from England in the early 1940s young Bert encouraged his father's writing and even suggested that he look into self-publishing. In 1950 my grandfather did just that and self-published a book titled "In Quest Of Beauty and which contains 50 of his favourite poems.

It seems that a talent for writing ran in the family and at school young Bert began to show signs of that talent. It was at De La Salle High School that Bert's teachers really began to be impressed with his writing ability and he was encouraged by teachers and especially family to develop that talent. After graduating from Del, Bert took journalism classes at the University of Toronto. By now though it was the 1930s and the depression had hit hard. Money was never plentiful in the Warr house. Frank, Bert and the two eldest sisters, Mary and Marjory and Emily too, once she was old enough, were counted on to help out by getting part time jobs when they could find work. I know that Mary being the oldest of the girls was the first to go out to work. She worked in The Old Mill Restaurant on Kipling Avenue and also worked at Simpsons department store on Yonge Street in downtown Toronto. Bert was very close to his sister Mary and she obviously idolised him. Bert's letters are full of support, guidance and much gentle teasing for his younger sister for whom he seems to have taken on the dual roles of hero, and mentor.

My grandfather Bertram Howard had of course grown up in England at the height of the British Empire's strength. He came from a middle class family and no doubt had typical British middle class ideas and views, Britannia Rules the Waves etc. At that time there was a strong belief held by many if not most of the British that they were superior to just about everyone else and their empire was proof of that. Bertram Warr would have been brought up in that atmosphere. When he emigrated to Toronto in 1903 he found himself in a city whose people were mostly British and who thought the same. Toronto and Canada were part of the British empire and that empire was the biggest and the best in the world. The British empire is long gone of course, the two world wars and the economic as well as political realities of the rights of people to self-determination have seen it off. However you still see even today an echo of those ideas of the superiority of the British nation and British people amongst some. At its worst it rears its ugly face in the skinheads and other far right violent neo-Nazi groups and at its gentlest and most benign it is on full display at the royal Albert Hall on the Last Night Of The Proms when the whole crowd sings along with such songs as "Land Of Hope and Glory."

in 1914 came the harsh reality and brutality of WW1 and following that the great depression. By that time, if he hadn't been before my grandfather had begun to believe in socialism and passed his ideas of social justice for the working class along to his children. Bert and Frank being the eldest were more involved and got exposed to these ideas earlier than the girls. However the girls became involved in charity work and social programs designed by the Catholic Church to help the local community through these rough times as soon as they were old enough. In his letters home from England Bert refers to Mary as a socialist like him. Bert fully supported Mary's position, and in his role of teacher and mentor often suggests books with socialist leanings which he thinks Mary should read. Mary worked for several organisations that supported the working man. She was also very active in the Catholic Church and worked with, and ran at least one of their organisations that was set up to help the local families of the congregation. During the early part of the war Mary served on a war council and Bert wrote home in May 1940 about this new work. "No one told me that Mary Warr has a new job. What the heck is a socialist like her doing on a war council? The money is fine $18.00 per week. Her work on the forum is more worthwhile, but I suppose she has to make a living."

Mary maintained her socialist beliefs her whole life but often voted for the whomever she thought was the best candidate regardless of their political affiliation. Emily was very much the same in that regard, voting her conscience and the candidate rather than along strict party lines. For her part Marjory after she moved to California never did take out U.S. citizenship and so never had the opportunity to vote in elections. They were all devout Roman Catholics throughout their lives and that organisation tends to be very conservative however it maintains a very strong network of charities set up to help the poor and downtrodden. Mary never lost those ideas of social justice that she had learned from her parents and brothers in her youth and continued to support various charities throughout her life. When they got old enough Marjory and Emily went out to work as well. Little Cecelia was still only 16 by the time the war ended and times were better and she didn't have to go out to work.

As well as journalism classes Bert studied bookkeeping and worked in an office. The extra money coming into the house must have helped, but right from the start Bert chaffed at the tedium and dull routine of office work. Office work was not for Bert and he longed to be able to pursue his dream of becoming a poet. But he carried on studying and working to help out.

By the spring of 1938 at the age of 20, Bert had had enough of office work, left the bookkeepers and Toronto, and headed to the Muskoka region of Ontario's cottage country where he found work for the summer as a porter at The

Bigwin Inn resort on Lake Of Bays. By this time Bert was showing real signs of his talent for writing. Bert and his father were having major disagreements about writing and to top it off Bert had by this time announced to the family that he was now agnostic and did not want to be a practicing Catholic anymore. This announcement rocked his mother as she was so devout in her faith. She took a dim view of her second eldest rebelling against what she believed was the true faith and this caused even more friction between Bert and his parents. Even at this early age Bert was flirting with socialism and his poetry reflected his beliefs. He was a Modernist. Modernists in poetry believed that poems should be about social justice and help point the way to achieving a more just society for all members of that society, rich and poor, ruling class and working class alike. My grandad was more traditional in his views about poetry. He believed the duty of the poet was to point out the beauty of nature, love and the world around us. Bert and his father would have long, often very heated discussions about these two opposing views of poetry. Naturally this caused friction between Bert and his parents. In addition Bert was disillusioned with the staid and conservative attitudes of the Canadian Author Society. Without membership in this group though, getting published in Canada as a young poet was not easy. All of these things no doubt played a part in Bert's decision to escape to the countryside where he could take time to think about just where he wanted his life to go. Bert's adventure in Muskoka was as much about escaping from parental attitudes as it was about escaping to an exciting summer of work and play in the idyllic countryside of cottage country in Southern Ontario.

Bert was 20 years old when he left home to go to Muskoka. He had grown in to a fine young man of 5ft 10 inches tall and was of slim build. His sister Mary said that Bert had his mother's hazel eyes, a mop of chestnut hair and a keen wit. Earle Birney said of Bert that there is a fine sensitivity in his face and strength and calm and affection. Bert has also been described as a man with a stern face but with very kind eyes. The kind of eyes that have seen a lifetime of stories.

Suddenly with a sharp eyebrow raise comes a soft smile painted across his face which reveals his compassion and kindness. With slicked back hair and a dimple on the right side of his cheek he seems to capture the intense stare any young man/soldier would hope to portray.

In the years to come this callow youth with a huge potential and the drive to carry it off would grow into a fine intellectual and maturing poet. Bert arrived in England in 1939 still living his grand adventure begun in Muskoka, and he spent the next few years learning, writing and developing his ideas of social justice. By the time Bert arrived in England he had the beginnings of the socialist ideas which he would continue to develop through his contacts with the literary and intellectual scene of London and the refugees whom he knew and helped. Alongside this he still had many of the ideas of the typical provincial lad from Toronto that Britain and the British were the best. These ideas though were not deeply held and seemingly were a veneer that he threw off as he matured. In Halifax he told us of the grocer who gave him credit and didn't want payment until after Bert had found work in England. He hastened to add "and him a jew." An early letter of Bert's from England also relates the following - "I accidentally stepped into a protest by 10,000 (or so it seemed) communists all screaming out we demand arms for Spain. There were about 1,500 police to handle them and quite a bit of pushing and wrestling. They seemed to be mostly bespectacled Jews. There was hardly an Englishman among them." Interestingly this is the only mention in any of Bert's letters of the Spanish civil war which was a cause celebre of many serious socialist of the time.

A second passage from another letter home from Bert's early days in England, which unfortunately survives as only a fragment dovetails nicely with this. This fragment helps illustrate that Bert was at this time still feeling the excitement of living his dream and not yet settling down to the business of the hard work that making that dream would entail. The second excerpt is about the IRA bombing campaign known as the S-Plan. Bert doesn't refer to it as that but that is what it is known as to us. Bert, dismissively refers to the bombers as "an organised gang of tramps from the north of Ireland." He wrote that they were doing their best to blow London to smithereens. His interest seems to be mainly that they have blown up tube stations and power stations close to Shepard's Bush. He then goes on to say the police are guarding Parliament, Buckingham Palace and other important buildings. Then the letter cuts off because the last pages are missing, but again there is no hint in what does survive of any opinion pro or coin about the bombing campaign.

Bert's derisive dismissal of what was a major undertaking by the IRA (300 explosions/acts of sabotage, 10 deaths, 96 injuries between the start of the campaign in 1939 and it's end in 1940) at once acts to allay any fears the family back home may have, but also shows no interest in the social justice/injustice of the ideas behind the campaign.

Both of these statements show that at this time Bert held a very broad stereotyped view typical of many British people and people of British descent of the Jewish people. Bert also exhibited a typical attitude to women at this time namely, male chauvinism. Writing about a concert that he attended early in the war he says that the performance was spoiled because there were too many women in the orchestra. It is tempting to extend these views we have of Bert to include the British view of everyone who was not British being inferior, but the evidence is not there for this and that is probably not fair to Bert. Because in the long run we know that Bert was not like that. He was a kind, helpful and, above all else, tolerant person ready to help anyone and everyone whom he thought he could. We know that both of these statements are misleading, both Phil Pinkus and Phil Sketchler were Jewish and Bert greatly respected and admired Pinkus. And of course Bert continually supported and encouraged his sisters and Patricia Ledward, to get educated and be as active and positive in the community as possible. Bert worked hard to help all the refugees, men and

22

women that he could. Many of his friends and the people he socialised with, especially the Austrian and Hungarian refugees that he met at Mrs Senjem's dinner parties were of course Jewish. I believe that those statements were nothing more than the residual thoughts of attitudes that he encountered growing up in Toronto in the 1930s where the idea of Rule Britannia was so prominent. Once exposed to the reality of empire and the people in it through his years in London Bert's true nature of social equality for everyone regardless of religion, race or sex came through.

While we cannot perhaps consider Bert to have been a man of action he certainly did not hesitate to act once he had made up his mind about something. He didn't hesitate to travel to England to live his dream. He wasted no time hanging around home after returning to Toronto from Bigwin. It was a short five days before setting out for Halifax and then on to England. He wanted to be a writer and saw that his best chance would be to go study in England so he did. Similarly once he had decided that being a conscientious objector would mean sitting on the sidelines working on a farm or going to a prison and effectively not accomplishing anything for the duration of the war he acted and decided to fight his fight not the fight that the corrupt politicians and ruling class wanted. It may be only a matter of semantics but it is an important point that Bert stuck to his beliefs and went off to war on his own terms. He spent the early war years defining himself as a socialist and eventually a conscientious objector, however Bert was uneasy with this status. He looked around and, yes he saw the corruption of the British leadership and was loathe to fight for them when he believed they were mainly interested in maintaining the status quo of the British Empire remaining a world power and stuffing their pockets with war profits to boot. He also saw the great suffering that the bombings were causing the people of London. The very working class people that he was determined to help and the idea of going off to a work farm or prison as he would have had to have done had he maintained his status as a conscientious objector, was not something that he felt could do. He needed to make a stand and so he decided to join the military when called up and fight for the cause he believed in, namely to help the people. This eventually led him of course to volunteer for aircrew duty in the RAFVR.

He also had leadership qualities as evidenced by 158 Squadron sending him on a Bomb Leaders course in preparation for taking over the duties of Bomb Leader for the squadron. Bert's leadership was not the razzle dazzle follow me sort. By all accounts he was a very quiet, thoughtful person keeping to himself in most social settings but he must have been looked at as a leader within his crew, someone you could rely upon to help out whenever needed and to make the right decisions under pressure when it mattered most. Otherwise he would not have been sent on the Bomb Aimers course.

Chapter 3: Bigwin Inn, Big Dreams

The Bigwin Inn Resort was on Bigwin Island in Lake of Bays about 250Km north of Toronto in Muskoka, the heart of Ontario's cottage country. The resort was built in 1915 by local Hunstville businessman C. W. Shaw. Shaw's resort did a roaring business. By mid 1930s it had gained an international reputation and had become the resort of choice in the area for socialites, politicians and even royalty. Among many others, Clark Gable and Carol Lombard visited as did Earnest Hemingway and H.G. Wells. Princess Juliana of The Netherlands once came to the island for a stay and the Rockefellers were regularly seen about the place too. Big bands such as The Duke Ellington Band and The Count Basie Band often played in the inn's Octagonal restaurant which doubled as the dance hall. Shaw would often get permission from the band leader to sit in with the band and play his trumpet. I can't help but wondering if Shaw was any good or not. Did he play quietly in the background or did he blast it out? In any event the big bands seemed to have survived Shaw's jamming with them. They carried on and they came back to the resort year after year, so he couldn't have disrupted things too much.

 In mid May of 1938 the big arrival at Bigwin Inn was Bertram Warr. To get to the resort Bert would probably have hitch-hiked from Toronto 235 km to the south. Then he would have taken the big old wooden ferry across from the mainland to the island, docking at the resort's private dock. Bert worked at the resort all through the spring and summer of 1938. When he first arrived from the crowded, dirty, city in May he was ill and was taking medication. The fresh air and good food that he got at the resort soon had him feeling much better. By summer's end he was the picture of health. Work at the resort was often hard, particularly before the resort opened for the season. When Bert first arrived he was told that he would be a porter for the season, that is if he was kept on. Whether or not he was kept on depended on how hard he worked before the resort opened. His employment also depended on the whims of Shaw, who was

25

picky about who he kept around the place and who he let go. Usually though he kept the hard workers but if he took a dislike to someone, hard worker or not he wouldn't hesitate to get rid of them. In the weeks before the resort opened Bert worked as an odd job man. That meant doing anything and everything that needed doing to help Shaw meet his opening day deadline of mid-June. This meant that Bert was up at 6 AM every morning and often worked until 7 at night. At 7 all the workers stopped for the day and headed off to have dinner and a good night's sleep ready for the next day's 6 AM reveille. It didn't take Bert long to figure out Shaw's penchant for getting rid of slackers or anyone he took a dislike to. So Bert kept his head down and worked hard, doing everything that was asked of him.

He must have been a good worker because a couple of weeks before the resort opened his boss told him that he was sure to be kept on for the season. According to Bert, Shaw was a tough old bird who fired staff at the drop of a hat. Bert writes that most of the staff were scared stiff of "Old Weevil as they call Shaw. He takes delight in firing people." Once when Shaw was in a bad mood he ran into one long serving bellboy and fired the fellow simply because the lad had been there for 4 seasons and "Old Weevil" was tired of seeing him around the place. Bert wrote though that "He doesn't bother me but he does think I'm too saucy when I answer him."

For his first 3 weeks work, paid pro-rated at the end of the month, Bert received the princely sum of $20.19 cents. Although a full months pay would not have amounted to much more, only $25. Not surprisingly Bert was usually broke and he was looking forward to the tips he hoped he would get once there were actually guests at the resort.

Partway through the season he wrote home that an ice cream seller had opened up at the hotel. In the sweltering heat of a Muskoka summer, cold, fresh ice cream was too much to resist. Bert told the folks at home that now he really would be broke after buying ice creams every day.

26

Bert seems to have always been short of money and getting in debt by borrowing a little cash from the other lads. This trait would be something that he would carry with him all the way to England and right up to his death. Mrs Senjem, Bert's Hungarian refugee friend, tried to get him to save money. She did manage to get him to open a bank account but there was never much money in it. At the time of his death his bank account held £5. She never did manage to get him to be more careful with his money and Bert would be constantly in debt his whole time in England.

Bert continued to work hard doing odd jobs before the resort opened for the season. Once he was tasked with getting rid of a family of mice that had nested in a linen drawer of one of the resort's out buildings. The mice were frightening the waitresses and kitchen staff. Bert wrote that it "was mice work if you can get it." That thought sums up Bert's attitude to his whole Bigwin experience. Once the resort opened Bert began his work as a porter, which according to him was the best job at the place. "I'm my own boss and tips are good. We have almost as good a time as the guests. We go swimming, use sailboats and launches and go canoeing on the lake. We pay 15 cents an hour to rent a canoe, that's half what the guests pay."

His only complaints about the place were having to put up with the swarms of mosquitoes and black flies which were everywhere. Typical of the Muskoka region and actually most of rural southern Ontario in general, Bigwin Island suffered from plagues of these flying pests. Bert wrote home tongue in cheek that he was losing weight in spite of being well fed because the black flies take a pound of flesh each time they bite. Swarms of mosquitoes and black flies have always been a plague in cottage country in southern Ontario.

Bert also wasn't thrilled with having to wash his clothes in the sink in his room. This was only a temporary inconvenience though because once the resort opened the laundry opened as well. Bert complained that " I have to look respectable every day and wear a clean shirt, just as bad as at the office." That was pretty much the only similarity between working in the dull, stuffy office in Toronto and working in the idyllic rural setting of the resort. Bert was having the time of his life at the resort and seems to have looked at the whole thing as one long working holiday that was as much an adventure as it was a job.

The day of the hotel opening rapidly approached. The first guests that season were a convention of the Lyons Club. Before the Lyons Club arrived Bert was confirmed in his porter's job and fitted for a uniform. he wrote that "We look like admirals of the fleet." Bert was to work as an outdoor porter. That entailed taking tickets at the cinema, acting as doorman at conventions and looking after the beds and rooms of 50 of the staff. He was also always on call for any other jobs that might pop up and needed doing.

The lifeblood of the resort seems to have been conventions. When there was a convention all the rooms were full. Conventions were usually rowdy affairs with the booze flowing freely and the place jumping. Very often, in between conventions most of the rooms were empty and there was very little going on. During these down times Shaw, always looking for ways to save a penny, would lay off most of the waitresses in the restaurant. Upwards of 50 of them would continue to get room and board but no pay until the next convention arrived and they were rehired.

There were no newspapers at the resort so Bert got the family to send him the Star Weekly magazine which helped him keep up with the goings on back home in Toronto. The family would continue to send Bert the Star Weekly for the rest of his life. When he was in England he looked forward to getting these weekly magazines very much. During some of his lonelier times in London they were a very welcome link to familiar places and times. He would often head over to the Canadian High Commission at Canada House in Trafalgar Square where he could read the Star Weekly, The

Globe and Mail and other Canadian newspapers and magazines from all around the country.

Most of the time work at the resort was routine but occasionally something out of ordinary would happen. Once an old lady died at hotel and Bert was horrified to see how the staff managed moving the body. They wanted to ensure that guests in the restaurant were none the wiser so "They lugged her out the back door and across the golf course to one of the freight docks. A launch took her to the mainland from there." For a young lad of 20 seeing a dead body in the hotel where he worked must have been a bit of a shock to say the least. Bert can't have seen too many dead bodies before except at funerals. Death at resorts and hotels, while not usually a common occurrence, is not unknown. I'm sure the long term staff were well practiced at moving corpses and getting them to the mainland with the minimum of fuss and without attracting the attention of the guests at the resort.

In July a fellow Bert knew in Toronto named John Francis Sweeney wrote him a letter asking if Bert could put in a word with the bosses about getting him a job. Against his better judgement Bert agreed. There were several fellows getting fired by "Old Weevil " Shaw so Bert wrote home that "There might be an opening for the big lug. I hated to recommend the big palooka but he might be alright. I sent him a telegram so he might be here by Monday" Even at this young age Bert was helping out people when he could even when his better judgement warned him against it. Bert appears to think that this Sweeney fellow was pretty lazy and in all likelihood would let him down. Sure enough Sweeney did just that. "Sweeney arrived Sunday. Instead of getting up early Monday to go to work he slept in. The lazy hulk. He worked Tuesday helping the plumber and complained loud and long about feeling tired. He is on night work now (Wednesday night) washing floors and is going to return to the city on Sunday. What a dope for me to recommend to the boss." In spite of Sweeney letting him down Bert would continue for the rest of his life to help everyone that he could. This was especially true once he got to England and floods of refugees fleeing from the Nazis were pouring in to London.

In spite of Sweeney letting him down and making him look bad to the bosses Bert's position at Bigwin remained secure because he was a hard worker who was willing to do whatever was asked of him, and in a cheery manner. He worked hard and enjoyed his time off too. On days off there were plenty of trips to the nearest big town, Huntsville, 23KM from Bigwin. The lads and most likely some of the girls too would go to Huntsville for meals out and to go to the movies. They usually hitch-hiked to town after crossing from the island to the mainland on the steamer. One time they did rent a car, but that ended badly when they managed to run out of gas on the way back. They had to walk in the rain to the nearest gas station to get a bucket of fuel. Bert wrote that it wasn't too bad because it was only 2 miles.

Once Bert hitch hiked to the small town of Baysville 10 KM away where his sister Mary was spending time on vacation. Mary had taken a job in Toronto with a real estate firm where she was making $13 per week. Impressed, Bert wrote that "Now that is money!" It was double what he was making at Bigwin but then Mary wasn't having the adventure that Bert was plus she was stuck in an office in the city, one of Bert's worst nightmares. I think that in spite of Mary's riches and his debts Bert was much happier in Bigwin than he was in an office. He was having the time of his life and making a little money too.

Before the resort opened a boat load of about 80 new waitresses arrived one day and like most 20 year old lads Bert seems to have had his eye on one or two of them. But he never writes of them again in his letters to his parents. So whether or not Bert had a summer romance on Bigwin will forever remain a mystery. Although Bert had a girlfriend named Hazel back in Toronto he doesn't seem to have been very close to her. He only mentions Hazel once in a letter home in mid-summer and at that all he wrote was that he really should write to her soon. Hazel or HK as Bert calls her in his letters rarely gets a mention but occasionally he does write in his letters home from England that he must write to HK. We learn next to nothing about Hazel other than she seems to have been an actress on the stage and a singer as well. But that is much more than we ever learn about any other girl in Bert's life apart from Patricia Ledward. Bert met Patricia on one of his university courses in London and it is an open question as to whether or not there was a romance between the two. It seems that besides HK and Patricia Ledward Bert did have a few other girlfriends. In one of her letters to Mary after Bert had died, Nora Senjem wrote that "Bert had lent his typewriter to one of his girlfriends." But in his letters home Bert never mentions any of them.

In spite of his agnostic beliefs Bert wrote to his parents that everyone went to the Catholic church by boat to attend masses. In a later letter though, he wrote that there was only one other lad on the island who was a catholic and who went to the church. I wonder how often Bert actually went to mass considering his beliefs. Bert may have been trying to ease his deeply religious mother's mind by writing to her about going to church. After all, he never wrote anything indicating how frequently he made the trip across the lake to the little church. If so, it was a tactic that he would use again in England once the war had started and he was serving on active duty in the RAFVR (Royal Air Force Volunteer Reserve). He never did tell his family that he was flying on active duty. Instead he led them to believe that he was working in a non-combat roll.

Bert's time at Bigwin was most notable for two reasons. First, it was at Bigwin that Bert was to meet a friend who would change his life forever. When he first arrived at the resort Bert bunked in a shack with several others lads and took his meals in the kitchen. But once he was taken on for the season he was moved to a room in the Caddy House at the golf course where there were only two to a room. Bert's roommate in his Caddy House room was a fellow named

Phil Pinkus. Pinkus, also from Toronto, had spent time travelling in the U.S.A. and, like Bert, also wanted to be a writer. The two lads had a common goal and that seems to have been a basis at least initially for their friendship. Pinkus had the idea that he wanted to go to England and it seems that right away Bert was intrigued. Pinkus was using his time at Bigwin to earn enough money to buy a ticket on an ocean liner and head to England where he planned on joining the RAF. Pinkus wanted to do a basic 4 year tour in the RAF which he said paid very well. He planned on using the money he hoped he would be able to save from his pay to pay for journalism classes at university. Bert had absolutely no desire to join any military organisation but the idea of going to England where he could learn about writing in one of London's world class universities and try his luck in its vibrant literary scene must have been too tempting to resist. He would be free of family religious pressures and the stifling restrictions of the Canadian Authors Association.

The other notable thing about Bert's time at Bigwin is that it seems to have been a golden summer for Bert, his last golden time. One last carefree period as an adolescent before he actually did go to England and settle into the business of becoming a serious writer. Bert's letters home from this time are very light and full of the joys of that summer. He talks about canoeing and swimming on the lake and hitch-hiking or borrowing cars to go Huntsville with the lads for nights out. In one letter near the end of summer Bert writes to the family that "This is no place to come to read or study. It's too noisy, I haven't been able to really concentrate all summer." I suspect though that Bert's lack of concentration all that summer was due to something else. Perhaps on some level he knew that he was turning a corner at Bigwin. At Bigwin he was free from the tedium of office work, the demands of study, and family religious pressures over his agnosticism. Also he was not butting heads with his father over their conflicting ideas about poetry. Perhaps he knew that at the end of the summer, whether or not he went to England it would be back to those and other just as difficult realities.

How difficult would it have been on the huge expanse of the resort or in fact the whole island for that matter, for Bert to have found a quiet corner somewhere to read and study? Surely if his heart had really been in it and he had the right mind set he would have found somewhere quiet that he could study for an hour or two most days. I think that perhaps Bert was not ready to study that summer and was more than happy to have one last golden summer of fun before getting serious about life and writing.

Bert and Pinkus continued to dream of heading to England after the season at Bigwin was over in September. All through that summer the two boys must have spent many evenings in their room at the Caddy House talking about and planning their big journey long after lights out. In September when the summer season and their jobs at Bigwin were ending, Bert and Pinkus decided to put their plans in operation. Bert arrived home in Toronto on September 14th full of his plans for travel to England and no doubt excited and eager to be on the road. Because Bert was back at home there are naturally enough no letters from the time just before he left for England. His sister Mary's diary is strangely empty for the 5 days that Bert was at home and if Bert had a diary it is now long lost to us. There can be no doubt though that Bert was excited and itching to get on the road and start living his dream. For Bert's Family it was another matter. The lone forlorn entry in Mary's diary 5 days later on September 19th, the day Bert left the family home for the last time simply and sadly reads "Bert Left." Little could Mary or any of the rest of the family Bert was leaving behind, have known that, that was the last time any of them would ever see him.

Chapter 4: On The Road

Bert and Pinkus started off with enthusiasm and high hopes but not much else. The pair had very little money and planned to hitchhike the entire 1100 miles (1770Km) to Nova Scotia, they didn't arrive in Halifax until October 9th, nearly a month after setting out from Toronto on September 19th. Whatever adventures they had along the way are lost to us now. Bert doesn't seem to have written any letters during the trip to Halifax. If he did none of them have survived. The first we hear from him is a letter that he wrote October 10th the day after he and Pinkus arrived in Halifax. Bert wrote that they had stopped briefly in St John New Brunswick where they had hoped to be able to board a ship to England. There weren't any ships in port at St John that were headed to England so they decided to push on to Halifax as they didn't much like St John anyway.

Bert's trip to Halifax is a bit confusing. Did he hitch-hike with Pinkus to Montreal where Pinkus then stowed away on a ship to St John? We know that Pinkus stowed away on a ship in Montreal from a newspaper article about him written when he was in the RAF and stationed in India. Did Bert stow away as well or did he hitch-hike to St John on his own where the two then met up again? Or did the two lads start out from Toronto separately and meet up in St John from where they then proceeded to hitch-hike together to Halifax? We know that Bert and Pinkus definitely arrived in Halifax together from the letter Bert wrote home on Oct 10th. "Arrived in Halifax Sunday afternoon (09 Oct '38). We have located in a housekeeping room in the residential part of the city."

Pinkus met a fellow named Phil Sketchler who was stowing away on the same boat from Montreal as Pinkus. Pinkus and Sketchler must have arrived in St John together. Did Sketchler also go with the lads from St John to Halifax or did he set off on his own arriving in the Nova Scotian capital separately? Sketchler, had similar plans to Pinkus. He wanted to go to England where he planned to join the

British army and spend his life as a career military man. It seems that when they got to Halifax Sketchler did not share the room with Bert and Pinkus but went his own way as Bert doesn't mention him again until after Sketchler has arrived in England.

In any event the lads arrived in Halifax that October where they found plenty of ships bound for England. Now though the two were nearly flat broke and didn't have the money the tickets for the trip cost. They spent no more than a day looking for accommodation because they arrived on the Sunday and by Monday they were settled in their housekeeping room. Most places they looked at were asking for the princely sum of $6 per week for a room which was out of their price range. They finally found an affordable place. Initially the landlady wanted $5 a week but the boys talked her down to $3. The room's furnishings were basic but the place was clean and had a kitchen with everything they needed to make and eat meals apart from the food, that they would have to supply themselves. A kindly Jewish fellow who ran the local grocery offered to let them have groceries on credit. Amazingly he was willing to wait for payment until the boys were in England and had found work there.

In the wider world at the end of September Britain, France, Germany and Italy signed the Munich Agreement. This agreement which amounted to a complete betrayal of the Czech people by Britain and France called for Germany to annex a portion of the Czech Republic called the Sudetenland. Hitler's excuse for this land grab was that there were 3 million ethnic Germans living in Sudetenland. This agreement was signed 30 September. That same day arriving back in London British Prime Minister Neville Chamberlain claimed the agreement meant "Peace for our time." Of course this was complete nonsense because all it did was appease Hitler and feed his desire for more and more expansion. Chamberlain was so desperate to avoid war that in spite of all of Hitler's double dealings he took Hitler's word that he would make no further demands for territory in Europe. In fact less than a year later the Munich agreement and the idea of peace for our time was shown to be a complete mockery because the Germans invaded Poland. This of course led to declarations of war against Germany by both Britain and France and marked the beginning of World War II. Winston Churchill who at the time the Munich Agreement was signed was not in the government was one of the few people to be opposed appeasing Hitler. He called the Munich Agreement an unmitigated disaster. Churchill said of Chamberlain "You were given the choice between war and dishonour. You chose dishonour and you will have war." Chamberlain's naivete in following this path of appeasement was playing directly in to Hitler's hands. The more concessions Hitler could wring out of the British and the French without the use of military force the stronger his hand got.

Bert and Pinkus had more immediate things to worry about than the annexing by Germany of some unknown part of a little known country in far off Eastern Europe. Winter was coming and it was starting to get cold in Halifax, especially at night. One of their main worries was just trying to stay warm at night. Their rooms may have been comfortable but they were cold. The houses in Halifax seem to have been largely timber framed and very badly insulated. In December Bert wrote that before going to bed he and Pinkus put on all their clothes including their shoes and gloves. Then they climbed into their beds pulled up their covers and were quite warm. That whole passage in Bert's letter seems to sum up to me Bert's attitude to this whole time. He was continuing his last golden summer of youth and going on a big adventure to England to top it off. There is a sense of youthful excitement and the awareness of what an exciting experience the whole thing was in spite of their trouble finding a ship to carry them to England on the cheap.

As far as Bert was concerned the sooner they could find passage the better. He didn't think much of Halifax and wrote that "The more I see of these other cities the more I

36

appreciate Toronto. Halifax is a very dead city. The best thing about the place is the weather. St John and Halifax are both poor and dirty. Halifax is swarming with children most of whom are unwashed. The houses are all wooden and look like they haven't seen any paint since they were built. They are nice and clean on the inside though. The people just don't seem to care about the outside but Maritmers* are very friendly and eager to help whenever they can."

Pinkus found work but Bert doesn't say doing what. He does say though that Pinkus was not paid any money for working and that he was given meals as payment instead. That form of payment seems to have been fairly common for those dark days of the great depression. Bert took on more than one job where payment was not in cash but in the form of food. In fact Bert's first job in Halifax was washing dishes in the kitchen of a local restaurant for which initially he wasn't being paid either. He too was getting free food instead of cash. That situation must have changed though because Bert wrote that when the restaurant wasn't busy he was laid off and so he didn't get paid. Bert's money had to pay the rent on the room and the lads daily expenses then anything left over presumably was put aside and earmarked for buying the tickets for their passage. Whatever the case, with Pinkus being paid in food and Bert possibly still being at least partially paid in food, cash was in short supply. They were not saving enough for their tickets and were still stuck in Halifax.

*Maritimers are what Canadians call the folks who live in the East coast provinces of New Brunswick, Nova Scotia and Prince Edward Island.

They carried on working all through November and by the time early December rolled around it looked likely that they would be spending Christmas in Halifax still trying to find a way to cross the ocean. Bert was hoping to start seasonal work over the busy Christmas shopping period in Eatons. Eatons ran a big Canada wide chain of department stores and at the time were one of the biggest retailers in the country. Bert says jobs were plentiful even if money for doing the jobs was not. He started working in the Carlton Hotel and that did pay a wage, however meagre. By a happy coincidence the dietician at the hotel had worked with Bert that summer at Bigwin and Bert perhaps feeling a little lonely or homesick or both wrote "So I'm practically among family."

They carried on in these jobs for some weeks and Bert spent his 21st birthday on December 7th still stuck in Halifax. For his birthday the family sent him a card with money in it. The mail must have been a lot a safer in those days because they regularly sent money back and forth in letters and it would seem they sent relatively large sums. The family sending Bert cash through the post continued even after Bert was in England and the money always seems to have arrived safe and sound. In any event the money came in very handy because Bert, broke as usual went out and bought all the family Christmas presents with it and posted it back that way. That was typical of Bert. He was always generous and not in the least bit selfish. He would give until he had nothing more to give and then he would borrow money and end up giving that away as well to someone whom he thought had a greater need for it than he did. He was generous to a fault and under present circumstances when he and Pinkus were desperately trying to save enough money to buy tickets for their passage he would have been better off being a bit more selfish. I'm sure that the family wold rather he had spent his birthday money on himself or put it aside with the rest of the money that he was saving for the ticket for his passage instead of using it to buy them Christmas presents.

Bert and Pinkus tried everything by hook and by crook to get passage on an England bound ship. They went to see the shipping master at Halifax harbour and "pestered him every day." Someone told them of a man in the Norwegian embassy who seemed to be able to get people over to Europe and they went to see him to see if he could help. Bert even went to St Mary's Basilica, the Roman Catholic

Cathedral in Halifax and enlisted the help of a priest. This priest gave Bert the names of a couple of people from the congregation who were in the shipping business. But none of that came to anything and they remained stuck in Halifax.

At one point they were pinning their hopes on a specific ship out of Boston which was arriving soon with 500 head of cattle in its holds. The lads were hoping that the cargo company would hire local men to go on the crossing to look after the cattle. That was a cheaper option than brining in experienced cow hands from Montreal as they sometimes did instead. That hope seems to have fizzled out because Bert only wrote about this in one letter and never mentions it again.

Phil Sketchler fed up with trying to save enough money to book a ticket on a liner decided to try stowing away. After all it had worked for him in Montreal so why not Halifax as well? Somehow he managed it and arrived in Liverpool where he was promptly arrested and detained by the authorities. He was put on trial and remarkably despite not even having a passport he was allowed to stay. He promptly joined the British Army Medical Corps, which of course had been his plan all along. He sent several letters to Bert trying to convince him to join up too. Bert's attitude to the military had not changed though, he wanted no part of it. Bert could be quite short with those he thought deserved it and he thought Sketchler a fool for joining the army and wrote "What a dope he turned out to be." It wasn't the fact that Sketchler had joined up that made Bert think him a fool. After all Pinkus wanted to join the RAF and Bert didn't think he was a fool. However Pinkus had plans to use the military as a means to an end to save the money he would need to take classes in journalism, which was his real ambition. For Phil Sketchler joining the military was the extent of his ambition. Bert thought Sketchler a fool because joining the military was the extent of his ambition. Sketchler seemed content to have joined the military and was more than happy to make a career toiling away as a junior NCO with no further ambition than perhaps one day reaching the lofty heights of sergeant or Warrant Officer. To Bert who hated the very idea of the military even then, such a career was unthinkable, not to mention extremely limited in its ambition and anyone who wanted that sort of life was a "dope."

Bert and Pinkus had been in Halifax since October 9th and it was now mid-December and they were no closer to getting to England than the day they arrived. With the news that Sketchler sent back the wheels began turning. Bert and Pinkus weren't saving much money so why not try their luck stowing away too? After all it had worked for Sketchler and it had worked for Pinkus out of Montreal. What did they have to lose?

With that in their minds, on December 23rd 1938 Bert and Pinkus made their way to Halifax harbour. They planned on stowing away on a cargo ship named the Beaverdale but members of her crew warned the boys off and told them they had no hope of getting aboard. Determined and undeterred they made their way to the Cunard Liner passenger ship Ausonia. Ausonia was scheduled to leave port that day, Christmas Eve. They snuck onboard her, found an empty passenger cabin where they stowed their bags and spent the night in this cabin undetected. At noon on Christmas Eve the ship set off. Bert and Pinkus were on their way to England at last. But it was not to be. After sailing about ten miles they were discovered and Bert wrote "We were politely asked to leave."

They were put aboard the pilot boat which was still alongside the liner. After two hours of pitching up and down on the waves they were then put aboard a Norwegian freighter which was sailing to Halifax. Back in Halifax harbour the lads were put ashore, disappointed and slightly seasick but undefeated. Was it the optimism of youth or dogged determination? It was now dinner time and options for sailing that day were fast running out. They didn't give up though, and were determined to try again. After a wash

and a shave, in of all places a local post office, Bert and
Pinkus headed straight back to the harbour. There they
boarded their third ship, the Canadian Pacific passenger
liner Montrose. They repeated the strategy they had used
when they had boarded the Ausonia and stowed their bags
in an unused stateroom. This time though instead of staying
put they mingled with the fair paying passengers in the
liner's lounges.

The Montrose set off at midnight on Christmas Eve.
Perhaps not quite as convinced of his agnosticism as he
would have people believe Bert went to midnight Mass.
Was he just seeing Christmas in or did he also say a prayer
or two that he and Pinkus would be successful this time and
finally make it to England? After all, he was already at mass
so why not? Of course another possibility is that he didn't
go to mass at all but merely wrote to his parents that he did,
trying to ease his mother's mind. He could just as well have
stayed in his cabin or gone to a passenger lounge to
welcome Christmas in with Pinkus and the rest of the
passengers, who must have been in a festive mood and
having a high time of it. Whatever the case, Bert and Pinkus
must have been holding their breathes and keeping their
fingers crossed as the ship left the dock. Would it be a case
of third time lucky? This time they made it past the pilot
boat and were headed out to sea. After they were out on the
open seas they left the passenger lounges and the ship's
chapel behind and spent a restful night in their cabin. On
Christmas morning Bert opened his cards from home and
opened his lone Christmas present, a shaving kit. This was a
gift from the housekeeper at the Carlton Hotel in Halifax
where Bert had worked. Cards and present finished with
they then left their cabin and presented themselves to the
captain. Maybe the captain was just a nice fellow or maybe
he was full of the Christmas spirit because as Bert wrote,
the captain "wished us a Merry Christmas, complimented
us on the neat way we had worked it and then sent us down
to dinner." The lads were allowed to stay on board and were
set to work earning their crossing as stewards. Bert was
thoroughly enjoying his great adventure "We have scrubbed

and polished our way across the Atlantic, brass, floors, stairs and decks galore, however it was fun." They were given one of the unused cabins to themselves and supplied with clean clothes and linen. Bert, possibly not believing all of this good luck wrote "To top it off we were forced to accept afternoon tea every day - some treatment for stowaways!"

Chapter 5: London: It's A Wonderful Joint

Bert and Pinkus worked hard during the crossing which
took about a week. Every day they would scrub decks,
polish brass and take on whatever task the crew set for them
with an unbridled enthusiasm. It was a one big adventure
and they were enjoying it fully. The Montrose docked in
Liverpool on new years day 1939. Bert wrote that they
expected to be shipped right back to Canada but possibly
because they had worked so hard during the crossing their
friend the captain again came to the rescue. Once they had
docked the local company lawyers along with the harbour
customs officials and the captain sat in the captain's office
on the ship. As the two lads stood before this array of
officialdom they expected the worst and thought they would
be trooped off to the next ship heading back to Canada,
turfed out on their ears. However the captain put in a good
word for the them with the officials and to Burt and Pinkus'
amazement agreed to let them stay. The company lawyers
and the immigration men wished the pair good luck and
shook their hands as they went ashore.

They spent that night in a local hotel and wasted little time,
setting off for London the next day. Of course as they had
almost no money they planned to hitchhike. They managed
to pick up a lift from a truck which took them the whole
way. They arrived in London in the dead of night but that
didn't stop the lorrie driver from taking the lads on a tour of
the capital before he dropped them at a rooming house at 6
in the morning. London, even in the dead of night must
have been an almost overwhelming site for two boys from
the back waters of provincial Toronto in the 1930s.

They stayed at those rooms for several days if not weeks.
Pinkus only stayed until he enlisted in the RAF. After
which he was sent for six months training in Ayrshire in
Scotland. Bert wrote home that Pinkus tried dozens of times
to get him to enlist in the RAF as well but Bert's attitude to
the military had not changed, he wanted no part of being in
uniform. Bert seems to have respected Pinkus'es decision

though and thought well of him. This was in stark contrast
to his feelings about Phil Sketchley whom we know Bert
thought was a dope. I think that this was probably because
Pinkus was using the RAF as a means to an end not an end
in itself whereas for Sketchley his ambitions seem to have
only extended to enlistment and to enlist and have a career
as a lowly enlisted man. Pinkus wanted to stay in the RAF
for 4 years saving as much of his pay as possible, a figure
which Bert puts at roughly $1500 CDN (roughly $28,000
CDN in 2023) for the four years. Pinkus planned using
those savings to pay for journalism classes leading to him
becoming a writer. It is obvious to see how Bert would
respect that career ambition if not the method of getting
there and how he thought the worst of Sketchley's lack of
ambition. Pinkus and Bert stayed in touch over the next few
years and on one occasion Pinkus even came to London on
leave to visit Bert, but he soon disappears from our story
and Bert stops mentioning him in letters home. I don't even
know if he survived the war. The last we hear of him,
Pinkus is serving as a navigator on RAF aircraft in the
Punjab in India in 1942 and that information comes from a
newspaper clipping that Aunt Mary had saved.

 Bert's initial impressions of London were that "It's a
wonderful joint – it would take years to see it all but it rains
all the time, the houses are cold and the people drink tea all
the time." He was thoroughly enjoying himself and found
work right away. London was emerging from the depression
and Bert says the help wanted sections of the papers were
full of several columns of ads every evening. He was
working within 3 days of arriving in London. He had found
work washing dishes at a Lyons Corner House cafeteria in
the heart of Piccadilly. The job paid 38 shillings and 6 pence
a week. That's about £1.90. He found accommodation in
Tubman Street in Shepards Bush and that set him back 10
shillings a week but included having his laundry done,
leaving him 28 shillings and 6 pence to get by on. The job
was meant to be a stop gap just to get some money coming
in until he could find something else. He was applying for
other work straight away and was hoping to get on at a

publisher's soon. In the event though Bert was to work at Lyons for several months and be thoroughly fed up with washing dishes by the time he did find other work. Lyons was half an hour travel from the rooms in Tadmore Street and Bert worked from noon until as late as 10 PM some days. He worked when the restaurant was busy and was given the day off without pay when things were slow.

Lyons Corner House Café in Piccadilly was somewhat of an institution for locals. My wife Tracy's family has deep roots in East End London that extend far back in to the city's past. She tells me that for her grandparents and other family members during the tough years of the depression a trip to the café in Piccadilly was a special treat. It's nice to think that perhaps one day while Bert was busy washing dishes in the kitchen out front Tracy's grandparents were enjoying a cup of Lyon's special mix tea. If Bert happened to do any bussing that day perhaps they could have even had a chance meeting. Perhaps Bert passed by their table or maybe they were sitting near the kitchen and caught a glimpse of him arms deep in soapy water. The odds are against such a meeting but you never know.

At some point between the last week of April and the middle of June Bert left Lyon's and took a job working as a bookkeeper at an Oyster company in Billingsgate Fish Market. He went to work in the London offices of The Whitstable Oyster Fishery Company which is still in business today. By the time he had that job he was taking three classes a week at Birkbeck College University of London in Bloomsbury Camden. At Birkbeck Bert took classes in journalism and literature. He was working hard learning his craft and honing his writing skills and developing his philosophy.

As well as changing jobs and starting school Bert also changed addresses. He moved from the Shepherds Bush rooms at Tadmore Street to 181 Sutherland Avenue in Maida Vale a few blocks west of Regents Park. It's not known how long Bert stayed at the rooms in Sutherland

Avenue. His landlady there, Mrs Bush sold those rooms and moved to new rooms at Lanark Mansions and Bert moved with her.

His old landlady at the Tadmore Street rooms whom he had once thought so kindly of came in for some withering criticism. Across the envelope of one of his letters from home she had written "Please Mr Warr give your family your new address. I can't keep forwarding your mail." A reasonable request one would have thought. However Bert thought otherwise and angrily wrote the family calling her " a disagreeable old wretch." Bert could be quite short and cutting with those he thought deserved it and he didn't often mince his words.

Although far from home Bert wasn't entirely alone and cut off. His cousin Joan Withers from Bristol was lodging at the same rooming house as he was. Joan was the daughter of his father's sister Emily Isobel and her husband Richard Withers. Richard was a member of the family the Warr's were in the forage and hay business with. She was born 02 February 1918, only a couple of months younger than Bert, and she was only 20 when she came to live in London. Just when Joan started lodging at the same address as Bert isn't clear but a good guess is that it was when he was at Mrs Burns rooms in Sutherland Avenue. It was definitely by April of 39 because Bert wrote home on April 21 that he, Joan and Rashbrook went to Hampstead Heath together. Rashbrook was Alfred Rashbrook known to one and all as "Tiny." Joan and Tiny were married in the afternoon of Saturday 16th of September 1940. The ceremony took place in between air raid warnings. The reception was held at a restaurant in London but Bert doesn't say where. The wedding and meal were both a huge success. There were 14 people at the reception meal. Their aunt Queen and Joan's brother Roy both came up from Bristol along with some other unnamed relatives and Rashbrook's family came down from Gloucester for the celebration as well. Presumably Joan and Tiny then left for a honeymoon but again Bert's letters don't say one way or the other.

The Withers seemed to have been very well off because Bert tongue in cheek wrote home 18 Febraury 1940 that "Joan Withers has returned to London after being away for two weeks. Only her spring holiday of course and quite exclusive of her summer ones." Bert, Joan and Tiny had many days out together exploring and enjoying the parks and countryside around London. After Tiny and Joan were married Rashbrook enlisted in the army and was eventually posted to a base near Maidenhead in Kent.It was the early days of the war and most young men were enlisting ion one branch of the military or another. In early June Joan left London and went to live in Maidenhead near Rashbrook's base so that she could be near him. That letter written on 6 June 1941 is the last time Bert mentions Joan or Tiny in any of his surviving letters. I do know that Joan and Tiny had two children but I don't know any other details about them. By that time Bert was only a few weeks away from enlisting himself and from the time he enlists his letters are mainly concerned with his training and leave etc. Bert also spent time with his Aunt Emily Isobel who was known as Queen. She came to London several times usually staying in Joan's rooms and had Bert down to her house in Pill, Bristol for Christmases and other holidays. Aunt Queen never married and lived alone in her cottage in the countryside near Bristol, close to the rest of the family. On her visits to London Bert and Joan kept her busy going to concerts and plays and visiting galleries etc. She seems to have loved her visits but was always happy at the end of her short two week breaks to be returning to the tranquil life that she enjoyed in the countryside.

In a sense, once Pinkus left for the RAF Bert was alone. He was still very much enjoying living his dream but he was not yet taking any courses and was working at a menial job where the prospects and social contacts were limited. True, his cousin Joan Withers was living in the same flats as Bert but really, she was a stranger. There is no mention of her in any of the surviving letters grandpa Warr got from his relatives back home so she was as much a stranger to Bert

and the family as she is to us all these years later. We have
no photographs of her either. In his letters home Bert for
his part does nothing to to enlighten the family as to what
Joan was like. He includes no descriptions of what she
looks like nor any of what her personality was like. Instead
he tells us of what Joan and Tiny were doing from time to
time especially if it involved him. He talks about trips to the
countryside that he took with Joan and Tiny and dinner
parties and breakfasts that they shared, but he gives us
nothing more.

This is true of Bert's letters in general. There is an aloofness
and an almost cold reporting style to his letter writing to his
family. From what he says we do get the sense that he cared
deeply for the family but there is a distance too. Affection
does come through sometimes in his letters when he writes
to his sisters especially Cecelia, the youngest but even then
there also seems to be a coolness, a lack of ability to express
deep feeling.

After Pinkus left, Bert was alone, a stranger in a strange
land. His one concrete link with home had been Pinkus.
Now he was on his own in the great city. He was still having
a great adventure but the loneliness of his life was also
weighing on him from time to time. Where Bert's letters let
us down in this regard we can still get a very good sense of
what Bert was feeling by turning to his poetry. He wrote
several poems in his early days in London that express his
feelings in ways that he was unable to in his letters home.
He had a sensitive soul, the soul of a poet and the best way
that we can now get to know him is through his poetry

The opening lines of the poem "In The Dark" written
around this time give us a glimpse of how Bert was feeling.

> *Many months ago in this city,*
> *Ears closed to me like faces folding,*
> *And I, as blood dashed from sudden wound,*
> *Appealed without a sound.*

We really get a sense of Bert's feelings of isolation and loneliness from these lines. The last line is especially telling I think. "I ... appealed without a sound." That would seem to seem to sum up Bert's social life in a nutshell. Mrs Nora Senjem who had known Bert almost since he first arrived in England as related in a letter Frank wrote to the family after Bert was killed, and after he had visited her tells us "I should like to collect all the details that I have of Bert, unfortunately this is very little, our mutual friends know less about him than I do. Everybody without exception liked him and appreciated him for his very decent and sweet nature. He was always very quiet in society and spoke very little." Bert it seems was as closed a book around his London acquaintances as he was in his letters home. The family were still sending the Star Weekly magazine to Bert on a regular basis and this was a very welcome link to Toronto and the family. He loved reading about the Toronto Maple Leafs his favourite ice hockey team in the NHL and the colour comics also seem to have been a favourite. Joan and Tiny also seemed to have loved those comics as did the landlady's young son. Bert wrote that on a Sunday morning the landlady would serve her lodgers their breakfasts in bed. After having eaten a hearty full English breakfast, traditionally consisting of fried eggs, bacon, english sausage, fried tomatoes and often blood pudding, he would relax and read the Star Weekly and the comics, while still in bed. Bert would send the comics in to Joan's room where she and Tiny were laying in bed also and they too would read the comics before sending them on to the landlady's young lad. Bert was certainly still enjoying living and studying in England but he was also at times at least feeling home sick and lonely. This really isn't surprising as in early 1939 Bert was not yet 21 years old. He was pretty much on his own, living thousands of miles away from home, in a place that although familiar was still strange. One time Bert went for a walk through Hyde Park which is one of the biggest and nicest parks in London a city noted for its parks. Bert ever eager to fly the flag of home and perhaps also feeling homesick wrote that "It's a nice treat to walk through

Hyde Park these days. It's not a bad place but High Park in Toronto has it beat by miles."

In contrast the letters that Frank sent home after he arrived in England in early 1943 are very warm and full of information about the people in his life. He talks openly and often of his friends and the family back home really engaging with their questions and answering them in terms we would expect in the letters from a loving son and brother to the folks back home. Getting to know Frank and Bert is of course impossible but through his letters it seems at least possible to catch more than a glimpse of who Frank was as a person more so than we get from from Bert's letters. Bert's letters and essays etc, tell us very little about Bert the man, focusing instead on Bert the intellectual. This is especially true of his essays. It is from Bert's poetry that we must try to catch glimpses of his feelings and who he was as a person.

Mrs Burns, Bert and Joan's landlady at Tadmark Street found herself struggling financially and was forced to sell up or abandon her flats there and move to a smaller holding at Lanark Mansions in Maida Vale, just around the corner from the EMI studios, which were to become famous as the recording studios the Beatles used for most of the 1960s. Bert and Joan moved with Mrs Burns to Lanark mansions. Mrs Burns was to remain Bert's landlady for the remainder of his short life. He stayed at her rooms every time he came to London after he joined the RAF too. They had a friendly relationship just as with Mrs Senjem, Mrs Burns seems to have taken Bert under her wing and been a bit of a mother hen to him. She would bring him breakfast in bed when he slept late on days off work and she looked after him when he had colds, which he seemed to have perpetually before he joined the RAF. For their part Bert and Joan when they had lunches, teas or dinners would often invite Mrs Burns to join them. It wasn't all smooth sailing though as at one point Bert and Joan staged a mini revolution when Mrs Burns announced that she would have to raise the rent. Bert and Joan were both outraged and refused to pay. This was during the blitz when there were plenty of empty apartment building buildings full of empty flats. Mrs Burns told them it was necessary because of the rising cost of gas and electricity. To which they both howled that that was not their problem. They must have gotten this issue resolved though because they both continued to live at Lanark Mansions and relations with Mrs Burns suffered no long-term damage because she continued to look after Burt and they still included her in their dinners

Bert continued to take his classes at Birkbeck all throughout that summer. One of the courses that he took was a literature course given by the well-respected poet Gwendolyn Murphy of whom Robert Graves was to write to Bert "I'm glad that you went to her class. She is no fool and humble and willing to learn from those who know."

It was at one of these courses, very probably Gwendolyn Murphy's, that Bert was to meet Patricia Ledward. Patricia, daughter of renowned sculpture Gilbert Ledward was a fellow student and would become a noted author, broadcaster, editor and a minor poet. The pair became became close friends for a time and also may have worked together for Favil Press the publishing company responsible for the "Resurgam" Younger Poets series an edition of which was published with 14 of Bert's poems in it. Bert and Patricia both had broadsheets published in that series by Favil Press in 1941. Bert never explicitly says so in his letters home but it is very probable that he and Patricia were more than just friends. In one letter home during the war he does say that Patricia is "chasing" him but that he has managed escape. He did not want to commit to any relationship during the uncertainty caused by the war. Who knows what would have been for Bert and Patricia had Bert lived through the war?

As that summer of 1939 rolled along, the last summer of peace before the second world war, there were increasing numbers of refugees fleeing the Nazi persecutions and terrors making their way to London. Bert volunteered to help at least one of these organisations. Between his

51

university connections and the connections he made amongst the refugees he soon found himself involved in London's world of art and culture. Bert spent many evenings at the home of his good friend Mrs Senjem. Mrs Senjem herself was a refugee. She had fled with her daughter from Hungary leaving behind her husband and her son. She would often have dinner parties and other gatherings of artists and intellectuals. It was at this time that Bert really began to become serious about his social beliefs. Bert's last youthful adventure wasn't ending but it was changing as Bert himself was changing. Bert was beginning believe it was not enough to hold Modernist views and to write Modernist poetry but it was also important to put those beliefs and views into practice. He was learning and beginning to become a serious thinker and writer. Much of Bert's ideology was picked up at college and he was no doubt also learning much more at Mrs Senjem's gatherings from the artists and other deep thinkers who attended. However a lot of what Bert was learning and writing about he was developing by looking inside and examining his own emotions, ideas and feelings. This introspection revealed a young man who cared deeply about the injustice and suffering of the downtrodden and working classes who had suffered so much under the years of the great depression. Bert was outraged by what he saw and looking around at the extreme wealth and seeming indifference of the ruling and upper classes of England was determined to use his poetry to try to help bring about at least some easing of the pain and suffering and a levelling of the playing field.

By mid-May of 1939 Bert had left Lyons Corner House and had begun the more agreeable work as a bookkeeper at the Whitstable Oyster Company. Although as we know Bert was not a fan of office work it was a step up from washing dishes and besides he finished work most days by noon which gave him plenty of time in the afternoons for writing and studying for his courses. Time which it seems that he used diligently. Bert's output of poems and essay from this time is the most prolific of his short life. Most of Bert's surviving poems and all but one or two of his work that was published during his lifetime date from the period between when he began taking university courses in London in the summer of 1939 and his very early RAF days in the summer of 1941.

Chapter 6: And War Begins

Unfortunately no letter's of Bert's have survived from the time between June and November 1939. So we don't know what his thoughts or actions were during the time directly leading up to and the start of the war in early September. What we can be sure of though is that Bert continued taking classes at university and pursued his writing and involvement with refugees groups and socialist organisations.

On September 01 Poland was invaded by Germany. Germany's stated reason for the invasion was to bring the German ethnic population of Poland and the free city of Danzig into the Reich but its real reason for the invasion was territorial expansion, a desire to dominate Europe and to become a real world empire. In a surprise move the USSR which had entered into a secret agreement with Nazi Germany attacked the Poles from the east. On the third of September Britain and France both having guaranteed that they would support Polish independence, delivered ultimatums to the German government demanding that the invasion be halted. The deadlines for these ultimatums passed with no comment from Germany, nor any cessation of the invasion, therefore both Britain and France declared war on Germany. In the following few days many other nations including, Australia, Canada and New Zealand quickly followed suite, declaring war on Germany themselves. The Second World War had begun and for the second time in less than 25 years the world found itself at war. At this point however these declarations of war by France and Britain were empty in themselves as the two nations could do very little to help the Polish. The Nazi invasion raced ahead and by the third week of September it was obvious that Poland could no longer resist the invaders as large sections of her country had already fallen to German troops. Poland formally surrendered on Sept 27 was divided between the Germans and the Soviets and was to be occupied by both of these for the next 5 plus years of the war.

All we know of Bert at this time was that he had thrown himself into his studies and his poetry. Raised as a Roman Catholic he had become sceptical and as we know had declared that he was agnostic and now he also considered himself to be a socialist, however he still wanted to see the principles of the New Testament taken seriously. He believed that it was the duty of the socialist poet to hold a mirror up to society showing it all of its failings and flaws, pointing the way to a better world, making men higher and finer and above all to help people keep a warm heart and open mind. Bert's honesty and humility also led him to reflect that "it is not so much the urge to create for art's sake which motivates me but rather the desire for success and honours … my desire is to become impervious to economic success."

Bert's idealism pushed him to try to write for all the right reasons, namely his beliefs. But being human he also couldn't help feel pride and satisfaction when he had work published and was recognised as an up-and-coming writer with great potential. Of course he also needed to eat and pay the rent and he wanted to be in a position to be able to support himself through his writing instead of having to work at office jobs. On the one hand he wanted to write for purely idealistic reasons and on the other hand he wanted to make enough money to write for a living. Most of all though Bert wanted his writing to matter. He wanted to make a difference through his poems and essays, to inspire people to action and to work for a better world. Poems such as his Working Class were meant to not only make people think but to move them to strive to make things better.

Bert's beliefs led him to a socialist outlook that the end of the war would usher in a new age, sweeping away all the dictators, profiteers and gangsters that he believed were running things not only in Germany but in the U.K and Russia as well. This idea of a sweeping change to usher in a new kinder gentler age to borrow a phrase from George W Bush, was something that a lot of socialists and communists of the time believed. Real change though rarely if ever sweeps in overnight. Human progress is slow and real deep and meaningful change takes time, decades if not hundreds and even thousands of years. We have become used to technological changes occurring at an ever faster pace but people can't change that fast and there is no way that our social and moral norms can keep pace with it. Certainly in the early 1940s technological change was not occurring as fast as it does now but the war effort definitely saw the beginning of this technological revolution.

Bert's idea of sweeping social changes after the war were idealistic and unrealistic but his beliefs that "we are fighting the war for the wrong reasons" was not entirely wrong. Britain not only declared war on Germany because of its moral obligation to safeguard the rights of the much smaller and weaker Poland against a much bigger and more powerful aggressor but also to safeguard its position on the world stage. Germany's real reason for the invasion was territorial expansion and acquisition of resources. Britain as well as wanting to help maintain Poland's independence, was interested in maintaining her position as a leading power in the world and ensuring that her empire remained strong and intact. In many ways Britain's part in the defeat of the Axis in WW2 was a Pyrrhic victory. Germany, Italy and Japan were ultimately defeated, regaining freedom for the many millions of peoples throughout the world who had been subjugated and enslaved by these powers but everything or almost everything else that Britain was fighting for she lost. He empire was broken up and she had piled up so much debt fighting the war that her status as a world power was greatly eroded. The end of the war ushered in an era of social justice and social awakening although not on the scale that Bert would have hoped for but at least enough so that countries such as India, Rhodesia and others were in a position to gain independence and self-government. The era of great empires and colonialism was ending and there was a growing realisation that the people of the so called third world had the same abilities and rights as the hitherto thought to be superior peoples of Western

Europe and America. Many people believe that the decay and erosion of Britain's empire actually began at the end of WW1 being caused by the heavy debt that she incurred fighting that war. That is probably true but one thing for sure is that the process was completed by the cost in money, resources and manpower of WW2.

However this was not evident in 1940 and the U.K. government continued to carry out their strategies for fighting the Nazis who were trying to muscle in on her place as a world power both economically and in terms of actual lands under her direct control. The Nazis however were not only trying to build an empire they were carrying out a program of extermination and enslavement of any and all whom they deemed racially inferior. The allies opposition to the axis was very much from the moral high ground more so than any desire to maintain the status quo.

In the winter of 1940 Bert's socialist ideas were becoming more entrenched and more formed and he began thinking of himself as a conscientious objector. In February he wrote that "The war goes merrily along. The politicians plead to the people to make sacrifices while they go on like a lot of Al Capones. This is just another big business racket and however just the cause these ghouls are only interested in filling their pockets." Bert may be correct in his assessment of the motives of the ruling classes and businessmen but the U.K. government and its people were also keenly aware of the atrocities being committed by the SS in the cities of Poland and there was a very real sense of moral outrage and a feeling that the war was being fought against a truly evil regime.

It was at this time that Bert became involved with a socialist publication titled "Free Expression." During the early stages of the war this group either came into existence or tried greatly to expand their very limited influence. They believed that the freedom of the individual was paramount and they were against all restrictions of personal freedom. They were especially opposed to the restrictions brought about by the Emergency Powers Act passed just before the outbreak of WWII. The Emergency Powers Act gave the U.K. Government special powers to take almost any action necessary to carry out the war successfully. In practice this meant that these powers controlled many aspects of everyday life during the war – including blackouts and food rationing.

Bert also became involved with the socialist/communist gathering called "The People's Convention." The People's Convention was a conference that was proposed by the Communist Party of Great Britain in 1940–1941. Its organisers attempted to convince the Labour Party and trade union members that the government was only for the rich and was dominated by those whose appeasement of Hitler had "caused" the Second World War, were opposed to the Soviet Union, and who were profiteering from the war. The conventions literature never explicitly came out and stated that the convention was communist backed but all the same it was pretty obvious that it was. Bert tried to attend a meeting of the convention in Manchester. As usual he had no money so he had to try to hitch -hike to the meeting. He couldn't get timely rides and had to give up and return to London and never did attend any of the groups meetings. Bert was socialist but he never was a communist. He thought that Stalin was just as evil as Hitler and he was just as opposed to Stain's regime as he was to Nazi Germany. Bert was equally convinced that members of the current U.K. government and others of the ruling class and big business were profiteering from the war. He believed that they needed to be stopped from making fortunes from the toils and misery of the common man.

Bert was more convinced than ever of the untrustworthiness of the press and its role as little more than a propaganda agent for the government. After all it's not for nothing that they say the first casualty of war is the truth. All of the warring nations used the press to put out propaganda to greater and lesser extents. Bert believed though that the British press in particular was a tool of the ruling class used to keep the workers down. When "Yet A Little Onwards", Bert's broadsheet of 14 poems, was published in 1941 the press got his personal details wrong, which of course did nothing to change his mind about them. The press clipping reads " Mr Bertram Warr, a 23 year old Canadian wrote the third and latest pamphlet. He calls it "Yes, A Little Onwards." (Note they even got the name of the broadsheet wrong substituting the word Yes for the word Yet) Mr Warr came to this country three years ago. His first job was as a dishwasher in a restaurant. He is now a member of an ambulance unit in London.

Bert makes no mention of the typo but he very strongly objects to the reporter writing that he served in an ambulance unit. "It is a horrid lie that I am serving in an ambulance unit. I intended to but was flung out the door wherever I applied."

These feelings about the press did not lessen and by the autumn of 1940 in the heat of the Blitz, Bert was still commenting in letters home about how the press, especially the American press were greatly exaggerating the destruction being caused by the German bombs in London.

In spite of this mistrust of the press Bert made frequent trips to Canada House, then the Canadian High Commission, now the Canadian Embassy located in Trafalgar Square London, to read the Canadian newspapers. Apart from letters from home this was the best way catch up with the news of what was happening back home. Bert's visits to Canada House to read the papers also allowed him to catch up with news about his beloved Toronto Maple Leafs. In the early months of Bert's arrival in England he quite often writes home about how the Leafs are doing in the league and in the playoffs but as he becomes more politically aware and active his interest in sport seems to vanish. Or maybe it was just that the war made caring about hockey and the Leafs a very low priority. Certainly as Bert developed his socialist ideas and as his feelings of being a conscientious objector on political grounds grow we hear no more about the Leafs. Bert's time was taken up by more important things than sports and boyhood teams and dreams. His political ideas, his writing and of course the war were the focus of his life now. The last we read about the Leafs in Bert's letters is in a letter that Bert wrote home about a BBC broadcast on the 9th of April. The BBC had broadcast a recording of the NHL playoff hockey game between the Toronto Maple Leafs and the New York Rangers. The broadcast was especially for Canadian troops already stationed in Britain. The match featured the iconic Foster Hewitt calling the play by play. Bert wrote that it was like old times hearing Foster call out his "he shoots he scores" catch phrase. It must have been a bittersweet experience for Bert sitting alone in his room listening to a voice so deeply connected to home and family. This is the last time that Bert mentions hockey or the Leafs in any of his surviving letters. Life for Bert was becoming to serious for such things as sports. The Maple Leafs were part of his old, last exciting youthful adventure which he was now leaving behind for the serious literary intellectual that he was becoming.

By March Bert's feelings had grown even stronger and he declared he was "now a socialist and against the war as it is for capitalist profits only. " And in somewhat dramatic fashion he declared " I should prefer to shoot Chamberlain and company as there is not one public figure in whom I have the slightest trust." Censorship could not have been in effect at this time or at least not very effectively yet because that is the sort of statement, tongue in cheek though it was, that would elicit a rasing of eyebrows in official circles and probably occasion a visit from the plain clothes boys. In fact Bert does get a visit from one of these fellows at a later date in connection with another letter but more about that later. He continues in the same letter "Am officially opposed on political grounds, so will not fight. The ruling class here is rotten but I thought it worthwhile using their army in my personal fight against the horrible huns! But I have made up my mind that killing Germans was a silly way to solve the problem. I am the only unit of the British Empire which is officially not at war."

Bert laid out his thoughts and feelings about the war in two unpublished essays. They were both written in the early months of the war when Bert was still wrestling with his conscience as to what role he would play, if any in the conflict. The first was probably written before he had decided not to go back home. It is very short and is untitled. In it Bert lays out his feelings about the war.

He declares that from an intellectual point of view he is against fighting in the war because "we are not guided by ethics." He believes the war is a struggle for power between "the old intolerant champion," England and the challenger, the Nazis. He admits though that his emotions, ironically spurred on by the very press and newspapers that he so mistrusts would lead him through an "unreasoning impulse to rush out as a crusader for right. I do not condemn my emotions. Their case is strong enough. Nazism is evil and its final abolition for ethical reasons is justifiable cause for the war." He resists these impulses to action though and maintains his intellectual position as a conscientious objector. Bert was perplexed by the British governments attitude towards the Soviet Union. "Why does the British government seek friendship with Russia? To Russia the partner in crime of Poland we extend the hand of friendship. Even after Poland, there came the crime of Finland and still we have no cause for friction with Russia. In Russia much more so even than in the Germany of Hitler, the blood purge has been employed to mould the nation into a unit. It is a fact that more people have been killed in Russia since the Third International assumed power, than have been killed in Germany since the coming of Hitler." This essay was written before Hitler launched Operation Barbarossa, the invasion of Soviet Russia on the 22 June 1941 so Bert's confusion is certainly understandable. On the one hand Britain is putting itself forward as a champion of virtue and democracy and on the other hand the British government is maintaining relations with one of the worst regimes in the world from the point of view of human rights. Bert declares "the position of the altruist, is therefore difficult. Conscious bidden he goes out to defend the right, but in order to carry out his task he is forced to ally himself with, and become the exploited instrument of a power whose motives he must as a lover of justice abhor. His position, together with the that of his fellows in the army, is simply that of a misguided fool. And is this not one of the damndest (sp) blackest tragedies of the war."

He carries on with a sobering thought that may very well be true of all military organisations past present and future. "The army itself embodies the spirit of Nazism. Have we not the same blind surrender of freedom of will, the will disciplined to the dictates of the Books of Regulations." He then extends this reasoning to embody the ruling of the state. "We may argue reasonably, that since such a system is proved of most efficiency in our own country in the fighting forces, a unit where the utmost cohesion is essential, then the same system, extended to the nation, should produce a similar efficiency in operation, and increased potentiality of each individual as part of the nation under a common discipline. Thus it must be considered whether or not in the Totalitarian State we do see evidence of the workings of evolution." Bert finishes this line of thinking with a thought that I think most of us can heartily agree with. He declares this "A sobering thought indeed."

The second essay was written sometime later, after Bert had taken his initial stand as a conscientious objector. This essay titled "Why I Object" begins with an explanation by Bert as to why he is in general against war and ends with his attempts to explain why he is specifically against taking direct action in this war. This essay expands on the ideas developed in the first essay. In it Bert works through the idea that all life is a struggle and not just during wartime but all the time. He believes that two kinds of people fare badly in this struggle especially during wartime, the virtuous man and the coward. He admits to being afraid of going to war and dying but he knows that this is not his overriding reason

62

for not going to war. We know that he did not lack for courage and he knew it too. His reasons for not going to war are more aligned to those of the virtuous; his belief in the corrupt nature of the ruling class and the government. He says that " I can look dispassionately at the lying presses, listen to the smoothing oil and large hypocrisies of the old men who rule, and consolidate my position with regard to what they represent. I hate them for their insincerity and greed, and acknowledge with awe the immense inhumanity of their dealings with the people. I see then the division between the nation and its leaders."

He carries on somewhat naively about the virtues of the masses "The decent idealism of the mass, geared to sacrifice and effort for good, exhorted and whipped into new energies contrasts itself with the desires of those men who seek only for selfish gain through their energies." As we well know there are more than enough people in the masses who along the lines of the business elite and the ruling classes equally act with only thoughts of selfish gain. Bert was still only 23 at this time and he was still to learn the harsh reality that greed and acting in self-interest are not the exclusive properties of those with high social status and financial security, however that may be, at this time Bert was deeply affected by his beliefs and acted in good faith to follow them by declaring himself a socialist and a conscientious objector. I get the feeling with both essays that they were written perhaps as much to work through and clarify his thoughts and feelings to himself as they were to any potential reader. This may be especially true as neither of these essays was ever published.

Note: In order that the reader may get as full a picture as possible and decide for themselves, as much as they can, about, Bert's motivations for becoming a conscientious objector transcripts of both of these unpublished essays can be found in Appendix VII. However when reading these one must bear in mind that the fullest picture that we can obtain of Bert's stance must include his comments from his surviving letters. For that the reader will be limited to my interpretations of these as the letters are far to numerous too reprint in full here.

Chapter 7 Bert Begins to be Noticed

That winter of 1940 was the calm before the storm. The U.K. was at war with Germany but there was not yet a lot of action involving British forces. That doesn't mean however that there wasn't a lot going on. In November in a blatant bid at expansion the USSR invaded Finland in what became known as the winter war. The Fins fought valiantly but ultimately fruitlessly as they were hopelessly outnumbered. After inflicting many heavy defeats on the huge but badly organised Soviet forces Finland was forced to surrender on 13 March 1940.

In January of 1940 the UK government introduced rationing of food. Bert wrote that "everyone has a ration book which consists of little tickets torn off by the by the person from whom we buy the rationed goods. Thus when you buy a meal in a restaurant the cashier takes one ticket from your ration book." Disillusioned by the leadership though he was, Bert was still very patriotic in his way and willing to do his bit to defeat the evil of the Nazis. Bert's description of rationing continues " A very good system. O well it's all for good old liberty and democracy, I suppose, I hope I hope I hope." Not entirely convinced that the best interests of liberty and democracy were being served by the leadership in another letter he wrote that people were "Starving for butter. Grocers can't get supplies from big business. It's a racket, one of many."

Rationing was introduced as a direct result of shortages caused by the what came to be known as the Battle Of The Atlantic. The United Kingdom required more than a million tons of imported food and other materials per week to survive. The Battle of the Atlantic pitted the German U-Boats, surface ships and Luftwaffe aircraft against the heavily protected conveys of Allied shipping. The North Atlantic conveys were protected by war ships and aircraft of Britain, Canada and the U.S.A. The Battle Of The Atlantic ran from virtually the start of the war in September 1939 until the defeat of the Nazis in May 1945 making it the longest continuous campaign of the entire war. At the height of the battle in June of 1942 the Germans were sinking upwards of 124 allied merchant vessels per month. This total gradually decreased as the Allied navies and airforces gained the upper hand and by June of 1943 the germans were sinking only an average of 4 ships per month and losing a large number of U-Boats to the improved naval escort system. The Canadian navy became specialist at U-Boat tracking and sinking using their large number of Corvette anti submarine ships which were extremely effective at finding and sinking the German U-Boats. By the end of the war Canada had the 4th largest navy in the world and most of its ships were specialised for use against submarines.

During the Blitz and the winter of 1940 Bert continued to take classes at university and he continued to write poetry. By now the literary world was starting to notice him. He had several poems printed in the Poetry Quarterly and two of his poems, "War Widow" and "The Heart To Carry On" were included in the anthology "Poems Of The Forces" that noted poet Henry Treece was publishing.

In September of 1940 a broadsheet of 14 of Bert's poems was printed and sold for one shilling, which was about 5 pence. He wasn't about to get rich but he was being noticed. His publisher sent several of his poems to the noted writer Robert Graves. Graves was impressed and wrote to Bert saying " It was a great pleasure in times like these to know that there was another poet about. As you must be aware it is always a small number. So to find your poems was a great pleasure. I shall tell the other poets about them." Graves wanted to bring Bert into his literary circle and suggested that Bert get in touch with a friend of Grave's, Alan Hodge who worked in Whitehall and with whom Graves worked on books.

Graves finishes his second and last letter to Bert with the sentence "Please send me poems whenever." However Bert never contacted Graves again and he wrote home that he lost the contact details of Grave"s friend Alan Hodge. So even though he had wanted to could not contact him. Clearly this is not true because Hodge's contact details are included in Grave's second letter the original of which still exists amongst Bert's papers. Mary Connolly said that Bert did not keep in contact with Graves because Bert wanted to maintain independence from any group. This explanation doesn't ring entirely true either. I think there is another reason that Bert didn't carry on his correspondence with Graves. One of Bert's literary heroes was the World War I poet Wilfred Owen. Graves knew Owen personally and in his second letter to Bert Graves spoke poorly of Owen and said that "if he had lived I would have had to break off my friendship with him just as I did with Siegfried Sassoon."

For Graves to write disparagingly about Wilfred Owen and Sassoon as well, was probably just too much for Bert to take and more than enough for Bert to not want to have anything more to do with him. Owen was one of Bert's most cherished poetry heroes. He also thought very highly of Sassoon. In one of his university notebooks Bert wrote that "Owen and Sassoon were the two great poets produced by the war."

In a letter home dated 25 April 1941 Bert, ever mindful of mentoring his sister Mary wrote "Has Mary read Wilfred Owen Yet. He is miles above Rupert Brooke. Tell her to compare an anthology of the last war with this one. The poets last time were not at all socially knowing. They groped about not understanding the place of war in history. This time they know but I must admit it doesn't make them write very good stuff."

This quote is interesting for a number of points. first of all it would seem that one of the things that Bert admired most about Owen was that his poetry was helping to shape and evolve poetry into the modernist style. Owen was a poet whose graphic descriptions of the horrors of war did much to help advance poetry into the modernist style that Bert was a disciple of. Wilfred Owen was one of the best British

67

poets of the first world war. He was a lieutenant in the Lancashire Fusiliers and served in France from december 1916 until his death. He was killed in November 1918 just one week before the armistice. Most of his poems were published posthumously and his reputation grew steadily after the Great war.

The second thing that stands out about this excerpt is that Bert thought that although many modern poets may be themselves adherents of the modernist style most of them were not very good. That is a sentiment shared by Robert Graves when he writes to Bert that it was a pleasure finding out that there is another poet about and that at any given time there are not that many truly good poets about.

Bert's poem "Poets In Time Of War" is a poem that Bert dedicated to Wilfred Owen and its inclusion by Bert's editor among the poems that he sent to Robert Graves and Graves response to its inclusion is what led Bert to turn his back on Robert Graves.

> *Poets In Time Of War*
> *(In Memory Of Wilfred Owen)*
>
> *Poets, who in time of war*
> *Divide in visionary horror*
> *Soul's dream from body's missions*
> *Knowing a holier connections*
> *Than the will to destruction*
> *Compelling the boy in arms to kill his broither*
>
> *All who tell the grave story*
> *Of love, the sad esentialiality*
> *Of pain, whom no bitterness*
> *Bars from life's true lovliness*
> *Whose words are a tenderness*
> *Of hands, caressing maimed humanity*

Spirits who dream and move onward
Leaving to us your dreams gathered
And resounding forever in the air-
O, believe us this bodily despair
Stuns not our spirits, for there,
Serenely, our visionary heritage has flowered

In any event, whatever the reason, Bert did not maintain contact with Robert Graves and his circle. Bert seemed determined to go his own way and remain true to his principles and his conscience.
He carried on taking courses at university and working with the various refugee and socialist organisations that he was involved with. Even as the Blitz carried on night after night as the Luftwaffe tried desperately to destroy the RAF and pave the way for the German invasion of England. In a letter home dated 16 Sept 1940 Bert wrote that "For the last four nights the anti-aircraft guns have fired almost the whole night through. It is one continual roar of guns mingled with the duller boom of bombs as as they fall."

He carries on as if that wasn't really anything out of the ordinary and adds the description of of his cousin Joan's wedding as mentioned above. "Joan and Tiny were married on Saturday (Saturday 14th September 1940) in between air raid alarms. It was a successful wedding. Aunt Queen and Roy, Joan's brother, came up from Bristol, and Rashbrook's parents from ColchesterAfter the ceremony we all tripped to a restaurant where a meal had been ordered for the whole fourteen of us. It was good, chicken etc. Have just heard a bomb come whistling down some distance away, but it must have been either a dud or a time bomb because it did not explode. The noise gives me a headache. It starts every night at about eight and ends about four in the morning." Bert ever ready to avoid the dull office routine of work finishes with "We do our sleeping when we can, go to work hours late in the morning and leave early, which is good."

Through the air raids of the blitz Bert continued his work at the oystery although at times this was a challenge. In the

69

building where he worked all the glass in the windows was blown out by a bomb that had blown up very close to the building. Bert had to work bundled up in his winter coat and hunkered down against the cold and rain pouring as the wind whipped them in through the broken windows, picking bits of glass out of the ledgers.

Life and work carried on in spite of the Luftwaffe raids. "They just began to repair the place today. Numbers of buildings in the vicinity were destroyed, it looks like war torn Spain. There is not much night life as everyone goes home early to sleep. Which is what I shall try to do now if the guns will stop for a few minutes. When I got back here to the flat in the afternoon of Monday the area was roped off as the police believed a time bomb had landed nearby. Everyone was evacuated and I went to a school for the night." In the true spirit of the Blitz Bert finishes this letter with the plucky fighting spirit we associate with this time. "Don't worry again as it is not half as bad as the American papers portray it. We just adapt ourselves to the new inconveniences." And perhaps more to reassure his family than anything else he finishes "No one is very upset and I am well and functioning."

On November 19 1939 Bert wrote home that "This week we must all register with a grocer for rationing of butter and bacon (which is eaten here in vast quantities and cannot be bought at a butcher store only at a grocers)." Everyone had to register for rationing at this time in spite of rationing not officially beginning until January 1940. In reality rationing doesn't seem to actually have come into effect, at least not for meat, until March. In a letter home dated March 10 1940 Bert wrote "Tomorrow rationing begins here. We are allowed 1/10 worth of meat in a week. That is enough for me as I only have Sunday dinner in the flat here and the rest of the time I eat bacon or sausages or something. Sausages are not rationed yet so we can eat all we want." He carries on in another letter written during the heart of the London Blitz "Starting tomorrow, the butter ration becomes 1/2 lb. instead of the meagre four ounces which has had to satisfy us until now. So many people are using margarine instead at 16 or 20 cents per lb that butter which sells at 35 cents per lb has been ignored and large stocks have accumulated." Somewhat humorously he adds "The margarine is not bad if eaten quickly so that you haven't time to taste it."

As the German attacks on the supply convoys began to bite, availability of meat has gone downhill drastically from Bert's initial optimistic report in March. "The meat situation is horrible. Instead of butcher's windows being crammed with great juicy looking roasts and steaks and chops, you see only plates of bilious looking insides of cows, old hunks of stewing meat, and a few scrawny looking chickens. Fowl are not rationed and turkey can be bought at about thirty cents a lb. Yesterday for dinner I splurged 40 cents on roast mutton and suet pudding. There was lots of it but that was the only point in its favour. All the taste had been boiled out of the meat, I suppose in the process of making it less leathery." The Germans were determined to starve Britain out and deny the British the supplies necessary to carry on the war. Using a combination of U-boats, aircraft and surface vessels the Germans kept a constant pressure on the convoys attempting to cross the Atlantic from Canada and the U.S. For their part their allies were just as determined to get the convoys through and adopted better and more effective tactics for convoy escorts. But in those dark days of the early 1940s the convoy losses were huge.

Rationing and constant nightly bombing along with the stress of worrying about the impending German invasion of Britain began to sap the spirit of Londoners. However demoralising as the meat rationing situation had become all was not bad on the rationing front. Bert wrote that "Oranges are very cheap here. Big ones cost only about 20 cents a dozen so occasionally I purchase one orange. "

In fact fruit and veg were never rationed but there were shortages of these especially anything that had to be shipped in from overseas. The government introduced a scheme designed to encourage people to grow their own vegetables wherever possible. The scheme became known as "Dig For Victory." Even so at the height of war and during the hardest times there were often long queues outside grocery stores as people lined up to try to collect their weekly rations. Often a person, usually a housewife, but occasionally a single man such as Bert would get to the front of the line after a long time spent queuing only to find out that the item they were lining up for had just run out, frustratingly leaving them to have to turn around and go home to try again tomorrow.

Under the rationing system each household had to register with only one grocer and could use their tickets in this shop only. When purchasing a rationed item along with the money the person had to give the grocer a ticket from the book. The same system was used in restaurants although it was not necessary to register with a particular restaurant so you could still eat where ever you wished on that score.

Germany relied heavily on Swedish iron ore for manufacturing the vast war machine that their armed forces ran on. In a bid to secure a safe trade route for this the Germans invaded Norway and Denmark on April 09. The British and French sent troops to Norway but they were really only token forces and the Norwegians were forced to surrender on June 10. The victory meant that the Germans had secured this much needed rich source of Swedish iron and a relatively safe route to bring these supplies into the Reich.

On the ninth of May the Germans launched their long anticipated attack and invaded France through the neutral countries of Holland and Belgium. The speed and organisation of the attack caught the French completely unprepared and their armies and those of the British were quickly overwhelmed and defeated. The British forces retreated to the coast near the port of Dunkirk were in one of the most daring operations of the war they were evacuated to the safety of home. Between the 26th of May and the 4th of June 336,000 British and allied troops were evacuated from the port and the beaches of Dunkirk and across the channel to the safety of England where they lived to fight another day.

On the 12th of May Bert writes that they all now have to carry gas masks wherever they go.
After Dunkirk the people of England, including Bert expected the Germans to invade at any time and sooner rather than later. Hitler did indeed plan to invade Britain and was building up an invasion force and the ships to carry it across the channel. Hitler's planned invasion of Britain was codenamed Operation Sea lion. Before he could put Sea lion into operation though Hitler wanted to have mastery of the skies over the channel and the U.K. itself. With that goal the Luftwaffe launched their bombing campaign that would rage throughout the summer and would go down in history known as the Battle Of Britain. Initially the Luftwaffe concentrated their attacks against RAF airfields, aircraft factories and radar stations. The Luftwaffe came very close to achieving their goal when they switched from primarily trying to cripple the RAF to terror bombing of British civilians. This switch in tactics was one of the luckiest things that occurred for the British in this early part of the war. The change in targets was designed by Hitler to cause wide spread disruption, confusion and chaos in London leading to a mass evacuation of the British capital. Hitler hoped that in this way he could force the British to agree to an armistice, ending British participation in the war and therefore eliminating the need to invade the island. This change in tactics proved to be a huge blunder and gave the RAF a much needed respite and allowing them to recover. In fact this change in Luftwaffe targets ended any hope that the Germans would attain the air supremacy over British skies and now neither the forced armistice that Hitler preferred over invasion nor invasion itself were realistic goals. In truth the ideas of a forced armistice was never realistic in any event. The British had no intention of entertaining any such thing at any time. By Oct 1940 Operation Sea Lion was postponed indefinitely. Churchill never seriously worried about the Germans actually

invading. He believed that a cross channel seaborne
invasion of Britain by the Germans was always beyond their
capability to carry out successfully. Churchill was happy to
have the people believe that invasion could come at anytime
believing that it kept them on their toes and in a high state
of readiness for whatever was actually to come. Of course
the people didn't know this however and all through the
summer months they waited anxiously and more than a little
nervelessly for the invasion.

Writing home Bert, somewhat tongue in cheek but with a
note of the seriousness and worry about the future that
everyone in Britain was feeling at the time, that he was now
taking a course at college in German in order to be able to
welcome Hitler properly when he arrives. It seems though
that as worried as the people were about being invaded that
the picture we have been handed down of the feelings of the
time are correct and that for the most part people did indeed
keep calm and carry on. Bert writes that every Tuesday he
goes to the Globe Theatre where Alec Guinness or some
other celebrity holds a poetry reading. He also went to
Swanley with Mrs Senjem and her daughter for a day out.
Mrs Senjem was also living in the flats at Lanark Mansions
and that is how he met her and her daughter, they were
neighbours. It may have been primarily through Mrs
Senjem and her connections to the refugees that Bert got
involved with that group of intellectuals and artists that
were so influential on him.

As the summer wore on the invasion which always seemed
imminent never happened. The Luftwaffe never were able
to gain the air superiority over the RAF that Hitler deemed
necessary before the invasion could take place. Without
absolute control of the skies the invasion forces in the
barges would be sitting ducks to the RAF fighter and
bombers.

Giving up on his planned forced armistice with or invasion
of Britain, Hitler let the Luftwaffe change its tactics and in
September the Luftwaffe began bombing London and the

other big cities of Britain in the terror bombing campaign that became known as the Blitz. Of course the people of Britain didn't know of the postponement of the invasion. Bert wrote on 9th of September that they expected the invasion tomorrow. As much as he disliked and mistrusted the government his patriotism and desire to see the evil of Nazism defeated prompted him to close that letter with the desperate "We expect to be invaded tomorrow, doubt if it will succeed, I hope, I hope, I hope."

The invasion never happened and by October Hitler put Operation Sea Lion on hold indefinitely. Hitler now planned on beating the Soviets first before turning and dealing with Britain. He wanted to deal with bolshevism which he hated almost as much as he hated the jews. He planned on invading the USSR in the spring of 1941 and had his generals make plans accordingly. He would turn and deal with Britain once the USSR was beaten and annexed to the Reich. Hitler and his generals had convinced themselves that they could inflict total defeat on the Soviets quickly and decisively. They had a total disdain for the ability of the read Army who they believed to be badly trained, badly equipped and led by generals even worse. And of course the Germans believed themselves racially superior to the Russians and therefore able to walk over their sub human inferior troops. That idea was of course nonsense. That would be a lesson the Nazis would soon learn and suffer much in the learning of it.

The Germans were well aware of the fate of Napoleon's Grand Armee outside Moscow but they decided the same fate wouldn't happen to them if they were clever and could envelope and destroy Russia's armies close to the frontiers. Of course no such thing happened. The Germans did inflict heavy defeats on the Soviet forces, took hundreds of thousands of prisoners and were able to push their invasion forward to Moscow. The Soviets two things in overwhelming abundance, a huge population and vast amounts of land. So of course in the end the same fate awaited the Germans as awaits any army foolish enough to fight a land war in Asia and they were ultimately utterly defeated. In spite of the Germans racial superiority they were ultimately soundly beaten by the sub human forces from Asia. Proving once and for all that ideas of one race being superior to another are pure nonsense. Of course this is a lesson still being learned today over and over again from Rwanda and South Africa with Apartheid to the USA with racial segregation to Palestine where the conflicts between the Israelis and Palestinians still rage and many, many other places around our world.

Bertram Warr: This is the photo that Bert had professionally taken in London shortly before he was killed

Bert and Frank late 1930s

Frank Warr: Rare colour photo of Frank. Date unknown but he looks very young

Bert and Frank: Circa 1920s

Bert looking cool in sunglasses and braces.

Frank and Al Hymus with unknown girl skiing. Frank was
very sporty. He skied, played golf, tennis and many other
sports.

Frank in a row boat looking somewhat uncomfortable in
suite and tie

Aunt Queen circa 1920s. Aunt Queen was Bert's father's sister. She lived in the district of Pill on Bristol and had Bert down to her house for holidays. She also used to often visit Joan and Bert in their flats at Lanark Mansions in Maida Vale London.

Bert's sister, my Aunt Mary: Mary was devoted to Bert and worked diligently to get a book of his poetry published. Acknowledgement to Life was published in 1970 ensuring that Bert's legacy lives on. The date this photo was taken is unknown but it was probably taken in the late 1940s or the early 1950s

Frank and the Warr "Glamour Girls" as he teasingly referred to his three eldest sisters. L-R Marjory, Frank, Emily and Mary. The date of this photo is unknown but must be sometime in late winter of 1942 because there is snow on the ground Frank has been in the RCAF long enough to have earned his sergeants stripes, which are clearly visible in the photo.

Frank and his mother Mary Teresa Warr winter of 1942 during Frank's aircrew training at Malton airport. Frank would ship out for over seas a few months later in September and was killed on Oct 02 1943 flying his one and only op as a navigator in a wellington with RCAF 424 squadron out of North Africa.

Frank training for aircrew Malton airport. L-R Willy Wilson, "General Grant" and Frank. General Grant was Frank's best friend in the airforce and the two shipped out together for duty overseas.

Frank his childhood friend Al Hymus. Hymus grew up with both Bert and Frank. He joined the army and was in England at the same time that Frank was. There two spent an almost comical amount of time trying to meet up. They finally managed a visit during the August bank holiday weekend of 1943 when they were able to spend a couple of days together palling around. It was to be the last time they would see each other.

Halifax MKII with 158 Squadron's designation of NP and the call sign of N for November. This was the type of aircraft that Bert flew all of his combat operations in. Note the rudder with the pointed leading edge. This is what caused the aircraft to go into uncontrollable rolls when the pilot went hard over rudder often resulting in fatal crashes.

Halifax Bomb Aimer position: As the aircraft approached the target the bomb aimer lay prone looking out through the perspex nose cone through his bomb aiming scope. He would direct the pilot to the target via radio intercom and once over the target give the signal to drop the bombs. At this point an automatic camera would fire off taking a photo of where the bombs landed. Until the camera had flashed the aircraft had to remain flying straight and true over the target and this presented the ack-ack and night fighters with a plum target.

The wreckage of Bert's Halifax DT635 NP-F. The aircraft was shot down by Major Werner Strieb flying a Messerschmidt BF109 for his third kill of the night April 03 1943. On crashing the aircraft broke in two at its mid section. The front of the aircraft hit the ground so hard that identification of the three bodies in the nose was not possible.

So violent was the crash of Bert's aircraft that the pilot Dennis Cole was thrown clear of the aircraft and through the roof of this neighbouring barn where his body was found still strapped into his seat.

A page from Bert Bert's flight logbook late March 1943 listing 6 training flights and 3 combat flights flown. Note the combat missions are shown in red and were flown to targets in Nurnberg, Stuttgart and Berlin.

Photographed on board
R.M.S. "QUEEN MARY."

Grandma Warr and my mom, Cecilia (Babs) on the Queen
Mary in 1948 on their way to England for a holiday and to
meet with John Gawsworth about his progress or rather lack
of, in getting a book of Bert's poems published.

Grandma Warr in mourning for Bert and Frank, "her boys"

Bertram Howard Warr, my grandpa, circa 1950s with
Skippy the family dog

The 158 Squadron memorial on the edge of the old runway
at the site of RAF Lissett Yorkshire

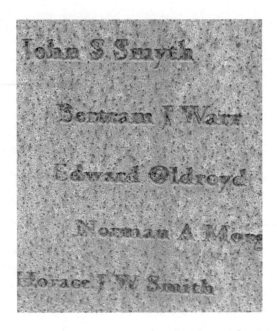

Closeup view of Bert's name on the 158 Memorial at Lissett
Yorkshire. 158 Squadron lost 851 men during the course of
the war which of course is 158 backwards.

Chapter 8: Bert Takes A Stand

On May 10th Neville Chamberlain resigned and was replaced as Prime Minister by Winston Churchill. In a letter home Bert related the change in PM "the old wolf Chamberlain has crawled halfway out the door at last. He is still cluttering up the place though as leader of the Conservative party. Churchill is held in good repute by the man in street chiefly because he makes fighting speeches like Hitler. I am trying to discover some other reason for his fame." Churchill did indeed make rousing inspiring speeches. On his first address to parliament after becoming P.M. he made his famous blood and sweat speech.

"I have nothing to offer but blood, toil, tears, and sweat. You ask, what is our policy? I will say: It is to wage war, by sea, land and air, with all our might and with all the strength that God can give us; to wage war against a monstrous tyranny, never surpassed in the dark and lamentable catalogue of human crime. That is our policy. You ask, what is our aim? I can answer in one word: Victory. Victory at all costs—Victory in spite of all terror— Victory, however long and hard the road may be, for without victory there is no survival."

Several days later Churchill made another of his famous rousing speeches remembered now mostly for these lines.

"We shall fight on the beaches, we shall fight on the landing grounds, we shall fight in the fields and in the streets, we shall fight in the hills; we shall never surrender."

Churchill made this speech on June 10th once it became obvious that the battle for France was lost and just 8 days before the French signed the armistice with the Nazis. Rousing stuff indeed. And while Churchill may also to have been one of the Al Capone's that Bert so loathed, the lines from his speech to parliament "a monstrous tyranny never surpassed in the dark and lamentable catalogue of human crime" show that Churchill was equally aware of, and felt

the moral responsibility to defeat the Nazis that Bert
believed was the only valid reason for war.

 All through these tense summer months of 1940, Bert
wrestled with his conscience. Initially he decided to go back
home to Canada. His first thought was to try to get back
home, acting as a chaperon to children who were to be
evacuated from the U.K. to Canada ahead of the invasion.
As the summer wore on however and the invasion didn't
happen this plan was never enacted. Many children from
wealthy families were evacuated but that was paid for by
their families and there was never any general overseas
evacuation of children from less affluent families. A plan to
evacuate as many children as possible from cities was
carried out. These evacuations were to villages and farms
within the U.K. however and not for any locations overseas.

By August the bombings of London began and what became
known as the London Blitz had begun. The Blitz had a very
profound effect on Bert. As he witnessed more and more of
the suffering caused by the bombing, Bert's compassion and
his ideas of social justice led him to change his mind about
going back to Canada. At the end of October 1940 he wrote
"I feel I should stay here now and help the people who are
suffering under the bombing. It would be unfair to leave just
now when I can be of use in a difficult time." This must
have been a very difficult time for Bert as he wrestled with
his conscience. On the one hand he was completely against
joining the military and fighting for the corrupt ruling class
of Britain. But Bert was desperate to do his bit to help end
the Nazi evil, especially the terror bombing of the Blitz
which was causing so much suffering among the working
class of the country. Bert's solution was a compromise. He
would try and join the Red Cross or a London Ambulance
crew. That way he would be helping the war cause but he
would not be fighting for the corrupt government and he
wouldn't have to join a military unit.

We don't know how Bert celebrated his 23rd birthday on
Dec 07 1941. The Japanese marked the occasion by

bombing the American fleet at Pearl Harbour, sinking 4
battleships and damaging 4 others. All the battleships were
later raised and returned to service apart from the USS
Arizona. The attack also damaged or sank three cruisers and
three destroyers. 180 American aircraft were also destroyed.
2,403 Americans were killed and a further 1,178 were
wounded. President Franklin Roosevelt, in his address to
the American people the next day said the day would live in
infamy. The British and the Americans both declared war on
Japan on December 8th. The British declared war because
the Japanese had also attacked the British colonies in
Malaysia and Singapore. Germany and Italy declared war
on the US on December 11th, bringing the US into the war
in Europe, which of course ultimately ensured the defeat of
the Axis powers. The US probably would have been drawn
into the European war in any event, but this rash act by Italy
and Germany ensured it happened sooner rather than later
thereby sowing the seeds of their own destruction by
awakening the sleeping giant that of the U.S. industrial
might. The U.S. had already been sending a lot of military
aid to England through the lend lease program but now they
would gear the majority industrial output and huge
population to fighting and winning the war. For Hitler and
the Axis powers it was only a matter of time. The only
possible way that they could now win would be to win the
race to build the atomic bomb, but Germany was hopelessly
behind in that race. Hitler put more stock in the rockets of
the V1 and V2 programs and jet aircraft than he did in
building an atomic bomb. The V weapons and jets could of
course make a difference but they were not game winners.
That dubious distinction would be left to the atomic
weapons; a single one which could destroy an entire city.

Still convinced that fighting for the bunch of Al Capones in
the British government would be wrong Bert tried to carry
out his plan to try to join the Red Cross or an ambulance
crew. Fate had other plans for Bert though. When he
attempted to join ambulance crews in London he wrote " I
was flung out the door wherever I applied." This was
because he was physically fit and of military age.

Bert was still determined to help and when he was notified in mid-January 1941 that we has to be conscripted for military duty he decided to accept this fate and go and fight. Bert's conscientious objector stand was very complicated. His pacifism was not based around the idea of the sanctity of life it was very much more a political stance. He believed very strongly that the Nazis were evil and had to be stopped. What Bert objected to was that the people in charge in the United Kingdom were not fighting the Nazis based around any ethical or moral reasons for stopping the them. They were fighting purely for capitalism and the continuation of empire which would maintain the status quo. The rich and the ruling class would continue to get richer and continue to rule on the backs of the working class man who was having to bear the brunt of the fighting and yet not receiving any benefit. Bert wanted to see an end to this. So he decided that he wouldn't fight for the politicians and ruling class. He would fight to help end the suffering of the common folk and to help bring about the social changes he believed were necessary and now thought could only be achieved through winning the war. In his essay about the war as we know, Bert wrote that the monstrous inhumanity of the Nazis stirred in him a feeling that it was his duty to help to avenge the innocent. However he had been resisting the impulse to rush out as a crusader for the repressed. " I do not condemn my emotions, their case is strong enough, Nazism is evil and its final abolition is justifiable cause for the war. But we are not fighting for any ethical reasons. We fight to maintain the status of the UK as a dominant economic and political power against the challenger who would usurp this position. Justice and right are not on our side because although the cause is just the motives of our rulers are corrupt."

Furthermore Bert continued to struggle with the idea of Russia as an ally. We know that he believed that Stalin was even more evil than Hitler and he had a real problem with the UK allying itself with him in the fight. The Russian front was essential to the defeat of Nazism. Hitler could not tolerate the communist state to his east and for him the essential struggle was not just against Britain and the western allies but was an ideological struggle between fascism and communism and his ideas of world domination by the German Reich. Politically Churchill and the west took the view of the USSR that the enemy of my enemy is my friend and were more than happy to see the USSR face the brunt of the attack while they prepared for the opening of the second front and the liberation of Western Europe. The U.K. and the U.S.A. did everything they could to keep the Soviet Union supplied with food, and weapons through convoys. It looked very much, especially in the early days of Hitler's invasion of Russia, that the Soviet armies would collapse in utter defeat and Hitler would make short work of his invasion leaving him free to turn his full attention once again to England. U.K. and U.S. support for the Soviets was essential for the war effort.

All these ideas and thoughts played through Bert's mind that whole winter of 1940-41. They ultimately led him to decide that when the time came and he was called up, he would opt to volunteer for duty as air crew in RAF Bomber command rather than take the conscientious objector route and go to jail or a work farm. all the men who flew in RAF bombers were volunteers. Bert's conviction that the people were worth fighting for and it was the people that he would go to war for is expressed in his poetry. He wrote several poems about the suffering that the blitz brought to the people of London. "Stenpney 1941" being the best example of his thoughts and observations of all that was happening to the people of the East End at the time and "War Widow" about the terrible effects of war on those left behind by the fighting man as he went off to die in battle.

I believe that in his heart Bert had wanted to join the fight all along but that he had resisted because of his position as a socialist and his opposition to the corrupt ruling classes which led him to declare that he was a conscientious objector. It seems to me that it is almost with relief that Bert finds that he can join the fight by declaring that he will fight for the common folk, to help end their suffering and not

97

fight for the Al Capones who make up the government and the ruling class. On the one hand he wanted to be a person who followed his intellect and didn't let his emotions rule him, but equally he was raring to enter the fray and do his bit to end the evil of Nazism. After all he had already publicly and emphatically declared himself a conscientious objector. At this point it would have been the easy road to accept a prison sentence or being assigned to work on a farm or down a mine for the duration. By making this decision Bert was able to follow his heart and not his head and enlist and join the fight without losing face. He still deplored the idea of actually joining the military. The idea of joining any military organisation was something that he had long resisted, but he was now willing and able to rise above these thoughts and enter the battle. Of course this is just my opinion, however it is an opinion reached after extensive study of all of Bert's surviving letters, notes and essays.

At about the time Bert was making up his mind to stand and fight a curious article that he had written was published in the March 1941 edition of the Free Expression magazine. Bert wrote the article on 12 February 1941. So presumably the visit from the government agent had taken place sometime in December 1940 or January 1941. Free Expression was the voice of a group who were interested in complete freedom of the individual and seem to have come into existence primarily to oppose the introduction of the Emergency Services Act. We don't know how Bert became involved with them but it is a good bet that it was through The People's Convention which he continued to be associated with. Bert writes about a visit he had from a plain clothes agent of the government's security services. At that time the man would probably have been in the Secret Service which was the forerunner of MI5. Bert gets the visit because of a letter he had written to America in which he had declared himself somewhat left of left and containing certain phrases that were flagged by the censor as indicating that Bert was a potential danger to security.

In the article titled - Warr is Visited - Bert relates that he was visited by a British plainclothesman from the C.I.D. (Criminal Investigation Department, a unit which investigates serious or potentially serious crimes) at his flat one afternoon. During the war the UK had about 10,000 censors who routinely read civilian mail looking for anything that could aid the enemy or that was a potential or actual security risk. The article is written somewhat tongue in cheek about a serious event that could have had very serious consequences for Bert had the agent been more officious and not seen that Bert posed no security threat whatsoever. The fellow read from a note book two statements attributed to Bert from his letter. " I am a communist" and "Heil the revolution." Either of those would have raised a red flag with the censors. The article continues with Bert's somewhat startled reply "Yers" having immediately remembered having written in the letter "A spectre is haunting Europe, the spectre of communism." Bert called both statements equally majestically silly and admitted to the agent that yes he had written heil the revolution but not written "I am a communist" which statement Bert attributes possibly to an overzealous police report.

The agent looked surprised, wrote in his notebook and matter of factly stated " You know of course how careful we must be these days in tracking down and dealing with what are known as subversive influences in this country. Bert wrote that "His voice smiled charmingly but his metallic eyes looked at Warr as though he were the personification of the subversive influences itself."

The interview continues and the agent tells Bert that it's his job to investigate by visiting anyone who makes such statements and then, putting Bert squarely under the gun asks him if would care to explain what he meant by them. Bert, perhaps scrambling a little at this point related that he held with the Marxism conception of history, and that the revolution to which he had "heiled" was already in progress, and its result would be a better world. The agent seemed satisfied, with this because he replied "After all that is what we are fighting for, a better world. but I have read Marx-part of my job. I can't say that I agree with the Russian way of changing the world. Do you mean a revolution stirred up by foreign agitators, a bloody revolution?"

"The eyes looked at Bert again. Evidently the young man placed much importance in the answer to this question." Bert in his typically humorously, yet to the point and adroit, way wrote "revolution that said please and was without blood he tolerated; revolution with a mess on the pavement, nicht gut, "'ere, wat's awl this abaht? Warr attempting circumspection mumbled about means and ends and justice."

Next the agent, keeping the pressure up homes in for the kill, and bluntly asks if Bert is is a member of the communist party of Britain or of any other organisation financed by a foreign power?" To which Bert answers a truthful "No."

Wrapping things up and taking note of Bert's identity and military service cards, the agent asks where Bert lived and worked and how long he had been living in England and oh, by the way what did Bert think about Churchill's performance in the house that day? The agent rather ominously tells Bert that they have an eye too, on the young Austrian refugee lady in America to whom Bert had written the letter in the first place. "There seems to be nothing wrong but you never know." Ending the interview here the agent shakes Bert's hand and rushes off to play a chess match that he had booked at his club, leaving Bert with plenty to think and worry about. Bert had to worry about himself and his Austrian friend in the U.S. who through his careless words he may have dropped into big trouble. That must have been the end of the affair because Bert never mentions another visit from this agent nor any of his colleagues and of course Bert does enlist and does go off to fight. It would be anther 4 months before Bert was actually called up and enlisted in the RAF.

100

Note: For a full reproduction of this interesting article please see appendix 6.

A couple of months later, in May 1941 one of the more bizarre incidents of the war took place. On May 10 1941 deputy Fuhrer Rudolf Hess flew in a specially prepared Messerschmidt BF110 from Germany to Scotland. He managed to evade several pursuing Spitfires and crashed his aircraft in a farmer's field south of Glasgow. He told the farmer who found him still struggling to get out of his parachute that he had a message for the Duke Of Hamilton. Hess was apparently worried about Germany having to fight a two front war once Operation Barbarossa, the invasion of the USSR, was launched and he saw his flight and attempt at negotiation with the British as a way to prevent this. Hess claimed that he had a message from Hitler and that Hitler wanted to reach out to the British and make peace. None of this was true. Hitler, through the German press called Hess a madman who was deluded and deranged and that Hess had acted entirely on his own initiative with no prior knowledge by Hitler of his intentions. The British authorities of course investigated the claims that Hess was making. Once it became obvious that he carried no authority to negotiate, he was imprisoned as a POW. Hess was initially taken to Buchanan Castle which was near where is aircraft had crash landed and later to the Tower of London. He remained at the Tower Of London until he attempted suicide by jumping over a railing to the pavement below. Hess wasn't successful in his suicide attempt merely breaking a femur. On 26 June 1942 after a 12 week convalescence he was moved to Maindiff Court Hospital near Abergavenny in Monmouthshire Wales. He remained at Maindiff until the end of the war after which he was transferred to Nuremberg where the top Nazis were being tried for war crimes. Hess was convicted at Nuremberg of crimes against peace and conspiracy with other German leaders to commit crimes. He was sentenced to life in prison and spent the rest of his life in Spandau prison, the allied military prison in Berlin. He died by suicide at the age of 93 on 17 August 1987 while still in Spandau.

Bert wrote about the Hess incident in his letter home dated 14 May 1941. "As you are probably aware Rudolph Hess, the Nazi has come here. Nothing much is known of his reasons for deserting Hitler, but it seems that he has run out on the rest of the gang. Some people say he has seen the error of his ways and has experienced a sudden conversion to the way of god. It must have been a sudden conversion because, for three weeks ago, in a speech at some celebration he mouthed the fiercest threats and heaped abuse on England. One of his choice remarks was to the effect that England has had only a taste of what the Nazis intend doing to her in the aerial war. He planned the assassination of Dolfuss, some of the jewish pogroms, is responsible for the horrible Dachau concentration camp and throughout his career has been an ardent Hitlerite. He seems to have friends here among the higher ups of the titled world, who when he arrived here began to plead for him. I suppose they will plead for Hitler also when the time comes, but I doubt that their pleas will avail them any good. Feeling is much too strong this time. There will be no more castles at Doorn."

Castles at Doorn is a reference to the manor house in the Netherlands where Kaiser Wilhelm II lived in exile after the first world war. Bert who was never one to miss an opportunity to make his feelings about the corrupt nature of the ruling classes of Britain must have been delighted when it became known that several members of the nobility where willing to plead for Hess a man who was as evil as any in Hitler's gang.

May 1941 was a busy month for the war, not only did it see the Rudolph Hess incident, but this was also when the German battleship Bismarck was sunk. On 23 May, the Bismarck and heavy cruiser Prince Eugen sailed for the Atlantic, planning to attack allied shipping. The British sent the battleships HMS Hood and Prince of Wales in pursuit along with several cruisers. The British ships intercepted the two German ships in the straits of Denmark, which is between Iceland and Greenland and immediately engaged them. During the battle the Hood was sunk and the Bismark took damage to her fuel supply lines. Because of this damage, Bismarck made for France where her captain was hoping to get her repaired. The Prince Of Wales broke off the attack and the British lost contact with the Bismarck and Prince Eugen. On 26 May the Bismarck and Prince Eugen were spotted by an RAF Catalina of RAF Coastal command making for the Atlantic. By this time the RN aircraft carrier Ark Royal had joined the pursuit. Ark Royal launched 15 Swordfish aircraft and these attacked the Bismarck, damaging her steering so that now she could only sail in a large circle. By this time there were several more Royal Navy ships and two Polish ships pursuing the Bismarck. Her crew were unable to make any repairs to her steering and the writing was on the wall. It was only a matter of time now. The commander of the Bismarck, Admiral Lütjens sent a message to the German command base "Ship unmanoeuvrable. We will fight to the last shell. Long live the Fuhrer." Lütjens didn't have long to wait, the Royal Navy ships King George V, Rodney, Dorsetshire and Norfolk located the Bismarck and attacked. Together they scored some 400 hits on Bismarck sinking her on the morning of 27 May. The Bismarck had been sunk without ever having attacked let alone sunk any allied shipping. The sinking of the Bismarck and the Hood effectively marked the end of the age of the battleship. This was now the age of the aircraft carrier.

In early 1941, whilst waiting to be called up, Bert worked as a fire watcher during air raids. For the most part, this work was a walk in the park. Bert was assigned to lead a crew who were watching over an area centred around a hotel. Night after night during air raids they would guard their charges. On nights when there were no raids they would find empty rooms in the hotel and get some well-deserved sleep. Bert couldn't believe his luck, getting paid to sleep. What could be better?

His crew did have a few adventures though. Once, he had to extinguish an incendiary bomb by dumping a bag of sand on it and Bert says it just petered out. Granted not the most exciting event of the war but during this duty he did have at least a couple of incidents which were more exciting than that. One time during a raid, while watching a huge fire in the distance, a Luftwaffe bomber started circling overhead and dropped two bombs very close to where Bert and his friends were standing. They all had to throw themselves to the ground. Ever calm and cool under fire Bert's biggest concern over that incident seems to have been that he tore his trousers and got a scraped knee.

On another night, whilst on duty with an old cockney fellow Bert notes that there were a number of bombs dropped very close to them. They sounded like a rushing express train as they fell. Bert was impressed by the calmness of this old fellow who didn't move throughout. So Bert didn't move either, thinking the fellow a typical Tommy, cool under fire. The next day Bert mentioned the old boy to a colleague. The fellow replied that - "Yes old George is a good enough bloke, a pity though he's stone deaf!"

Chapter 9: To The Aerodrome: RAF Training

The last few weeks before he was called up Bert more or less just cooled his heels. He quit work at the oystery on the 26th of July but continued working with the People's Convention and he continued his job fire watching during the nights. He wrote home that "since May 10th, the date of the last blitz there has been no serious raid. I am able to sleep nights now. It is a very pleasant way to make money, eating supper and sleeping at a hotel and being paid £3.10 a week."

And that is how Bert spent the last few days of life as a civilian that he would ever enjoy. He enlisted in the RAF at Euston in London on Monday 4th of August 1941.

The next year was a whirlwind of training for him. His first two weeks of training were at or near Euston and he returned every evening at 6PM after training had finished for the day to sleep at his flat at Lanark Mansions. Bert's flat was only a five minute walk from the training centre. On August 7th he wrote "Have been working for the king since Monday. The new state is satisfactory, most of the day being spent in one's own pursuits. For two weeks I shall be here during which time I shall be equipped and undergo numerous inoculations." Although far from happy with being in the military, Bert was resigned to the path he had chosen.

After his initial trining, Bert was sent to Scarborough for aircrew training and then on to Scotland for actual flight training. Once he got used to the military routine he seemed to, if not enjoy his life in the military, at least be more comfortable with it. It wasn't until he was sent to Scotland that his moral plummeted. He found that in his free time he couldn't concentrate enough to write any poetry and he didn't write anything from the time of his enlistment in August 1941 until the spring of 1942. Bert's letters home from his training days and his days with the squadron also do not mention his increasing despair concerning what he was being tasked to do and his falling morale, his increasing stress and his belief that he would not survive the war. Because he didn't tell his family that he was on active duty he couldn't write to them about all these misgivings and problems,. So there was no way the family could offer support, comforting words or any other help to Bert coping with these problems. Bert was of course very independent, but it must have been very difficult coping with these problems on his own when he had cut off his family who up until this time had been one of, if not his main support network.

Bert's letters home from the time he enlisted until his death continued to be full of questions about the family, the general goings on in the Warr household and to thank the family for the birthday, Christmas and other packages that they sent. Like all other wartime packages sent overseas by families, friends and organisations such as patriotic shop keepers, to sons, brothers and husbands the packages were full of cakes and other goodies thought to be in short supply in the barracks. Like most other fellows who received packages, Bert generously shared his care packages out with the other fellows of his unit. He routinely shared out everything except pipe tobacco, that special treat he kept for himself.

In his letters home Bert almost never mentions the name of any of the fellows that he is training with. Even later on, when he is serving at an active squadron we never learn the names of the men closest to him, namely the crew mates that he flew with. This is not surprising because he did not tell his family that he was flying let alone that he was flying combat missions. Of course they knew that he was in Bomber Command and posted to an active unit but just what he did there Bert never made clear. In one letter in answer to a question from the family, he even feigns surprise that they don't know what his job is. However he evades the question and doesn't tell them. He did this to spare them the nightly worry that all families with men on combat duty in the RAF faced. Is he flying tonight, did he make it back to base safely?

While this saved his parents the daily worry of wondering if Bert was safe, it was a false security. The grief it caused them when they got the telegram informing them he was listed as missing was far worse than if Bert had told his parents that he was flying operational missions from the beginning. When they did get the dreaded telegram, at one stroke they not only found out not only was he flying in combat, but that he was now missing. His aircraft having failed to return to base from his latest combat operation. It wasn't until after Bert was listed as missing that the family learned from Frank that Bert was in fact a bomb aimer and had been flying regular combat missions for months.

Most of the detailed descriptions of Bert's flying he wrote in letters to his ""Hungarian friend" Mrs Nora Senjem. Nora Senjem had fled Hungary from Nazi persecution with her daughter leaving behind her husband and young son. At her flat in London she hosted many social events and parties attended by many of the writers, musicians and artists of London's wartime refugee community. Bert was a regular attendee at these events. He and Mrs Senjem became very close. In fact she seems to have been viewed by him as a sort of mother figure and she seems to have had a similar view of Bert. She was very supportive and protective of Bert. When Bert wanted to have his portrait taken it was to Mrs Senjem that he turned for the name of a good photographer. In fact he even wrote to her asking that she buy him some underwear, "Jockey is the brand that I use," which she then posted to him at his base. When Bert returned to London on leave he usually stayed at his old flat at Lanark Mansions in Maida Vale but he spent a lot of time at Mrs Senjem's flat attending her dinner parties and other get togethers. She was a very important person in his life, this seems to be especially true of the time after he enlisted.

The weeks before he was called up were filled with worry that the long awaited German invasion of England was imminent. As late as June of 1941 it seems that the British public were still expecting the Germans to invade England

at some point. In a letter home on June 19 1941 Bert wrote
that although everyone still expected that the Germans
would invade England it looked like that would have to wait
until they had dealt with the USSR. By this time it was an
open secret that Hitler intended to turn on his Russian ally
and invade the Soviet Union. This seems to have been clear
to everyone except for Joseph Stalin. Against all the
evidence he seems to have been unwilling or unable to
believe that Germany would betray him and attack the
Soviet Union. Bert fully expected Germany to not only
invade Russia but to beat them fairly quickly and then turn
to deal with Britain. In fact that is exactly what Hitler
himself thought too. It seems that everyone believed in the
invincibility, or near invincibility of the German war
machine.

They wouldn't have too wait long to see that theory put to
the test because on 22 June 1941 Hitler's armies invaded the
USSR. They launched a surprise attack and, using the
Blitzkrieg tactics that had worked so well against the low
countries, France and Britain the year before, quickly made
huge gains of territory and defeated the Soviet forces
wherever they encountered them, killing and capturing tens
of thousands of Russian soldiers. The Nazis expected the
invasion to be over quickly and the Soviets to surrender.
The Soviets, in spite of being defeated in almost every
battle did not surrender and as they retreated adopted a
policy of scorched earth. As they retreated, the Soviet
armies burnt or destroyed crops, farm and factory
machinery and everything and anything else that might aid
the enemy. A steady stream of refugees followed the
retreating Soviet soldiers deeper into the country and away
form the advancing Germans. Many millions did not escape
though and this harsh policy was particularly hard on them,
condemning them to a winter of hardship and the prospect
of starvation during the extremes of a Soviet winter. As the
Nazi armies advanced their supply lines got longer and
longer and moving supplies and reinforcements to the front
lines became more and more of an issue as the invasion
progressed. The hoped for quick defeat of the Soviets did

not happen and it soon became evident that this invasion would not be over anytime soon. Hitler and his generals continued to believe that the next push or the one after that would result in the Soviets surrendering and that the war would be over before winter. The Germans and their allies the Fins, Romanians and Hungarians took Kiev and surrounded and laid siege to Leningrad. They pushed on to Moscow. They were certain that when they took Moscow Soviet resistance to the invasion would collapse and the war in the east would be over. Stalin had other ideas though and had no intention of ever surrendering to the hated Nazis. He arranged for virtually all of his armaments factories to be dismantled and moved further to the east, far from any threat from the invaders.

Also at this time the British, who were aiding the Soviets were starting to get supplies in to the ports of Archangel in the far north of the Soviet Union. The Soviets were manufacturing thousands of tanks, planes, artillery pieces and small arms each month and the convoy supplies send by the British and Americans were a major reason that Soviet war production was able to accomplish this. The new Soviet T34 tanks were better than any tanks the Germans had and the only weapons the Nazis had that could knock one of those beasts out of action were their big 88MM anti-aircraft guns and there were not many of them. In fact because of the swiftness of their advances and the fierceness of the fighting the German panzer divisions were exhausted by early September and were dangerously depleted and badly in need of rest, resupply and refitting. Hitler was in no mood to halt the advance though and ordered the army to push on to Moscow as soon as Kiev was taken and secure. He was sure that this would end the war in the east and he would have secured the oil, rubber and other vital supplies that he needed in the Caucusus.

In a letter home dated 27 June 1941 Bert says that he has one month left before being called up. He continued his fire watching job at night and was planning a week's holiday the second week of July. Evidently the man in the street in

Britain had been completely shielded from the reality of just how weak Britain's military situation was because Bert wonders why England doesn't invade France and open a second front. He quite rightly feels that such a move would be ideal now that the bulk of the German army is in Russia. What he doesn't seem to know is that the British were in no shape at this time to send any troops to France. It would have been a suicide mission and any force they did send would have been quickly defeated. Britain had its hands full with fighting Rommel's Afrika corps in North Africa and trying to keep him out of Tobruk. Rommel since his arrival in North Africa had won a series of stunning victories against the British forces there. So audacious was Rommel, and so stunning were his victories that he gained the reputation as the best general in the war on either side and earned him the nickname "The Desert Fox."

Ever willing to think the worst of the corrupt British government Bert thought " There is something phony about the whole thing. An opportunity like this and they (the British) remain on the defensive." Bert thought the British should invade France right away. He also thought it was "pathetic and amusing to see the British capitalist government wrestling with the formality of their attitude towards the much hated Bolsheviks of Russia." In a speech broadcast to the British people over the radio the day after Hitler's armies launched their attack on the USSR, Churchill says that he fully expects the Russian people to resist the best that they can but that he expects the Germans to deal them a crushing defeat and then to turn once again to thoughts of invading England. But that in the meantime Britain must do everything it can to support Russia in spite of the fact that their form of government goes against the principles of a free democracy. Churchill's overriding concern was stopping Hitler. In his speech he says "Hitler is a monster of wickedness, insatiable in his lust for blood and plunder. ... The Nazi regime is indistinguishable from the worst features of Communism. It is devoid of all theme and principle except appetite and racial domination. It excels in all forms of human wickedness, in the efficiency of its cruelty and ferocious aggression. No one has been a more consistent opponent of Communism than I have for the last twenty-five years. I will unsay no words that I've spoken about it. But all this fades away before the spectacle which is now unfolding." Churchill thereby makes it plain that the British will support the Soviet Union any way it can to stop the common enemy and do everything they can to stamp out the evil of the Nazi regime.

In Bert's letter home of the 7th August we get a rare glimpse of a tender moment between Bert and my mom, his youngest sister Cecelia, who would have been nearly ten by this time "Thanks for the letter and beautiful drawing from Cecelia Genevieve Agnes Warr (the sister of you know who). I have shown C's bit of art to our cat which is sitting on the bed now, but I am afraid the animal does not like it, as a most unhappy expression remained upon its face during the length of the inspection."

After the initial first two weeks of being kitted out and undergoing all the necessary medical examinations and inoculations and he had completed the basic six weeks of basic military training Bert was sent Scarborough on the Yorkshire coast. Here he began his aircrew training. Scarborough and environs is a beautiful area. Bert wrote that "I am sitting in a park, on a height overlooking the sea immediately below, writing this with my gas mask case as a table. It is warm and the sun is shining in a cloudless sky."

When he got to that unit his daily life would change drastically. Bert initially found the physical demands of training very difficult but he stuck with it and gradually his strength and endurance improved. He wrote that "from 6 in the morning until late in the evening we are in motion, school, drill and study and there is much else to occupy me, boots, buttons and sewing have become supreme in importance." So demanding did Bert find his training that during his free time in the evenings he didn't have either the will or the energy to write anything. He spent what free

111

time he did have relaxing by listening to the radio or going to concerts.

It seems that, all in all Bert enjoyed his time at Scarborough, although he found some of the classes he had to take tedious. This was especially true of military law of which he wrote - "the quantity is exceeded only by the absurdity."

Although he was finding it too difficult to write any poetry with the heavy training workload he was under, he did stay active in the literary world, giving lectures and teaching classes in some of the local Scarborough schools when time allowed.

One incident during Bert's time in Scarborough stands out. One day, while carrying out drill on a local road in in the town a Luftwaffe Junkers 88 appeared overhead. All the men of the unit dove for cover in the hedges lining the road as the German started his bomb run. They needn't have worried though because the fellow had poor aim and dropped his bomb harmlessly in the harbour. Bert's unit stayed put under cover in the hedges though because they thought that maybe the German would return to machine gun them but luckily a couple of Spitfires appeared overhead and drove him off.

In December of 1941 Bert was posted to West Freugh near Stranraer on the west coast of Scotland. Initially he found he liked the place and was thrilled to be starting flight training as a Navigator, but by the end of his 7 months in West Freugh he hated the place and couldn't wait to get back to civilisation, leaving behind the flies, the rivers of mud and the crowded barracks life.

Flight training was another matter though. After his first flight actually navigating an aircraft he wrote of the exhilaration that he felt and that he now knew "How thrilled Columbus was when he sighted the Americas. I experienced this thrill when we broke through a mass of clouds to see below the town for which we had set course. The disorder in the plane is enormous. Visualise a small area crowded with awesome pieces of metal, knobs instruments etc and Bert in the midst. A tremendous roaring of engines dulling my mind, attempting to read maps, converse with the pilot, find my pencil, which has rolled away again and last of all admire the view and all of this simultaneously!"

Bert seems to have had a cool indifference to personal safety during all this writing that "when we are coming in to land I think how interesting if we crash, doubtless I should die, that's all. I am not nervous." No doubt it was at least in part this calm coolness which would help him become a stalwart member of his bombers crew and mark him out for advancement once he was at an active squadron flying combat operations.

Chapter 10: Active Duty

During all these long months of training, although Bert had found that he was unable to do much writing, he was still in demand. Several anthologies of poems were published at this time which included some of his poems. These included a volume edited by his good friend Patricia Ledward, titled - Poems of This War. Four of Bert's poems were included in that anthology - War Widow, There Are Children In The Dusk, Poets In Time of War (Bert's tribute to Wilfred Owen) and Working Class which is now Bert's best known work.

By the summer of 1942 Bert had more than had enough of the mud and barracks life at West Fraugh and his spirits were very low. On leave in London he wrote "How pleased I am to be away from that awful hole in Scotland. The conditions are disgraceful and the food is terrible." Also at about this time his training as a navigator stopped and he was switched to training for a new position the RAF was introducing for its heavy bombers, the bomb aimer, and his spirits sank even lower. Bert said of this new work that "Some of the work is interesting but a large part is hideous to me and the most onerous of duties."

Bomb aimers had the responsibility of directing the aircraft the last few miles of the flight to the target and then pushing the button to actually release the bombs which would rain down death and destruction on the city below. At this stage of the war RAF bomb aiming was, in a word terrible. Because of the heavy losses they incurred carrying out daylight raids the RAF had stopped daylight raids all together and now only flew at night. The reason for this was that the RAF bombers were basically sitting ducks for the ack-ack and Luftwaffe fighters when they mounted daylight raids. The guns carried by RAF bombers were very ineffective against the armour of the German fighters. Unlike the American bombers which were armed with heavy 0.50 calibre machine guns, the RAF bombers were armed with much lighter 0.303 machine guns and in Wellingtons and Halifaxes only two of those giuns at that.

This was so that they could save weight in both ammunition for the guns, and for guns themselves, meaning they could carry a higher bomb load. By contrast not only did the American B17 carry heavier guns but it had 17 of them. The Americans did not bomb at night. They only bombed during the day when their crews could actually find and see the their targets. Of course this meant that the enemy could see them as well. But they believed that all the extra guns and the tight formations that their bombers flew more than made up for this.

Bombing only at night gave the poorly defended RAF bombers a better chance of survival because the German ground defences and fighters naturally found it more difficult to find and attack aircraft in the dark. It also made the job of the bomber crews more difficult. Not only was it far more difficult to even locate the target in the darkened, blacked out skies over occupied Europe but once they did find what they hoped was the right city, actually locating and hitting the target was literally a hit and miss exercise. As the time went on, improved tactics such as the introduction of the pathfinder squadrons and the introduction of targeting aids such as GEE greatly improved this. GEE was a radio navigation system which improved accuracy down to a few hundred metres at up to a range of 350 miles from the source of Gee signals. In spite of these improvements bombing at night was never an exact science. This lack of accuracy was the main reason that the RAF introduced area bombing which ultimately led to the very controversial fire bombings of cities such as Dresden. All that was still in the future though, but it is easy to see why the pacifist Bert was not thrilled to have his trade, changed from navigating, which he loved to bomb dropping which he hated. Also in these early days the bomb aimer often had to man a gun in the nose of the aircraft close to his bombing station. So Bert would have had to learn to fire this gun. These nose guns were never very effective though mainly because German fighters rarely, if ever attacked from the front plus the gun was still the small calibre and ineffectual 0.303 gun. The Luftwaffe preferred to attack from behind the bomber or, better yet, to come up from below their target, attacking the bombers at their weakest spots. Bert would have hated firing this gun, however he had made his decision to do his bit to help the war effort and he carried on no matter the personal cost.

Although Bert hated the life and came to hate his training at West Fraugh even more, it was here that he began to emerge from the mental fog that he had been in. His writers block began to clear and he began writing poetry again. It was also at this time that he met fellow poet John Gawsworth and I can't help but believe that the two events are related. When Bert had enlisted his life changed dramatically. He had been living the life of a budding intellectual, taking university courses, working for various poetry and Socialist magazines and at Mrs Senjem's dinners and parties, surrounded by talented artists and writers. For Bert those must have been intellectually exciting and stimulating times. Then suddenly he lost all that and he and he was thrown into the dull, repetitious world of military training with its tedious discipline, rules and regulations. No doubt the thrill and challenge of flight training alleviated a great deal of this tedium but that was of course not on the same plain as his previous life from an artistic point of view. It is not surprising that someone of Bert's sensitivity struggled to not only cope with this new life but to try to carry on writing at anywhere near the levels he had been attaining prior to enlisting. At his first meeting Gawsworth Bert did not seem to warm particularly to the fellow writing that "Gawsworth has done quite a lot in poetry. He was told by the editor of Poetry Quarterly to get in touch with me. I'm afraid we have very little in common but he does know very much more about poets and poetry than I do."

As time went on Bert's opinion of Gawsworth changed. The two spent many evenings together and Bert even spent several weekends at the house in Glasgow of Gawsworth's friend Harry Isherwood where they whiled away the nights drinking and talking about poetry. By the time Gawsworth left the West Fraugh area at the end of January he and Bert had become good friends and Bert was sorry to see him go. "Gawsworth, the poetry person is to leave here shortly. I am afraid he has been most interesting company." Bert did meet Gawsworth again at least once when Gawsworth was investigating a suicide that had taken place at his camp and they kept up a regular correspondence. Once while on leave in London Bert even visited the home of Gawsworth's mother.

Although Bert and Gawsworth were not to meet again they planned several literary projects together for after the war. Gawsworth admired Bert and his poetry very much and after the war worked very hard to get a book of Bert's poems published. Sadly though, that project did not come off and seems to have ended in acrimony between Gawsworth and the Warr family, particularly Bert's mother who doesn't seem to have thought much of Gawsworth at all. The ending of this project to get Bert's poetry published in book form was especially hard on Aunty Mary who was desperate to get the project completed and see her brother's work in book form. Although very disappointed Mary did not give up. But it take another 25 years before she would see her efforts pay off and gert a book of Bert's work finally published.

Gawsworth himself was an extraordinary character. His real name was Terence Armstrong, John Gawsworth was a pen name. Gawsworth was born in London in 1912 and grew up in the Notting Hill and Holland Park regions of the city.

Amongst his accomplishments Gawsworth could list being a Freeman of London. He was awarded the Benson Medal of The Royal Society Of Literature in 1939. He was a founding editor of The English Digest poetry magazine and editor of the Literary Digest. Poet Laureate John Mansfield said of Gawsworth that " He was one of the most beautiful and promising of our writers."

Gawsworth served in the RAF in North Africa, Sicily and Italy after leaving Scotland. He started his RAF career as an

A/C 2, the lowest rank in that force and by the time he left the RAF after a stint in India he had worked his way up the ranks to being a commissioned officer.

The most extraordinary thing about this extraordinary character though was that he was the king of the tiny Caribbean Island of Redonda. This came about because Gawsworth was very good friends with the former king of the island, the writer M.P. Shiels who had been proclaimed king quite randomly by his father in the mid 1930s. The title was pretty much meaningless. This king had no powers and was king in name only. Gawsworth would hold his royal court from his home in Notting Hill every year on January 29th, his birthday. At his court each each year he would create Dukes from literary people who over the past year had help perpetuate the memory of Shiels.

He said of his reign "It is purely an intellectual aristocracy." When asked by a reporter if he ever planned on visiting his kingdom he replied "Great scot whatever for."

For Bert once Gawsworth left he found life in West Fraugh as tedious and awful as ever. Things were about to change for the better for him though because in June of 1942 Bert was promoted to Sgt and he was posted to RAF Kinloss on the north east coast of Scotland. The promotion to sergeant and new posting brought with it better quarters and much better food. Bert found Kinloss to be a beautiful place and a very welcome change from West Fraugh. "I am now a sergeant responsible and respected. One's lot improves a lot in the RAF with such a promotion."

Part of Bert's hatred of West Freugh grew out the tedium and lack of privacy of barracks life. The men were in huts witch contained twenty beds each. Privacy and quiet for writing and studying were non-existent. Both Kinloss and East Moor, and indeed all three of the bases that 158 Squadron operated out of during Bert's time on the squadron, operated a system of accommodation and aircraft hangarage known as dispersal. In this system aircraft were not parked together but instead parked separately around the airfield on hard stands with plenty of room between them. Similarly the men were quartered in huts scattered around the base or sometimes even off the base in private homes and hotels etc. Many of the administration and other buildings such as the messes and latrines etc of the base were similarly dispersed around the airfield. Spreading things out like this was done to minimize damage and death as much as possible in the event that the base was bombed.

The men would either walk or ride bikes to get around between their quarters, the mess and administration buildings such as the briefing room etc. Being billeted in these quiet quarters came as a real shot in the arm for Bert. Now that he was a sergeant he had his own private room and that alone improved his mood. "Am not working much and have many pleasant hours reading in my room, which I cherish having endured so long the barrack room existence." The room came complete with a desk where Bert could write and a fireplace to keep him warm during the cold Scottish summer nights. Coal was almost impossible to come by because of rationing but there was plenty of good wood in the woods surrounding the billet. Now that he was in more settled surroundings and after his time spent with Gawsworth Bert found that he was able to start writing again. At first though Bert's efforts at writing poetry seemed to have been very tentative and awkward. He had spent nearly a year in training and much of it was hard times for him. Often during that time he had been pushed nearly to his limits both physically and mentally. Now though he could take some time to sit back and re-evaluate his attitude and try to find himself. "Am writing a little again, although I feel like a headless hen trying to establish what was, is now and will be later, it is all very confusing."

Bert was also helping write a play, a musical that was planned to be performed for the men at the camp by "a fellow" there who had experience producing. Bert only mentions the play once in his letters so whether or not they actually performed the play or not and what role(s) Bert

119

played in getting the play put on is one of those mysteries we have to live with.

It was now late June 1942 and at about this time brother Frank had enlisted. Bert was against this of course and was loath to see his brother have to endure what he went through during training but he did write "I wish the best of luck in his new work and hope that he can endure the life, it is horrible sometimes. " I think though that Frank with the active life he had lived, was probably much more suited to the physical demands of training than Bert was.

The war news in those early days of June was a mixture of good and bad. The Japanese attack on Pearl Harbour in December of 1941 had been the brain child of Japanese admiral Isoroku Yamamoto. At the time of the attack, Yamamoto believed the attack would give the Japanese at most a six month window in which their navy would dominate the Pacific. He hoped that during that time the Japanese military would have enough time to secure the defences of the empire in the Pacific and that a negotiated peace could be worked out with the Americans. Yamamoto believed that after this initial six month period the industrial might of the Americans would start to awaken and that they would begin to get the upper hand. Yamamoto was spot on with his prediction of six months. In early June the Americans launched an attack against the Japanese carrier fleet near Midway Island some 1400 miles west of Hawaii. The Japanese carrier fleet was comprised of six carriers but only four were present at the battle. The Americans attacked the Japanese with waves of aircraft off the carriers Yorktown, Hornet and Enterprise. The American attack caught the Japanese completely by surprise and three of the four Japanese carriers were set ablaze and ultimately had to be abandoned. The Americans didn't escape the battle completely unscathed. They lost the carrier Yorktown and the destroyer Hamman. The loss of the three carriers was a devastating blow to the Japanese and destroyed the power of their Pacific fleet. After this the American navy dominated the Pacific. The only realistic hope that the

120

Japanese had of winning the war against the Americans now was if they could hold out with the ground forces they had in the many islands that dotted the Pacific from their home islands eastward and southward towards the Philippines and Australia.

 The war news wasn't all rosy for the allies that June though because in the second week of that month Rommel's Afrika Korps took Tobruk in North Africa. This was a humiliating defeat for Britain and was a major blow to moral at home as well as being a disaster militarily. Rommel had come to Africa in January with a relatively small force of tanks and armoured cars and infantry. The Luftwaffe did dominate the skies over the area and, in combination with the Axis navies of Germany and Italy, they dominated the Med. However the British had a much larger ground force in North Africa than the Germans and they should have been able to defeat Rommel's small force. Rommel outgeneraled his British counterparts at every turn though. The British command was disorganised and not co-ordinated and they fought every battle piecemeal, getting beaten at nearly every turn. The defeat of the British and the fall of Tobruk cemented Rommel's reputation as one of the top generals of the war. Not only that but it opened the way for an all-out German assault on Egypt. The fall of Egypt would be a disaster for the allies and pave the way for the Germans to gain control of the whole of the Middle East, thus controlling not only the shipping of the area but also the all-important oil fields. The loss of Tobruk was a huge blow to moral at home. Bert in typical fashion saw this defeat in terms of the corruption and general incompetence of the ruling classes of Britain. His cynicism and contempt for the ruling class of Britain shine through in this quote from a letter he wrote home shortly after the fall of Tobruk was announced to the British public. " I compare the sportsmanlike surrender with the work of our eastern allies. They at least realise that the war is not a game at Eton and that there can be no more surrendering."
The battle of Midway and the fall of Tobruk had no impact on the day-to day life of Bert and his training his at Kinloss

continued. Kinloss was a very welcome improvement over West Fraugh. Bert was for the most part enjoying his flight training and of course he was also writing again. The general improvement of his surroundings at Kinloss added to the fact that with his promotion to sergeant he was getting better food and had better quarters led to him feeling stronger and getting healthier by the day.

This time at Kinloss was to be the last 2 months of his training. His next posting, in August, would be to the conversion unit for RAF 158 Squadron at Marston Moor. At Marston Moor newly trained crews were introduced to the heavy Halifax bomber and at that time they also usually were assigned to the crew they would fly active missions with. From Marston Moor on 24 September, Bert and his new crew were posted to 158 Squadron at RAF East Moor, just down the coast in Yorkshire from Scarborough where the year before he had begun his RAF training.

Before reporting to 158 though, Bert had ten days leave in London in early August. During this leave he doesn't seem to have relaxed and recharged, instead he seems to have spent the time rushing about here and there seeing people, watching plays and going to concerts. He stayed in his old room at Lanark mansions which he did on every leave that he took to London until the very end. I don't know whether or not Mrs Bush the landlady charged him rent or not or whether or not she kept his room empty and available to him any time that he needed it, but she always had the room ready for him when he came to London on leave.

While on leave over the August bank holiday (Long weekend) Bert went to the countryside around London, somewhere along the banks of the Thames to the west of London but Bert doesn't say where. He stayed with a writer friend whom he had taken some courses at college with and who was living in a converted bus. Bert wrote home that this friend was attempting to write a book "Which I fear will not be published as it is not good." It seems that bad book or not, Bert spent an enjoyable two days in the countryside.

122

At Kinloss Bert's training had been carried out in Whitworth Whitely aircraft and it was flying these aircraft that Bert was crewed for the first time with Dennis Cole, the man who was to be his pilot from that time on. Flying with Bert and Dennis were two other fellows who were to be part of the crew right up until the end, navigator Ron Stemp and wireless operator Albert Ward. Of these men we know precious little. Bert never mentions them in his letters home to the family because as we know he didn't want the family knowing he was on active combat flight duty. We do know that Dennis Cole enlisted at Euston, the same as Bert, and that he was originally from Alexandria in Egypt. Ronald Claude Stemp, the crew's navigator had enlisted at Oxford and Albert Ward, the crew's wireless operator had enlisted at Padgate in London. That Bert became close to his crew mates we know for a fact because of what he told Patricia Ledward "The members of the crew are strong and all for one another." There was a strong bond between members of all crews. They trained together, they flew together and more often than not when it was time to relax they all went to the same pubs, dances and restaurants, drinking and eating together. We don't get a sense of any of that camaraderie from any of Bert's letters home nor to Mrs Senjem. With the exceptions of John Gawsworth, Phil Pinkus and Al Sketchler, Bert never mentions the names of any of his friends, associates or other lads in any of his units.

Chapter 11 All For One Another

While Bert was enjoying his ten days of the leave, the British launched the disastrous Dieppe Raid. This raid, codenamed Operation Jubilee, was an amphibious attack on the German occupied port city of Dieppe. The plan was to attack and occupy the town for a short time, destroying as much German military infrastructure in that time as possible. The idea of the raid was to test the ability of the allies to launch an amphibious seaborne assault in preparation for the D-Day landings, which would be launched in two years. The fighting force was made up of over 6000, primarily Canadian infantry supported by a regiment of tanks, The Calgary Regiment. The Royal the navy and the RAF also supported the landings.

The attack was a disaster. The Germans had been warned by double agents that an attack in the area was likely to occur at any time and their troops in the area were on high alert. British aerial and naval support was wholly inadequate and offered little effective support to the troops on the beaches. Within ten hours of the landings, over 3,600 of the men who had been landed had been killed, wounded or captured. Furthermore, because the treads of the supporting tanks were not designed to operate on the pebble terrain that made up the beaches of the area, the tanks could not operate properly and they offered little support to the infantry.

The RAF had anticipated a Luftwaffe response of course but not on the scale that it actually occurred. The RAF lost 106 aircraft to ack-ack, fighters and accidents. Against this the Luftwaffe lost only 48 aircraft. The Royal Navy lost 33 landing craft and one destroyer.

Although loses were extremely high and the raid was wholly unsuccessful, this raid did teach the Allies valuable lessons about what to do and what not to do when attempting an amphibious landing against fortified and protected coasts. Hard lessons that would help enormously

in the future landings in Sicily, Italy and of course D-Day
itself.

After Bert returned from his ten days leave in London he
and his crew joined 158 squadron. First though they went to
165 Heavy Conversion Unit at Marston Moor in North
Yorkshire. This unit was where newly trained crew were
introduced to the aircraft they would be flying in at the
squadron. During their initial aircrew training, aircrews
trained on two engine medium bombers but now they would
be flying in the much bigger heavy four engine Halifax
MKII. At the conversion unit crews would make several
practice flights in the new type and generally become
familiar with the aircraft. Once the instructors were satisfied
a crew was competent on the aircraft they would be sent
along to the squadron proper and assigned to one of its
flights. Each squadron usually had three flights, A, B and C
and each flight usually comprised 8 aircraft, making 24
active aircraft for the entire squadron. Bert wrote that the
move to East Moor was his fourth move in 10 days. The
move from Kinloss to the conversion unit at Marston Moor
was one move. Marston Moor was just to the west of
Rufforth, which itself was just west of the city of York.
Then moving from the conversion unit to the squadron
proper was another move. What the other two moves were I
have no idea and Bert never says. At East Moor Bert was
again billeted in dispersed accommodation." We walk
hundreds of miles each day as this place is widely
dispersed. We have very pleasant private rooms in a wood."
Bert's main complaint about East Moor, apart from all the
walking was that there were swarms of flying insects
plaguing the area. "There are wasps and clusters of tiny flies
that get everywhere. They crawl in our ears and down our
necks. The wretches are everywhere." For a lad from
mosquito infested Southern Ontario this should not have
been too much to handle.

Once the men were at RAF East Moor they were joined by
2 air gunners, Bill Robinson and Cliff George Dawson. Like
Albert Ward both of these men had enlisted at Padgate.

125

Flight Engineer, Ron Gowing had enlisted at Cardington which is a suburb of Bedford to the south east of the city. Bedford itself is a few miles west of the university city of Cambridge in East Anglia. Gowing had trained at No 4 School of Technical Training in South Wales near Cardiff. The only member of Bert's crew that we have any but the most basic information about is Bill Robinson. This is thanks to Bill's daughter Patricia. Thanks to Patricia we know that Bill, the crew's Mid Upper Gunner (MUG) was born August 16 1916 in Eastham Wirral south of Liverpool. He was the youngest of 6 children, 4 boys and 2 girls. In civilian life he had been the manager of a butcher's shop. However when the war started this was a protected trade and therefore he would never be called up to join the fight. Determined to enlist and do his bit Bill quit work at the butcher's and went to work in a paper mill in Ellesemere Port. Bill was married to a girl named Violet. He had met and married Violet while he was still working as a butcher. Bill enlisted at Padgate and after his training he was posted to 158 and joined Dennis Cole's crew. Bill's daughter Patricia was born on 5th March 1943, less than a month before Bill was killed. Patricia tells us that amongst his belongings, which were returned to the family by the squadron, were several poems that he had written. I can't help but wonder if Bill had been influenced or encouraged by Bert to write poetry. From what we know about Bert I'm sure that he would have been more than happy to help out his fellow crew mate in any attempts he was making to write poetry.

And that is all that is now known about the six men who were on Bert's crew with him. Scant information to relate about the six men who, arguably were the most important people in Bert's life at this time, each relying heavily on the others to carry them through all the perils of combat operations and return safely to base after each flight. The men of a bomber crew were a close knit group. They trained together and flew together and most spent much of their off duty time socialising together. Bert's letters home make no mention of any of these fellows ever. It can be supposed that this may have been because Bert was keeping from the family the fact that he was on dangerous active flight duty. Less easy to explain is that none of his letters to Nora Senjem, who was aware of Bert's flight duties, ever mention any of Bert's crew mates either. It seems that Bert made a deliberate effort to keep his military and his civilian life completely separate.

While he was in London on leave, before reporting to 158 Squadron Bert had arranged to have his photo taken by a professional photographer friend of Mrs Senjem's. His desire to keep his two worlds apart can be seen in his letters home about this photo, which relate an awful lot of effort and preparation for having this photo taken. The photo gets mentioned in several letters home and caused him a lot of worry and bother. Mindful that he was gaining some fame through publication of his poems and anxious about his reputation he wrote home "Am getting photo done, will send copy but please do not send to the St Claire collection of faces (Note: that would have been St Claire Primary School, which all the Warr children had attended and indeed which at the time my mom, then in grade six would still have been attending). I object to being included because I am being publicised as a member of the fighting forces, a roll which is still and will always remain hateful to me. I make no capital out of my uniform, it is the mark of bestiality in this age."

There are not many photos of Bert and there is only one of him in uniform, the one he himself had done professionally in London. Cameras were banned on RAF bases for all but the official forces photographers at the time that Bert was flying. Many crews ignored this rule and there are plenty of photos of men and machines from RAF bases at this time. It seems though that Bert's crew took this order seriously because I know of no photos of Bert's crew. Of course it could be that there were photos taken by other members of the crew and Bert just never bothered to get copies. There certainly would have been official photos of training and perhaps even an official flight or squadron photo taken with the full approval of the base and squadron commanders. Not surprisingly, given his attitude towards the military and how he wanted the one photo that he did have taken treated, Bert never bothered to get copies of any of these.

It may seem strange to us in this age of instant digital photos and endless and quite often somewhat pointless pics taken on phones ad nauseam but in those days not everyone even had a camera, nor was interested in getting one. Bert's one and only professionally taken photo would have been to him a very big deal. It certainly seems that way at least by the amount of space in his letters home and to Mrs Senjem that he devotes to getting the photo taken and copies sent home.

On the other hand there are plenty of photos of brother Frank in uniform, many of them taken at home with his sisters, mother and even one with Skippy the family dog. There is one glaring exception though, there are no photos of Frank and his father, nor do I know of any photos of any of the other family members taken with their father at this time. As for Bert, there are only a couple of photos of him and Frank together and none of Bert and any of other members of the family. And very unfortunately there are no photos of Bert and Frank on leave in London together the last time that the two would see each other. This may have been because neither of the brothers had a camera or because they just didn't see the need to have photos taken of their time in London together. They may have thought why bother, as after all they would probably meet up many times over the course of the war.

Bert struggled with his role in the military, especially after he had his trade changed from the passive role of navigator to the fully engaged in the fight bomb aimer. Of all of the crew of a bomber it was the bomb aimer alone who was actively involved in the destruction of the target each and every flight. All the other members of the crew were there to ensure the bomb aimer could do his job and took no part in the actual dropping of the bombs. Even the gunners didn't

128

get involved each flight. They only fired their guns if an enemy fighter approached within their limited effective range. Bert had taken his stand and was doing his duty but the role he had ultimately been given was not one that he was proud of. The military was his life now but he struggled with this reality and fought his own internal struggle against it. He wanted his life very much to be defined by his writing and not by his role in the destruction of German cities. I don't think he would have wanted to be remembered as a war poet in spite of the number of his poems which had the war as a theme. Bert wanted his poetry to lead to social improvement for the lot of the common man. He still believed very strongly that the state leadership was corrupt and that the country was being led by a gang of criminals more interested in lining their own pockets and profiting from the war than caring for, or helping, the average working class man in the street. Bert believed the working class were carrying the huge burden of fighting the war but gaining nothing but pain, sorrow, misery and death from their struggles. He did believe that the Nazis had to be stopped but he also believed that the rulers of England should all be thrown out and the system of government and the social order completely revamped. It was still his hope that this would happen at the end of the war once Nazis and the fascists were defeated. He believed that a radical social change was needed and was coming after the war for the victors as well as the defeated, democracy or dictatorship. It was with this outlook that Bert at last began his real work in the RAF after more than a year's training.

Although Bert and his crew moved from Marston Moor to the main 158 Squadron base of East Moor in mid-September of 1942 it wasn't until 15th of October that they flew their first operation, a mission to bomb Cologne. They spent the time between moving to East moor and their first combat operation becoming more familiarised with the big Halifax bombers and flying training missions. In that month Bert and his crew flew 14 training missions before they finally saw action. That was a flight nearly every second day. After the crew's first operation, 10 more missions followed between mid October 1942 and January 1943, to places like Stuttgart, Duisberg, Lorient, Nuremberg and the dreaded Berlin. Naturally enough Bert makes no mention of these operations in his letters home, nor does he mention them in his letters to Nora Senjem. As a result we know nothing about any of these sorites apart from the entries in his flight logbook and the brief entries in the squadron ORB (Operations Record Book, which listed every single flight flown by the squadron and the outcome of that flight) and Bomber Command War Diaries. But as there are no entries of any exceptional incidents happening to Bert's crew in the squadron ORB for these ops we can assume that they were fairly routine. That is to say as routine as anything can be when you were flying into the teeth of occupied Europe with its thousands of bristling ack-ack batteries and buzzing Luftwaffe night fighters. The area of the Ruhr Valley alone had over 10,000 ack-ack batteries that bomber crews had to evade on every mission to cities there. Bomber crews had nicknamed the area "Happy Valley" because it was anything but.

The Halifax MK II bombers that Bert flew in were decent enough aircraft given their prewar design restrictions but they did have some serious flaws which made them very vulnerable to night fighter and ground attacks. They had small underpowered engines which limited the altitude the big aircraft could attain when it was fully loaded with fuel and bombs. In spite of the engineers best efforts to mask them, the exhaust flames of these engines lit up the area directly behind the aircraft like beacons calling out here I am come and kill me. Because, fully loaded the Halifax MKII had to fly lower and slower than the more powerful engined Lancaster it was an easier target for ack-ack batteries and night fighters. The loses of Halifax MK II aircraft for this part of the war were extremely high. The Halifax MK III aircraft eliminated all of these problems and more but Bert never got to fly in that aircraft. 158 squadron did fly the MK IIIs but not until late December of 1943, nearly nine months after he was killed.

Of all the targets in Nazi Germany Berlin was one of the most dreaded by aircrews because, not only did it involve a long flight deep into enemy territory, the Nazi capital was also one of the most heavily defended places on the planet. For a more detailed description and listing of all the operations that Bert flew with 158 Squadron see Appendix 2- Combat Operations Flown By Bertram War.

The time just before a mission was extremely intense for aircrew. During the long hours leading up to an operation nerves were stretched and there was a heightened anxiety as crews prepared for the operation and waited for take-off. Once they were in the air the men had to be on high alert for the whole operation until the wheels of their aircraft touched down safely back at base. Only after a safe return could the crews relax their frayed nerves for a few hours or a day or so until the whole thing started over again with preparation for the next mission.

Military flying was very different from any other branch of the service. The men of the army when in combat of course were at the front lines where they fought, ate and often slept in their fox holes far from any comforts of home. Likewise the navy man spent his time on his ship in the middle of the sea for days and sometimes weeks at a time. The airman though would live and work from his base in England leaving only to fly his missions deep into heavily defended enemy territory. This afforded the airman a unique way to recover and relax after battle that was denied to every other branch of the service while the men were in combat, the local pub. When the men were stood down they would often frequent the local pubs of the Lissett area to try to relax and let off some steam. Some of the favourite watering holes of 158 squadron crews were The Black Bull in Barnstrom, The Chestnut Horse and the Spa Ballroom in the nearby coastal resort town of Bridlington. All of which as of 2023 are still in operation in one form or another. Bridlington with the Spa Dance Hall and its promenade along the sea was a favourite destination of off duty crews from all the squadrons in the area. Bridlington at this time was a lively and jumping place almost any night of the week but especially at the weekend when there were dances at the Spa. The dances were attended by the local girls and the WAAFs (Woman's Auxiliary Air Force) of the various bases and stations in the area and many young crewmen from the RAF, RCAF, RAAF and RNZAF as well. Another very popular bar with all the aircrews was Betty's Bar in York which the crews affectionately called "The Dive." The men would spend many nights there drinking and socialising. Over the course of the war Betty's is said to have supplied over 20,000 meals and beverages to hungry and thirsty airmen. Betty's is still in operation but now it is called Betty's tea room and serves only tea and cakes, and no alcohol. Bert visited York on several occasions to see plays or go to concerts. No doubt he also found his way to Betty's for a meal and a quick beer or two or to relax with his pipe over a glass or two of whiskey. He never mentions going to Bridlington in his letters but since he was in the area from September 1942 until his death in early April 1943 it is a safe bet that he went there on occasion with his fellow crew mates as well as going to some of the other pubs in the area. In fact at least one of Bert's poems is set in a pub.

> Like a dew worm that has swalllowe
> a half-crown piece
> he washed his hands in the heat of the fire
> confident as a calendar
>
> Someone murmured "langwidge, langwidge,
> ladies present mind,"
> and immediately on hearing this
> all the ladies assumed outraged expressions.

This short fragment, all that remains of this poem now, evokes in my mind a wonderful image of a smoke filled, small, but comfortable, country pub crowded with locals and aircrew enjoying their drinks and shared conversations around the fireplace on a cold winter's night.

Of course the men would also socialise together in the Sergeants mess at the base where the rules were very relaxed so that all the members of a crew could be together, officers as well as enlisted men. We know from Nora Senjem's letters that when he was in London and he went to dinner parties and other gatherings at her flat Bert was very withdrawn. He would sit quietly smoking his pipe or a cigarette, sipping his drink and also drinking in and eagerly learning from the conversations of the writers, artists, musicians and others that were there. It is tempting to visualise Bert doing much the same thing in the RAF messes and pubs that the he went to with or without his crew. One can imagine him sitting quietly in a corner watching and listening to everything, drinking in not only his whiskey but all the local colour and conversation as well.

As time went on Bert increasingly struggled with the stress and strain of flying combat operations and the isolation from friends and colleagues that he was increasingly feeling. The poem Acknowledgement to Life ends with the very telling lines

> *"I am as lonely as the universe.*
> *I am the unit whole in no association with my parts."*

In spite of these internal struggles Bert continued his work flying and must have been very good at it, and even excelled at it, because he was earmarked for a leading role with the squadron. In mid-January 1943 he was sent on a Bomb Leaders course at RAF Station Mamby in Lincolnshire. Each squadron had trade leaders for each of the of crew positions. There was a Nav leader, Gunnery Leader etc. It was the Bomb Leader's job to answer to the Squadron CO (Commanding Officer) on issues regarding bomb aimers and their work and training. There was normally only one Bomb Leader per squadron. They were the coordinators of all of the bomb aimers at the squadron and, together with the other leaders they formed the working group of the CO. Sometimes these leaders were

133

part of the CO's crew. The CO didn't often fly but when he did he would hand pick his crew so that he got to fly with the cream of the squadron. If the CO's aircraft went missing many of the squadron's best men would be lost, leaving large boots to fill for the rest. In theory being a Bomb Leader would have been a safer role for Bert than being a regular Bomb Aimer because the Squadron Bomb leader did not fly as often as regular crew. In practice though this was not the case. The bombing section leaders of 158 Squadron had a tragic record of failing to return with 5 of the 7 who held that post being reported missing on operations during the course of the war. If we add Bert to that list as having completed the training but not yet having taken up the duty, this sad record becomes 6 out of 8 Bomb Leaders lost at 158. I don't know how this figure compares with other squadrons but it does seem that 158 Bomb Leaders had particularly bad luck. Squadron Leaders were all commissioned officers, so Bert's promotion would have been imminent.

Just before beginning this course Bert went to London on leave, where he met up with his brother Frank, newly arrived from Canada with RCAF's 424 squadron and soon to be heading to North Africa. The two brothers spent an enjoyable week together. Bert showed Frank the sights of the capital and Frank told Bert all that was going on with family and friends back home in Toronto. Bert had two weeks leave but Frank only had one week and soon had to return to his base at Bournemouth. It was the last time the two brothers ever saw each other. Frank would be killed flying a mission to Italy in October just six months after his brother was killed.

Chapter 12: And That Is How The End Would Come

Glad to be able to relax away from the squadron and the constant stress that combat operations brought, nonetheless Bert felt that he was living on borrowed time. He wrote that "I shall be astonished if I live to visit London again." The stress of flying and fighting in a bomber had taken a heavy toll on Bert psychologically. This along with the fact that he deplored the role of Bomb Aimer that he found himself forced to occupy instead of his preferred job as a navigator, had sapped his spirit. He had come to the realisation and acceptance of a fate that few in Bomber Command at that time would escape. During that part of the war flying in a Halifax squadron in Bomber Command was almost like a death sentence. Casualties were extremely high. The relief the men of a crew felt arriving safely back at base after an operation was too often tinged with sadness as one or more of their fellow crews did not return. This happened on flight after flight week after week. The men knew that it was likely that it was not a matter of if it would happen to them but only when it would happen to them.

In her poem titled "The Dead" dedicated to Bert, Patricia Ledward wrote that "Back from a raid on Germany you said: You're wrong to let the physical death fill you with such dread; believe me when I say only the tragedy is large, each death is small." Len Gasparini included this poem in Bert's book and it is on the very first page of "Acknowledgement too Life."

The Dead
(For Bertram Warr)
Back from a raid on Germany you said:
"You're wrong to let the physical death
Fill you with such dread;
Believe me when I say
Only the tragedy is large, each death is small,
In a bomber one is not alone,
Courage is met with quietness and all
The members of the crew are strong,

And all for one another,
That is how the end would come."

So many go it wasn't strange to hear
You'd not returned when Essen blazed
That April night last year
Although I wished a man with Owen's feeling
And the satire of Sassoon could write
Your epitaph-how you hated war,
How kind you were with the overwrought,
The refugee, the maimed, the old,
Could tell the irony and pity in your eyes,
When German boys bombed London.
You had a bitterness I never understood,
Did not believe in afterwards
When people planned in happy mood
You kept your silence although once you said
"The dead have all the luck you see."

Patricia Ledward
From Khaki and Blue (London: Resurgam Press, 1945)

125,000 men flew in RAF Bomber Command during World War 2, of those 55,000 were killed. That is a staggering 44%. Add to that another 8,400 wounded and you get an unbelievable casualty rate of over 51%. And at the time Bert was flying Bomber Command losses were at their highest point for the entire war. It's no wonder that Bert had a fatalistic attitude. The wonder is that Bert, or any of the men carried on flying at all.

In Patrica's poem Bert continues - "In a bomber one is not alone, courage is met with quietness and all the members of the crew are strong, and all for one another, and that is how the end would come." We can imagine that that is exactly how the end came for Bert and his crew mates. Returning from their successful raid against Essen every man would have stood by his station and done his duty and his best for his crew right up until the end. Bomber crews had a deep comradeship that we can never hope to understand. They

136

supported each other and drew strength from each other and I believe that is how they found the courage and strength and the heart to carry on in the face of almost certain death night after night.

Since the beginning of the war, Bomber Command had suffered from shortages of aircraft and changes to its orders. The first problem was finally being overcome in early 1943. The new four engine heavies, the Lancaster and Halifax were coming off the assembly lines in ever increasing numbers and, for the first time, Bomber Commands numbers were increasing. Gone were the days when a new squadron would be formed only to be sent off to Coastal Command or the Middle East. New squadrons were being formed and their strength was being added to the main force. New navigation aids such as OBOE, which was a similar system to GEE but more advanced. Special marker bombs for the pathfinders were also being added to help with the fight. The second problem was still an issue and between December 1942 and early March 1943 was to plague Bomber Command and no doubt play havoc with Bert's conscience as targets were switched from tactical bombing of factories, sub pens and similar, to area bombing of whole cities and back again, time and again.

The U-Boat war in the North Atlantic was raging, the allies were desperate to turn the tide in this struggle. Bomber Command received orders to divert a major portion of its nightly effort against the ports where the U-Boats were stationed. Not only were these ports French, which meant that for the first time the men of the squadrons would be bombing the towns of an ally but the orders were to carry out area bombing and not try to hit precise targets. This meant that there would be significant damage to the cities and many, many deaths of French civilians. They were specifically ordered to focus on the French ports of Lorient, St Nazaire, Brest and La Pallice. Bert was to go on two raids in early 1943 to Lorient. We can only imagine the anguish that this must have caused him. He was already having deep moral issues with being a bomb aimer in the

137

first place. Now add this extra torment of knowing that he was dropping his bombs not on the enemy but on the innocent French civilians who happened to have the bad luck to be living in a port city that the Germans had decided was to be a major U-Boat base.

I do not know when Bert began writing the unfinished essay which is the last work in Acknowledgement To Life. The essay is not dated and I can not find any reference to it any in any notes of Bert's that are left but it is tempting to think that it was begun around this time. This would have been one of the most difficult times for Bert mentally and from a moral standpoint he must have been very conflicted and tormented. That essay, expresses more than anything else that he wrote, the despair, and fatalism that he was feeling. In that essay Bert not only writes that he fully expects to die shortly, but that his death will be a welcome release from the moral abyss that he finds himself in because of the war and his role in it. It's a fair bet that Bert started working on that essay in late 1942 or early 1943.

Things were set to improve for Bert though. First off he went on his Bomb Leaders course in early March knowing that on his return he was due his commission and a promotion to a position which would mean less flying. There is reason to believe that Bert's mental outlook was improving with the prospect of being commissioned and being promoted within the squadron to the important position of Bomb Leader. His letters home at this time were more optimistic and he wrote repeatedly and impatiently about getting his commission. He was also very much looking forward to meeting up with Frank in London when they would both be on leave. He must have been missing his family very much. This would be the first time since he had left home over 4 years earlier that he would see any close family.

Secondly, in early March Bomber Command orders were changed yet again. They were now ordered to concentrate on bombing Germany's industrial heart land, the Ruhr Valley. Targets would still be area bombed but at least the crews could take solace in the knowledge that they were attacking the enemy, attempting to cripple his ability to supply and arm his troops by going after major industrial centres and not French civilians. Of course the Ruhr valley would not be the only target that Bomber command would go after. If it were, it would be too easy for the Germans to concentrate all their night fighters in that one area and make it very hot for the RAF bomber crews. They would of course hit other targets in Germany and Italy but the main effort for the next while was to be the Ruhr. It was an area that had a very high concentration of ack-ack batteries and extensive night fighter coverage but by flying operations to other areas as well the RAF had some hope of catching the Luftwaffe off guard at least some of the time.

At some point between arriving at 158 Squadron and his death on 03 April Bert wrote the poem from which the title of this book is taken. It is in many ways a sad poem with a forlorn almost desperate hope of survival in spite of the odds. Looked at another way though it can also be seen as a hopeful love poem. Written to the one who waits at home for the safe return of her loved one after the night's work over enemy territory had been safely carried out and the bombers had all returned safely home.

The Heart To Carry On

Every morning from this home
I go to the aerodrome.
And at evening I return
Save when work is to be done.
Then we share the separate night
Half a continent apart.

Many endure worse than we,
Division means by years and seas.
Home and lover are contained,
Even cursed within their breast.

Leaving you now with this kiss
May your sleep tonight be blest,
Shielded from the heart's alarms
Until morning I return.
Pray tomorrow I may be
Close, my love, within these arms,
And not lay dead in Germany.

Laying dead in Germany is, sadly exactly where Bert and his crew mates ended their short lives. This poem is not dated but it was obviously written after Bert had started flying combat operations. That it turned out to be somewhat prophetic is not surprising considering the casualty rates being suffered by Bomber Command in late 1942 and early 1943. However with Bert's completion of the Bomb Leader's course and his impending commission there was every hope that he would indeed survive and live through the war to pursue his dreams and work to reach the great potential that so many saw for him.

The news from the war in general was good too at this time. On the 02 February the beleaguered and surrounded German 6th Army at Stalingrad surrendered. The Nazi capture of Stalingrad turned out to be a high water mark of Hitler's invasion of the Soviet Union. After the Soviets recaptured Stalingrad they would push their advantage and continue pushing the Germans out of their territory and back eventually all the way to Berlin. In May in North Africa, Tunis fell to the allies and the defeated German troops Afrika Corp and their Italian allies were marched off to prison camps. More than 200,000 Axis soldiers had been captured. This defeat was as big a disaster for Hitler as the loss of the sixth army at Stalingrad. The defeat of the Axis powers in North Africa meant that the whole of the African continent was now liberated. The Italian African Empire was no more. Mussolini, Il Duce was now on veery thin ice and barely clinging on to power at all. The stage was now set for the Allies invasion of Sicily and the Italian mainland which was planned for the summer. The Allies invaded Sicily on 10 July 1943 and by 18 August, they controlled

140

the whole island. Preparing the way for an invasion of the Italian mainland. The Allies hoped that an invasion of Italy, would draw German troops away from the Soviet eastern front, and that is exactly what happened. Mussolini's grip on power in Italy was failing. Between these invasions, shortages of food, raw materials for factories and just about everything else, and coupled with the allied bombing of Italian cities the people had, had enough of Mussolini and Fascism. Italian king Victor Emmanuel sacked Mussolini on 18 July. The Allies invaded the mainland on 03 September 1943, and Italy surrendered on the 18th. As was hoped by Allied command this forced the Germans to redeploy troops from the eastern front to defend Italy for the remaining Axis powers. The Germans initially sent 25 divisions from the east to Italy. The battle for Italy would be a tough and bloody slog for the Allies. The Germans put up a determined defence, but the invasion had achieved its goal of forcing the Germans to weaken their eastern front by redeploying troops from there to Italy. Final liberation, and surrender of the last German troops in Italy was not until 02 May 1945, only five days before Germany itself surrendered ending the war in Europe.

Bert returned to flight duty as soon as he had returned to the squadron after completion of the bomb leaders course in March and flew on 4 more missions with his own crew, led by pilot Dennis Cole. Then on 29 March he flew an operation as bomb aimer to his squadron leader Wing Commander Hope. No doubt this mission was in part a chance for Wing Commander Hope to evaluate his soon to be new Bomb Leader. The mission which was to Berlin nearly ended in disaster as the aircraft was hit by flak and badly damaged. Wing Commander Hope managed to coax the wounded bird back to England and a safe landing back at base. It was a lucky escape.

For Bert and his crew mates luck would run out 5 nights later. On April 3rd 1943 on the return leg of a mission to Essen, Major Werner Streib, flying a Messerschmitt, closed in on Bert's Halifax and got it in his sights, bringing it down with deadly accurate fire for his third kill of the night. The aircraft crashed in a farmer's field near Pfalzdorf, 43 km north of Roermond from a height of 4.500 metres at 23.30 hrs with the loss of all hands. The men were less than an hour from a safe return to base. The aircraft slammed into the ground which such terrific force that pilot, Dennis Cole was thrown clear of the wreckage. Still strapped into his seat, he crashed through the roof of a nearby barn, seat and all. The aircraft had broken in to two pieces splitting apart at its mid-section. This was a trait of Halifax aircraft that had saved the life of more than one tail gunner in the past while the rest of the crew in the forward section were killed. On this night though rear gunner Leslie Watts was not so lucky and, the force of the crash was so intense that he died on impact along with the rest of his crew mates. The three men in the forward section of Bert's aircraft, namely, Bert, Wireless Operator Albert Ward and Navigator Ron Stemp could not be identified at the time and were initially interred in a communal grave together in the Stadtfreidhof, Munchen Gladbach cemetery. After the war the Commonwealth War Graves Commission (CWGC) re-interred the crew at Rheineberg War Cemetery just 40 KM west of their last target, Essen. The CWGC identified all seven of Bert's crew and now each man rests in his own grave.

As for the man who shot them down, Major Werner Strieb, he was one of the Luftwaffe's top fighter aces of the war. He claimed a total of 67 kills including the three on the night he brought down Bert's crew. On the very first day of the battle of France, May 10 1940, Streib, flying a Messerschmitt bf 110 heavy fighter, got his first kill, shooting down an RAF Bristol Blenheim. He was awarded the Iron Cross 2nd class for that kill. Streib was appointed *Geschwaderkommodore* (wing commander) of NJG night fighter squadron 1 on 1 July 1943 and continued to rack up kills of RAF aircraft at an impressive rate. On 23 March 1944, he was made Inspector of Night Fighters. Streib would stay in this post as *Oberst* (colonel) until the end of the war. Streib was awarded the Knight's Cross with Oak leaves and Swords. The Oak Leaves were presented to him by Hitler personally on 11 May 1943. Streib was often called 'Father of the *Nachtjagd'* (Night Fighters) and he was instrumental in developing the operational tactics used by the Nachtjagd during the early to mid-war years and he had a leading role in helping make the Luftwaffe's night fighters a very effective fighting force against the aircraft of RAF Bomber Command.

Werner Streib survived the war and after it ended he went in to the grocery business where he worked until 1956. Streib was then asked to join West Germany's Bundeswehr, the Federal Republic's military, where for three years he commanded Pilot School A. There he was responsible for training beginner pilots. Streib was promoted to *Brigadegeneral* and took up the post of *Inspizient Fliegende* (Inspector of Flying Forces). He retired from the miliary on 31 March 1966 and died in Munich on 31 March 1986 where he was buried with full military honours.

The dedicated men of RAF 158 Squadron continued to fly operational sorties against the enemy until the end of the war. The squadron flew its last operation of the war on April 25 1945. The mission was to knock out coastal batteries on the Frissian Island of Wangerooge. After the last of 158's aircraft touched down safely back at Lissett the squadron was stood down from Bomber Command. Shortly after the war ended the squadron was transferred to Transport Command before being disbanded entirely in December of 1945. Now the squadron exists only in the history books and memories of the crew and their families. Today the fields of the old Lissett airfield have been returned to farmland. The few wartime buildings that remain now house tractors and ploughs instead of bombers. Part of the old runway is now a wind farm. In a touching tribute to the sacrifices of the men of 158 each of the wind turbines is named after one of the Halifaxes of the Squadron. Now Friday The 13Th, Goofie's Gift, Zombie and the others help to light and warm local houses delivering power instead of bombs.

On the edge of the old airfield next to the road stands the poignant 158 Memorial to the 851 men who lost their lives flying with the squadron during the war. The memorial depicts the seven men of a Halifax Bomber crew in full flying gear as they return to base after a successful flight. Etched on both sides of the memorial is the name of each one of the fallen of the squadron. On the rear of the memorial on the far right hand side about midway down the crowded list is the name Bertram James Warr.

Chapter 13 Frank Warr

My uncle Frank Warr was born in 1916 one year before his brother Bert. Although the two were brothers they were very different from each. Frank stood 5'7 1/2 inches tall and on a good day pushed the scales at 150lbs. Frank had black hair and grey eyes and a narrow sharp nose. In many of his photos he looks like he has a sleepy, dreamy expression. Nothing could have been further from the truth. In his letters home we get a picture of an intelligent man with a sharp mind and a keen sense of humour. There is also a look of kindness in that face and in those eyes. In spite of his slight build he was very athletic and I would guess that he had an easier time in basic training than Bert, who found military life very tough going at first. Like Bert, Frank was very good academically however he did not pursue an academic career. From Bert's letters it can be guessed that Frank had leanings to the left politically just like the rest of the family. This was not surprising, the Warrs were a working class family during the depression years of the 1930s. Everyone had to chip in with whatever work they could get to keep the family household running. Socialism, with its promises of a more equitably spread wealth and a fair shake for the little guy would have been very appealing to a struggling family who were watching the rich get richer and the poor get poorer during the dirty thirties.

Frank left school at age 16 in 1932 after graduating from grade 12 at St Claire Elementary in Toronto. It seems though that he didn't find work until 1933 when he found employment at Mercer Bradford and Company. Mercer are a financial consulting firm who's offices are still located on Bay Street in the heart of Toronto's financial and banking district. Frank joined the firm as an office junior. He worked at Mercer for a year and left them to work at The National Trust Company of King Street. He worked at National Trust in the accounting department from 1934 until he enlisted in the RCAF in 1942. While working at National Trust he was taking night classes at U of T in accounting.

As with Bert, my primary sources for researching Frank were his letters home. But unlike Bert Frank was not a writer so there is not the additional source material of unpublished notebooks and published material to work from. Frank's surviving letters to the family naturally only begin after he left home for his overseas posting with the RCAF. This was in September 1942 when his training squadron was sent to Halifax Nova Scotia to await transport overseas to England. The unit's wait in Halifax turned out to be much longer than I would have thought and much longer than Frank and his mates wanted. They were stuck cooling their heals in Halifax from September 1942 until February of 1943, when they finally set sail for England on a troop transport. This unnamed ship would have part of one of the convoys that were escorted across the Atlantic by the navy in attempts to avoid the hunting packs of German U-boats. Frank's ship arrived safe and sound in Liverpool and he makes no mention of any encounters with German submarines along the way.

From family photos and his RCAF service record it can be guessed that Frank was a very active sportsman. There are photos of him rowing boats, skiing and golfing. His Service record lists sports that he was "extensively engaged in" as tennis, golf, skiing, baseball, skating and track, and sports that he "moderately participated in" as swimming, hockey, rugby, and riding. He was a very active person and it is easy to understand how the vigours of a military life and the thrill of flying would be attractive to him.

Not surprisingly Bert was against Frank enlisting. In a letter home written on 18 February 1940 Bert; ever mistrustful of governments wrote about the possibility of the Canadian government introducing conscription against their stated policy; he paraphrases Horace Greeley and advises Frank and all their friends "Head north young man" to avoid conscription. Of course Frank ignored this advice and volunteered for service anyway. In fact Frank seems to have been very keen to enlist and learn to fly. He joined the RCAF on March 25 1942 at No 1 M Depot Toronto. Frank did all of his training at Malton Airport which is now Pearson International and Toronto's main international airport. He carried out his flight training in Anson trainers. Frank qualified as a Navigator but also had some training in aerial photography and bomb aiming. Navigation was his primary trade and it was as a Navigator that he would do all his flight training in Wellingtons in, and it was as a navigator that he would fly his one and only combat mission, also flown in a Wellington. Frank seems to have taken to military life like a duck to water. He enjoyed the comradeship of squadron life and he loved flying.

Frank's letters home are much more relaxed than Bert's. While Bert's letters about family members are affectionate and at times teasing they can be stiff and at times rather impersonal. Frank's letters are much more playful especially when it came to writing about my mom, his youngest sister Cecelia. This is not surprising though. When Bert left home Cecelia was only 5 and when Frank left home she was nearly 10 but still considered the baby of the family. Frank had those extra five years of watching his little sister grow and being around her every day. When he got to England whenever Frank was close to the seaside he collected a few sea shells and saved them to send home to his little sister. He also enjoyed teasing his other three sisters, Marjory, Emily and Mary who he once playfully dubbed the "Warr Glamour Girls". Frank's letters home were often very light hearted. He often opens with something like "Dear mom, dad and brats." Once Emily and little Babs wrote to Frank asking if they could have his room for themselves and the family dog Skippy. Frank's reply was typical of him, "of course you can have my room, just don't go in it."

Frank also wrote more openly about his friends than Bert. It seems that his best friend during training was a big lad nicknamed General Grant. Frank and General Grant got up to all kinds of shenanigans during their training. Once while training in Scotland they were put in a decompression chamber together. The pressure was slowly decreased to simulate a rise in altitude to 30,000 feet. This was done to find out how an airman would respond to the low oxygen levels found at that extreme altitude. Of course there was a danger of getting the bends. If a person started to experience dizziness or pain they were to signal the device operator who would stop the test and get them out of there as quickly and safely as possible. Frank had to do just that because of an acute pain in his left shoulder. The test was stopped and a battered Frank was removed from the chamber safely, having failed to reach the test altitude. It turns out though that the cause of the pain in Frank's shoulder had nothing to do with the test and was caused because during the test run Frank and General Grant were repeatedly punching each other in the shoulder as hard as they could.

Another time while training in Scotland Frank and his unit were ordered to go on a long route march as part of their training. Evidently Frank didn't feel like going for a long walk that day because he just stepped out of line and started walking along beside his unit looking for all the world like he was going somewhere important on other business. He got away with that one and no one was any the wiser. Still in Scotland, while their unit was carrying out basic infantry defence training, Frank and his squad were on their way back to quarters after finishing for the day when they spotted a newly arrived unit moving up to start their first day's training. This training had a reputation for being very tough and Frank wanted to make sure the new unit started their day with this in mind. When Frank spotted the new unit marching towards them he decided to have a little fun. He got all the lads in his unit to start limping and leaning on each other as if they could barely make it back after the gruelling day's training they had just endured. He even got them to carry one fellow back as if he had a severe leg injury. The new unit must have been wondering what they were getting into as this sorry lot limped passed.

Before all this though Frank had to undergo all the basic military and flight training that all aircrew undertook. Frank did all his basic training in Malton close to home. He got to spend a lot of his free time visiting home and was able to

148

see family and friends right up until the time he and his unit were shipped out to go overseas. After leaving Malton in September of 1942 for Halifax Nova Scotia with his unit and finally leaving there in late January 1943 they arrived in England in early February and travelled to Bournemouth where they were to be billeted. Frank, never having been abroad before was bowled over by the beauty of the English countryside and Bournemouth. He wrote to his father that Bournemouth "most the beautiful town I have ever seen. I would like to spend the duration here."

Almost the first thing that Frank's unit did after settling into their new quarters was to go on a week's leave. This was at the time that Bert was just finishing his Bomb Leaders course and he was given two weeks leave before he had to rejoin 158 Squadron. The two brothers arranged to meet in London during their leave. Frank telephoned Bert to finalise the details of their planned visit. Frank relates that when Bert came on the phone that he didn't recognise his voice at first because Bert now had an English accent. After the two met up Frank wrote a letter home reporting to the family about his brother. Unusually Frank's letter is not very forthcoming with details. He merely says that Bert "looked well and of course a little older." It is probable that Frank, mindful of the fact that Bert had not told the family that he was flying combat missions was playing it safe by keeping his information about Bert rather general and vague so that he didn't inadvertently spill the beans revealing Bert's secret. He did make note though that Bert had left his adolescence behind, that he had grown and matured and become "a very fine chap and I suppose an intellectual." In a answer to a question asked by Mary Frank added that Bert "certainly had not become hard. A person of the sensitivity necessary to turn out such poetry could not be." I suppose that Mary asked this because she was worried that military training had changed her brother, and not for the better.

Frank's letter, while light on details about his brother does give a good report of all the things that he and Bert got up to while together in London. Bert showed Frank all the main tourist sites in London and had him round to his rooms at Lanark Mansions. Frank reported to the family that they went "Sight seeing and wandering around chatting. Saw Random Harvest and two other shows, went to a couple of dances and heard London Philharmonic at The Royal Albert Hall." Bert too reported to the family about the visit. He wrote home that "Frank was very well, not delighted to be away from home but I think he is interested in his work here." That statement strikes me as odd because as we have seen Frank seemed to be completely enjoying his adventure and being away from home. I'm sure that Frank was missing family and friends but from all his letters he seemed to have loved the whole experience of Airforce life and being overseas. It seems that both brothers were playing their cards very close to the vest when it came to telling the family what was actually going on. he does make sure to tell them that he showed Frank all the sights of London and including his rooms at Lanark Mansions. Bert also thanks the family for all the parcels that they sent over for him with Frank, four in total. And that is the extent of Bert's report home on the time he and Frank spent together in London. That week was the last time the two brothers would ever see each other.

On his return from his week's leave Frank's unit was detached from the RCAF and seconded to the RAF while they carried out their ground training. This involved a move to the north east coast of Scotland where they underwent the infantry training, during which Frank pulled off the tough training prank. After Scotland, Frank's unit had postings to bases near Stratford Upon Avon and Cornwall where he regularly went swimming in the ocean. Frank was obviously made of sterner stuff than me because the times that I have been to Cornwall doing anything more than wading slowly out into the frigid waters until the water was knee deep was about all I could ever manage. In fact most people who go swimming in the sea off Cornwall wear wet suites. Frank never even mentions the cold waters at all.

150

While he missed flying, Frank was thoroughly enjoying the experience and took every opportunity to take advantage of these postings to see and experience all that rural England had to offer. He went canoeing on the Avon near Stratford and of course went to see some Shakespeare plays in Stratford itself. He also managed to buy a bicycle and learned to ride that on the country roads. Surprisingly with his sporting background he had never ridden a bicycle before but, after a shaky start and a few falls, he was soon cycling around the leafy country lanes. The picture that Frank paints in his letters home at this time is very much contrary to Bert's report that Frank was not delighted to be away from home. He seemed to be thoroughly enjoying the whole experience.

Bert and Frank had a childhood friend named Al Hymus. They both mention him numerous times in their letters. In all the letters they both just call him Hymus, never Al. Calling people by only their last names in letters seems to have been a family habit. Bert often mentions, Pinkus but seldom, if ever Phil. Carrying this further Bert often mentions people by their last name or the even less personal habit of naming them by their nationality. He often mentions 'The Hungarian Lady," in his letters, meaning Mrs Nora Senjem. It is an odd, impersonal way of referring to friends and colleagues.

It seems that Hymus joined the army around the same time that Frank joined the RCAF and he was sent overseas to England at roughly the same time as Frank was. All through the winter, spring and summer months of 1943 Frank and Hymus tried to meet. But every time that they arranged to meet up something would happen and they kept missing each other for one reason or another. The tale begins to take on a tragi-comic feel. They would arrange to meet somewhere, usually in London, but on more than one occasion in another town while both were on leave only to have one of them show up on the wrong day or the wrong time or at the wrong place. More than once one or the other had their leave cancelled at the last minute yet again spoiling their chance to get together. Finally though Bert and Hymus did meet up. Frank had two weeks leave in late August just before he was to finally ship out to North Africa. He managed to track Hymus down at his base. The two spent some together there over one weekend. When Frank arrived at Hymus' base he found his friend in the middle of a baseball game against another squad. So Frank watched that game, then the two went off to the mess together to catch up on all that had been happening since they had last seen each other and to enjoy a beer or two. The next day, Saturday the lads travelled together to London. Frank wrote that they went to Madam Tussauds's and then to the movies together. After staying the night in London they went back to Hymus' base on the Sunday. They had intended to go for a long bike ride in the countryside but someone had stolen the bike that Hymus had arranged to borrow for Frank. Instead of the bike ride they ended up taking a long bus ride out into the country where they spent the afternoon hiking. On returning to the base Frank spent the evening beating Hymus at ping-pong and winning several rounds of beer from him in the process. Frank left on Monday to go to Bristol where he would stay with relatives until Friday when he returned to base. Those three days were the last time that Frank and Hymus the two childhood friends would see each other because shortly afterwards Frank left for North Africa from where he would never return. As with Pinkus we don't know whether or not Hymus survived the war.

Chapter 14: Frank's War

Shortly after Frank's leave his training outfit was again posted to Bournemouth. It was here that Frank got the news that Bert was reported as missing. Because the family were not aware what Bert's trade was or that he was flying in combat the telegram informing them that he was missing was a shock and no doubt contributed greatly to the extreme trauma the family experienced when they learned out of the blue that he was missing. Of course Frank had known was on active duty but he kept Bert's secret.

The family, probably primarily my grandmother and Mary had wanted Frank to transfer out of an active flying role. Now, with Bert missing they put enormous pressure on him to transfer out of Bomber Command. Frank was very reluctant to request a transfer as it involved not only a demotion from Sgt to AC2 but also the stigma of being classified LMF. The initials LMF stood for Lack Of Moral Fibre and basically labelled a man as a coward. To Frank the idea of a transfer under such a dark cloud was unthinkable. Also all indications from his letters suggest that Frank was having the time of his life in the RCAF. He loved the comradery of the lads in his unit and on his crew and he loved flying. However after the news that Bert was missing he bowed to family wishes and said that if the news about Bert was found to be bad he would request a transfer, but that he would not request the transfer if the news was good and Bert was reported as being alive and safe.

Classifying a man as LMF for whatever reason was not a decision taken lightly by the RAF or the RCAF. Today such a brutal policy would never be used. Much more is understood about PTSD etc and kinder and more humane methods are used to remove a man from a role that has traumatised him. An LMF classification also carried with it a great stigma of shame and cowardice in society. In this regard the RAF used it as a blunt club held over a man's head to keep him in line, albeit it was only used as a last resort. No one wanted to be branded LMF, lack of moral

153

fibre! Coward! There were many cases though where men, especially those in Bomber Command flying into almost certain death on a nightly basis did accept this fate. Of course in other cases the man was completely broken and the decision was inevitable. Let us not forget that all bomber aircrew were volunteers and no one entered bomber crew training who was not willing to lay down his life in this role. That some found extreme stress of the nightly trips into the hell over occupied Europe and Germany too much and were broken by the experience is not a surprise. Everyone has their breaking point. The wonder is that so many men did manage to carry on night after night and not only completed their missions but did so time and time again.

The decision to classify a man as LMF was always taken by a non flying officer, that is a desk jockey. Bomber crews themselves understood the pressures facing their unfortunate crew mate because they were right there with him every minute of every flight. Most crews would do everything they could to cover for their mate, to try to help him through this rough patch hoping his trauma was temporary and that next flight all would be well. There must have been many times when this was true. A man would lose his nerve under the extreme pressure and might bounce back next flight or the one after. However there were times when this did not happen and the crew would have no choice but to accept the man's breakdown and let him remove himself from flight duty by reporting himself to the MO as unable to carry on mentally.

For Frank the news that Bert was missing was a double blow. Not only did he have the worry that his brother was dead but he also now had to worry that he would be forced by family pressures to request a transfer out of bomber command. Frank did not want a transfer. He liked being in an active unit and being aircrew and of course he dreaded the idea of having to accept a classification as LMF. The time between Frank learning that Bert was missing and Bert being officially listed as dead on June 18 1943 must have been agonising mentally for Frank. Frank, true to his word bowed to family wishes after june 18 and agreed to ask for a transfer out of Bomber Command, out of active flying duty and into a safe and boring desk job with the extra stigma and humiliation of being classified as LMF.

For Frank's mother and father and the rest of the family things looked different. They knew that Bert was in the RAF but assumed him to be reasonably safe in a non-combat role as he not said otherwise. I'm not sure why they never asked. Perhaps they did and he fobbed them off with vague replies. So when Frank announced that he was going to fly combat duty the family wanted him to transfer, thinking only of keeping both brothers safely alive for the duration of the war. However before Bert's death they seem to have been willing not to press Frank to transfer after he learned of the double whammy of demotion and classification as LMF.

The double trauma of learning at the same instant that not only had Bert been flying combat missions but that he was now missing renewed the family pressure on Frank and they again began to press Frank to do the unthinkable and request a transfer. To them, a son and brother who was alive and safe was the most important thing and Frank's parents seemed more than willing to have him take the demotion and classification as LMF that such a transfer brought with it.

Frank spent the summer months of 1943 billeted in a hotel in Bournemouth which he still considered to be the prettiest town he ever saw. When Frank learned that Bert was missing Frank was actually at an OTU (Operational Training Unit) and getting ready to start flight training on Wellingtons in preparation for finally being returned to the RCAF and joining an active squadron. It was at the OTU that Frank, bowing to family wishes and pressures put in his request for a transfer. Naturally Frank's request was taken very seriously by the brass and further extended his stay in England and away from active flight duties. After he put in

155

his request Frank was immediately pulled from flight training. Instead of flying Frank spent his time in barracks and attending the many, many interviews the brass wanted while they assessed his request.

In July Frank got more leave and he went to visit the family in Bristol. He stayed with Uncle Dick, one of his father's brothers and Dick's wife Hattie. Uncle Dick showed Frank all around Bristol and the Warr family houses where they had grown up. Uncle Dick showed Frank the little school they had attended as children, the local pub "The Black Boy", a tree they called the stumps and had used while playing cricket when they were children. He also saw the suspension bridge and all the rest of the sights in that part of Bristol. They took a trip out to Pill where Frank explored a converted brewery the family had. Frank doesn't say what the brewery was converted into but presumably it was a house. He then went into Pill with Uncle Dick, Aunt Queen and her husband Uncle Rich and their son Jim and his wife. Aunt Queen and Uncle Dick took Frank in a little pony trap out to their cottage where he met Aunt Nell, cousin Peggy and her husband and their baby. It seems strange to think of people as late as the 1940s, even in the British countryside not having cars and using buggies pulled by horses and ponies but England and indeed most of Europe was still very rural and not many people had cars. Even those who did have cars would have had trouble getting enough petrol in those war days due to rationing. They stayed at the cottage overnight. It had rained on the trip out in the pony trap and they all were soaking wet. Frank was given a pair of Uncle Richard Withers pyjamas to sleep in while his clothes dried out. I guess that Uncle Richard was not a small man and of course Frank was very slight. Frank notes in his letter home that the pyjamas he was forced to wear "are quite copious." We can imagine Frank standing in the living room in front of the fire looking very much a like a boy in his dad's pyjamas, long sleeves and trouser legs hanging down and pyjama top billowing out. He must have been quite the sight.

156

Joan and Tiny, by this time married, were away in the forces as we know so Frank never had the chance to meet them. The next day they rounded up the pony in the field and Uncle Richard, Aunt Nell and Frank drove back into to Pill. From there Aunt Nell and Frank took a bus into Clevedon where Frank had the chance to thoroughly explore the promenade. In the afternoon Frank went with Aunt Nell to the farm of Aunt Queen's son John, which was a nice little place close to the water. Frank got a chance to taste some forbidden fruit in those rationing years. They had some fresh Devonshire cream for tea. It was forbidden to make cream for the duration as I it takes a lot of milk to produce. One of the Jersey cows had wandered off and they had been unable to milk it in time to send the milk to the dairy. When they did find the cow and milk her they made some fresh cream, a rare treat and one that they thoroughly enjoyed. On the Saturday Uncle Dick took Frank on the train to the coastal resort town of Weston Super Mare where he saw all the sights along the waterfront and went for a swim in a saltwater pool. They returned to Bristol in the evening on the bus where Frank spent the night before finishing his leave and heading back to camp. That had been the second week of his leave. He had spent the first week in London where he had met Mrs Senjem and had spent time finding out from her all that he could about what she knew of Bert.

Back at camp Frank sat around his billet while he awaited news of his transfer request. He does mention that there were dances at a nearby WAAF camp nearly every night and that he often went to these. At about this time he also started seeing "a nice little WAAF who was educated in a convent in Belgium." Frank doesn't tell the family this girl's name in his letter nor does he give any details as to where they went together except to say that he enjoyed her company, that she was a lot of fun to be with and that he wants to see her again when he returns from duty in Africa. This letter of course must have been written after Frank's request for transfer was turned down and he was returned to active flight duty.

157

As we know Frank loved flying and he loved the military life and being a navigator, and he was obviously very good at what he did. During his interviews this enthusiasm may have come across to the men asking the questions and taking his statements. While they considered his fate this was no doubt a factor in their decision to deny his request and return him to active duty. They wrote that Frank was willing, in fact even keen to return to active duty. I can't be sure but I can guess that it was grandma Warr who by this time was pressing the most for Frank to carry on with his transfer request. For her part Aunt Mary, once she realised that this request would tarnish Frank's reputation and mark him out as a coward fully supported his decision to accept a return to flying. Aunt Mary wrote that "Frank was so determined to be accepted for aircrew instead of being earmarked for a safe desk job that at his own expense he underwent an operation to remove a nasal blockage that would have prevented him being selected for air crew duty. He was a brave and keen young man who would not have deserved the shame and stigma that being declared LMF would have brought him." The rest of the family seem to have accepted this decision buy the authorities to deny Frank his transfer request but grandma Warr, for one, never forgot, nor forgave the Air Force for taking her boys from her.

We can only guess at the relief that Frank must have felt when his request for transfer was denied and he was returned to active flight status with the RCAF, but it must have been immense. Frank returned to duty and resumed his flight training on Wellingtons. After several weeks of this he was assigned to 424 Squadron. 424 was operating from a base in North Africa in Tunisia on the north east coast about 50Km west of the city Kairouan. They were there in support of the Allied invasions of Scilly and Italy. The allies invaded Sicily in July 1943 and main land Italy 03 September that same year. The Allies invaded Sicily on 10 July 1943 and by 18 August, they controlled the whole island. Preparing the way for an invasion of the Italian mainland. The Allies hoped that an invasion of Italy, would

158

draw German troops away from the Soviet eastern front, and that is exactly what happened. Mussolini's grip on power in Italy was failing. Between these invasions, shortages of food, raw materials for factories and just about everything else, coupled with the allied bombing of Italian cities the people had, had enough of Mussolini and Fascism. Italian king Victor Emmanuel sacked Mussolini on 18 July. The Allies invaded the mainland on 03 September 1943, and Italy surrendered on the 18th. As was hoped by Allied command this forced the Germans to redeploy troops from the eastern front to defend Italy for the remaining Axis powers. The Germans initially sent 25 divisions from the east to Italy. The battle for Italy would be a tough and bloody slog for the Allies. The Germans put up a determined defence, but the invasion had achieved its goals of both opening a second front and forcing the Germans to weaken their eastern front by redeploying troops from there to Italy. Final liberation, and surrender of the last German troops in Italy was not until 02 May 1945, only five days before Germany itself surrendered ending the war in Europe.

On his return to active flying duty, Frank was assigned to the crew with whom he had done his conversion training, namely, Pilot Andy Martin from Saskatchewan, J. R. Dack who was the air bomber (AB) and also from Saskatchewan, air gunner (AG) Dick Cote and Don Dodson who was the Wireless operator (WOP). Dodson was RAF. All the rest of the crew were RCAF. In his letters home Frank's enthusiasm for flying shines through. He was so excited to be returning to active flight duty that he positively gushes " We have the best crew and the best squadron." He wrote that before he had even reached the squadron who had been in Africa since June. The crew flew their Wellington to North Africa and joined the squadron on 15th September 1943. They didn't immediately go on active duty but spent a few days on leave in Morocco where Frank managed to visit Fez.

When they did join the squadron they continued to enjoy themselves "We made a lovely trip in trucks yesterday and

159

had a lovely swim in the Mare Nostrum. Lovely warm water and fine golden sand" (Mare Nostrum was the Roman name for the Mediterranean Sea). The water may have been warm and sand golden but there were also jelly fish and Frank got bitten by them twice. It didn't seem to bother him though because he carried on swimming and enjoyed his day. Of course while he was at the seaside he gathered some seashells for his little sister Babs. It is nice to consider that Frank and his crew mates had this one last day of fun at the sea just days before they took off into the night skies on their one and only combat operation and were never seen again.

Interestingly this day trip to the seaside is mentioned in the 424 squadron ORB. ORB entries are usually confined to relating transfers in and out of the unit and listing of crew and aircraft and their targets and bomb loads etc on particular ops. To make an entry about a squadron day out to the seaside was most unusual.

In his last letter home Frank relates how glad he is to be back in the RCAF and "in the best squadron out here." Poignantly and perhaps tempting fate the letter continues "I don't think you need to worry much about our safety here as the ops are not tough and we get them over in a hurry here which is good." And that was the last thing he ever wrote home.

Frank and his crew took off for their first and only combat operation on 01 Oct 1943. It was an op to bomb Formia, which is located halfway between Rome and Naples in southern Italy. In one of those strange quirks of fate, both Frank and Bert took their last flights in "F" for Freddie designated aircraft. Bomber Command aircraft all had manufacturer's serial numbers Bert's - Halifax II DT635 and Frank's Wellington HE795. In addition each squadron had it's own two letter code and each aircraft in the squadron was assigned a call letter. Bert"s Squadron number 158 had code NP and Bert's aircraft was therefore NP-F. Franks squadron had code QB and Frank's aircraft was therefore

160

QB-F. Frank's Wellington HE795 QB-F took off from base at 19:43 to bomb Formia in Italy. Nothing was ever again heard of this aircraft after take-off. It disappeared without trace.

Frank Warr Active duty Log: Frank's one and only combat mission

424 Sqn ORB entry: Lost: 01 Oct 1943. Op to bomb Formia. Wellington HE795 F.

T/O: 19:43. Nothing was ever heard of this aircraft after T/O

Crew: Pilot: Martin I A
Nav: Warr F
B/A: Dack JR
WOP: Dodson GD
A/G: Cote JR

The 424 ORB states that extensive searches failed to turn up any trace of the aircraft. The op was considered to be what was called a milk run. A milk run mission was about as safe an op as you could wish for. It was typically flown over very lightly defended areas and to an equally lightly defended target. On this occasion the enemy made no claims for having shot down any Allied aircraft. So what happened to Frank and his crew? Did they reach the target and carry out their mission and then crash on the return flight. Did they even make it to the target? It seems that they did and were then lost on the return leg of the op.

Aunt Mary persisted in trying to find out what happened to her brother Frank with a dogged determination which can only be explained by the deep love and close ties that the family shared. She managed to contact a fellow from RCAF 425 Alouette Squadron. 425 were also operating out of North Africa at the time in support of the Allied invasions. This man, named Alistair Craig, wrote back to Aunt Mary and told her what his crew had experienced and seen that night of Oct 2. He related that the weather was absolutely terrible. There were heavy thunder storms all over the area.

161

He said that several aircraft were even forced to abort their missions and turn back base because of the weather. However Alistair's crew carried on and bombed the target. The target, Formia was lightly defended so there was no ack-ack and there were no night fighters sent up because of the bad weather. Their bombing run went off without a hitch and Alistair's aircraft turned for home heading back out over the Med. It was over the sea that the pilot saw a flash and a huge explosion in the distance. He deduced that it could only have been caused by an aircraft being hit by lightning and then exploding. They flew to the area and made several low level passes over where they believed the aircraft must have come down but they saw nothing. They then continued back to base. The only report of any aircraft lost that night was of Frank's Wellington so the explosion Alistair's pilot witnessed must have been Frank's Wellington blowing up. Alistair continued in his letter " Francis and his crew would never have known what hit them as they would have been killed instantly in the explosion. I am sure that none of them would have been alive when the aircraft hit the water."

The loss of Frank's aircraft to a lightning strike on an operation which otherwise was a safe as any could ever hope to be was a strange and cruel quirk of fate. There are a good many unanswered questions about the op. Why did Frank's crew even attempt the mission? After all the weather was so bad that many more experienced crews didn't even take off or turned back before even reaching the target. Was it the determination of the new boys to prove themselves in combat or was it perhaps a lack of experience that a more seasoned crew would have had? What are the odds of a lightning strike so violent hitting the aircraft that it was completely destroyed? They must be very long. Looking through squadron ORBs I didn't find accounts of any other aircraft being lost in this fashion. I'm sure that a thorough examination of ORBs of all the squadrons operating over the Med would turn up accounts of aircraft being hit by lightning but very few would have been brought down by the strike, let alone have been completely destroyed by it.

The loss of Frank's aircraft in this way was a very unlucky, one in a million shot.

Chapter 15: Bert's Legacy

The news that Bert was missing in action and then finally
that he had been killed rocked the family. I don't think that
my grandparents ever fully got over Bert's death, followed a
scarce six months later by Frank's. The shock and the
trauma caused by the loss of "the boys" left deep wounds
that never fully healed. As we know Bert's family were only
vaguely aware what his trade in the Airforce had been and
they did not know that he was flying in combat. He didn't
want them to worry about him so he didn't tell them that he
was flying combat missions. They didn't seem to want to
press the issue and were more than happy to carry on
assuming that Bert's job in the RAF was in a non-combat
roll.

After they received of the telegram informing them that
Bert was missing the family held their collective breaths
waiting for official news one way or another. No one more
so than Frank, whose future stood to be affected the most by
whether or not Bert was alive or not. His promise to the
family that if the news was the worst that he would indeed
ask for a transfer from active flying duty weighed heavily
on him. They all figuratively held their breaths as the days
passed and they waited for official confirmation of Bert's
fate. There was every hope that Bert and his crew mates
survived the crash and had been taken as prisoners or else
had evaded capture and were hiding out with hopes of
trying to make their way back to England. Those days of
uncertainty must have been an agony for the family. Every
time there was a knock at the door they must have been
dreading that it would be the telegram informing them of
the worst.

Bert's aircraft was shot down on the night of April 3rd 1943
and it was on 18 April that he was officially declared to
have been killed in action. A Telegram from Air Ministry to
Frank and another one to the family informing them that
Bert was officially listed as having been killed was sent on
18 April 1943. In the usual terse style of telegrams and cold

official language of military messages the telegram sent to
Frank reads as follows:

*"Immediate from Air Ministry deeply regret to advise that
that according to information received through the
international Red Cross Committee your brother Sgt
Bertram James Warr is believed to have lost his life as a
result of air operations on 03 April 1943. stop. The Air
Council express their profound sympathy. His mother is
being informed Under Secretary of State. stop."*

The telegram sent to the family would have been very
similar, written in just as a cold and terse a manner. The
British had gotten confirmation of Bert and his crew's death
from the International Red Cross who had been informed by
the German authorities that none of the crew had survived
the crash.

On 05 May Frank true to his word put in a transfer request.
I'm sure he did so very reluctantly and with fingers crossed
that he would be turned down. A future blighted by a
classification as LMF was not something anyone would
want, let alone a man of Frank's quality and bravery. He
wanted to keep flying and didn't want to be chained to a
desk in a non flying role. In the short term he was
immediately pulled from training and put into a sort of
official limbo while his request was considered by the brass.
This left him cooling his heels in his billet. With nothing to
do but wait for whatever fate the powers that be deemed
was in store for him.

Frank took some of that downtime to write a letter home in
an attempt to ease the pain of his family. He wrote of his
impression of Bert when they met up on leave in London
that March "Bert had grown into a very fine chap and his
life in recent years had been interesting and eventful. In
giving it up we can hope it was not in vain. Flying is not
sordid warfare, clean and interesting. The dangers are not
terrifying but exhilarating. His main regret would have been
the pain and sorrow caused to you folks at home."

165

As well as causing chaos in Frank's life and devastating the family, the news of Bert's death resulted in a flurry of sympathetic letters to Bert's parents from family and friends. John Gawsworth wrote Bert's obituary in The Times Literary Supplement and in a letter to Bert's sister Mary dated Nov 29 1943 he introduced himself to her and sent the family his condolences. At this time he requested that they let him have Bert's manuscripts for editing and publishing in book form in England and Canada after the war. Of course in letters home Bert had often written of Gawsworth so they were at least familiar with him from those and knew that he was a friend they could trust. Bert had become close friends with Gawsworth. The pair had been planning on collaborating on a book after the war. Now Gawsworth wanted to carry on with his own project to keep Bert's memory alive.

John Gawsworth's obituary of Bert in the Times Literary Supplement August 7th 1943 ran as follows:

I have been informed through a member of his family that the loss of Bertram Warr, at the age of twenty five, on air operations, has been confirmed. It was my good fortune to be stationed for several months with this young but intellectually mature Canadian poet, the while he qualified as an air observer. Frail in appearance a very "parfait gentile" serious young man, it was difficult to imagine the self chosen vicissitudes he had endured: hitch-hiking across Canada, stowing away one Christmas Eve and landing in Liverpool with but ten shillings in his pocket, to starve at times, wash dishes and clerk at Billingsgate, solely because he desired to add to the literature of the mother country. His modesty would have it that it was but a mite that he had to offer. Alas that we will never know the full sum! Nevertheless he has his place and it is right and fitting that he should have found it under English imprints. A broadsheet of some dozen poems in the Favil Press Series of Resurgam Younger Poets (with a prose preface that clearly states his poetic principle), a few uncollected poems in Mr

Wrey Gardiner's Poetry Quarterly, and representation in
"Poems of The Forces" and Miss Patricia Ledward's
Cambridge University Press anthology of wartime verse:
such are his published beginnings. After the war I sincerely
hope it may be possible to issue a volume concurrently in
England and Canada, selected from the above and from his
assembled manuscripts.

Gawsworth thought a great deal of Bert and admired his
talent and potential so much so that not only did he want to
publish a book of Bert's poems but he also dedicated one of
his own poems to Bert. The poem is titled "Permanence."

Permanence
(For Bertram Warr)

The bomb obliterates.
The dream remains.
No thing may mankind utterly destroy.
Within the ether unity obtains.
A great loss often is a cause for joy.

Anarchy's triumph is a moments spell;
Culture's long travail augers longer life.
A poem slays more spirits than a shell.
An essay comforts longer than a wife.

How short our living we seldom know;
What seems beginnings like as not are ends.
Beneath life's current runs an underflow
That drags us down from fancies and from friends.

Who knows that laughter is
(When all else fails and falls)
The quintessence of bliss,
Though echoed under broken walls,

167

Sees symbols of a better day,
Achieves crustacean hardihood.
No heart insensible to clay
Creates for public good.

Gawsworth wanted to get all of Bert's manuscripts and papers that were in the care of Mrs Senjem and Patricia Ledward. The family agreed to this and Bert's sister Mary wrote letters to both these ladies asking that they send any papers of Bert's that they had to Gawsworth. The family and Mary especially, were very keen to have a book of Bert's poems published. Mary worked tirelessly to help Gawsworth with this project. And Gawsworth, true to his word worked long and hard himself on the project after the war when he had returned to civilian life. Sadly, Gawsworth's effort were ultimately fruitless and he was unable to see the project through. He never did publish a book of Bert's work.

Patricia Ledward also expressed interest in publishing a book of Bert's material. In her letter of condolence to Mary she offered to contact Mrs Senjem whom she knew had many of Bert's papers. This project of Patricia's came to nothing because Mary and her parents had already committed to Gawsworth's planned project. Bert must have had some contact with Patricia over the last months of his life. He had written home in July of 1941 that he had not seen nor heard from Patricia Ledward in over 6 months but at some point they must have seen each other because in her poem dedicated to Bert, Patricia relates words Bert had said to her about his expected death. In fact that poem reads as if they were having a conversation and not something taken from a letter. So it would seem likely that they had met up at some point after Bert had started flying combat operations with 158 Squadron.

At some point after the war Patricia seems to have had a change of heart about the papers and letters of Bert's that she had. When Aunt Mary, having decided that Gawsworth was the fellow to get a book of Bert's work published wrote to Patricia requesting that she send them any and all material of Bert's that she had, Patricia wrote back that she had destroyed everything, published and unpublished that she had held of Bert's. We can only speculate as to why she did this. Perhaps the pain of Bert's loss was too much for her. Perhaps she now found herself in a new relationship and either destroyed Bert's letters and papers at the request of her new fella or she wanted to cut ties with that part of her past. Obviously the decision to destroy any letters that Bert had sent her was her right and likewise destroying any of Bert's published work that she had was her right. Where I think Patricia crossed the line is in destroying all Bert's unpublished work and notes that she had. She should have sent these to the family. Whether or not any of this material was any good or not is beside the point. Legally all this material belonged to Bert's mother who held copyright on all his material. Sadly whatever, if any, unpublished papers of Bert's that Patricia Ledward held are now lost to us, likely all because of the whims of a broken heart.

Many others had comforting words of condolence for the family. Frank was in contact with Aunt Queen after Bert's death and from her he learned that Bert had told Joan Withers "I shall just about learn to fly then, one bomb and I shall be gone." Frank wrote that Aunt Queen also thought Bert "very loveable."

It is from Nora Senjem that we get the best idea of Bert's mental state in the months leading up to his death. Of course we know from his essay about dying that ends Acknowledge To Life that Bert was resigned to death. He was even to an extent ready and wanting to die because of the strains of flying combat. It is from Nora Senjem that we get an idea of how much this affected his thoughts and actions. Frank went to London and met Nora Senjem after Bert's death and afterwards wrote to the family what she had related to him about Bert. Nora Senjem herself also wrote to Aunt Mary several times. Frank wrote that Nora Senjem had known Bert since the first days of his arrival in

London from Canada. As I have related elsewhere Bert
seems to have considered her to be a sort of surrogate
mother or perhaps a very close aunt. That feeling was
mutual and Nora Senjem cared a great deal about Bert. She
related that Bert was always very careless with all his
things. Throwing away and giving away his money and
possessions to any needy person. Then he would end up
having to borrow money for his own needs. Consequently
he was always broke and in debt. Bert was not only careless
with his money but with pretty much everything else as
well, lending his typewriter to one of his girlfriends. One
time while in his cups in Scotland Bert had bought quite a
few records from a local shop. He seems to have just left the
whole lot of them somewhere in Kinloss or West Fraugh.
Mrs Senjem convinced Bert to open a bank account but he
only managed to save £5 in it. After he enlisted his friends
had quite a time keeping track of him. He would arrive in
London on leave suddenly and just as suddenly leave again
without the slightest warning. He was never now on time
for appointments if he kept them at all. It would seem that
military life was taking a toll on him right from the day he
enlisted.

In one of her letters to Mary, Nora Senjem wrote that she
wanted to collect all the details that she had concerning Bert
and pass them along to the family. She adds though that
these amount to very little real information and that their
mutual friends knew even less about Bert. As one would
expect in letters to his family after his death all comments
are very kind and positive and paint Bert's character in the
best light. Nora continues, writing that everybody without
exception liked him and appreciated him for his very decent
and sweet nature. He was always very quiet in society. At
parties and dinners he spoke very little but tried to help
everybody, usually beyond his means. This description
tallies with what Bert himself wrote in his letters home the
few times that he did mention dinner parties or other
gatherings at Mrs Senjem's house. It seems he was more
than content to sit in a quiet corner with his glass of
whiskey, perhaps puffing on a favourite pipe and enjoy the

170

conversation and other entertainment around him making very little effort to join in. But no doubt listening intently to the writers, deep thinkers and other artists who attended these gatherings at Mrs Senjem's house. Many of these people were refugee intellectuals and others that were high on the list of people that the Nazis wanted to persecute. They seem to have been primarily from Austria and Nora Senjem's native Hungary.

After the war, John Gawsworth Alan Crawley and Canadian poet Earl Birney published several of Bert's poems in their respective poetry magazines and in 1949 Birney read Bert's poem "The Heart Carry On" on his CBC radio show about poets of World War 2.

Once Gawsworth had made his way back to England from India after the war he proceeded to carry out his plans for publishing Bert's work in book form. He worked diligently, gathering manuscripts of as much of Bert's work, published and unpublished that he could find. He was in close contact with the family, specifically Aunt Mary. Although it was Grandma Warr who now owned the copyright to all of Bert's work it was Aunt Mary who looked after all the administration and correspondence etc. Gawsworth got permission from the family to carry on with his book project and they sent him all the papers of Bert's that they had. He also contacted Patricia Ledward and Nora Senjem and got all of Bert's papers that they had. How much material he got from Patricia Ledward is unknown because as we have seen she destroyed Bert's papers that were in her care. At this point unfortunately, Gawsworth's efforts stalled. He became ill and also was very much involved with other projects that were more urgent than getting Bert's book published and he put the project on a back burner. Even so there was great hope that Gawsworth's book would be published. Canadian poet Earle Birney was impressed with the selection of poems that Gawsworth was planning to include in the book. Writing to Aunt Mary he said "here is some fine work. The record of an original, honest and thoughtful mind of a young man who was already inwardly a developed poet, with a subtle yet easy way with him, imaginative but with his feet on the ground. I am eager to see it all published."

As Gawsworth's project languished and stalled Birney became more concerned as did Aunt Mary. On 22 September 1949 Aunt Mary wrote to Birney voicing her concerns which Birney seems to have shared. They were both worried about Gawsworth's choice of publisher and the excessive amount of time that he was taking to get the project to press. Aunt Mary wrote "I can't tell him that I don't want his edition, I do - sight unseen, but I owe it to Bert to ensure the finest publication."

In the summer of 1948 grandma Warr and my mom went to England on holiday. My mom would have been 16 at this time. At or near the top of their to do list was a meeting with Gawsworth. They had lunch with him and grandam Warr came away singularly unimpressed by this fellow. As Aunt Mary wrote to Birney "My mother considered that he was greatly concerned with his own affairs, new wife, sovereignty of his island, etc and placed little confidence that he would look after the work." Mary however didn't share this view as she adds "That it seems was unjust." It seems that Mary's assessment was right because Gawsworth's project did finally reach the stage when contracts were ready for signature and it seemed that publication was set to proceed. He sent a contract ready for signatures to the family but it had no cover letter and that of course raised major concerns. There must have been other things at play and other concerns about Gawsworth's project within the family but it seems that the fallout from the contract letter was the straw that broke this projects back. The family decided to cancel Gawsworth's project outright and Aunt Mary wrote to him requesting the return of all of Bert's papers. Gawsworth duly sent everything that he had of Bert's to Mary with nary a word surviving as to the why's and wherefores and that is the last we hear of John Gawsworth.

But this was not yet the end of Bert's legacy. Earle Birney in particular was very impressed with Bert's work and often included one or more of Bert's poems in his publications. Earle Birney was born in Calgary on 13 May 1903 and died of a heart attack at the age of 92 in Toronto. He grew up in Erickson B.C. and as a young man worked variously as a farm hand, a bank clerk and a park ranger. Entering university his plan was to get a degree in chemical engineering but after time at UBC, U of T, UC Berkley and the University of London he graduated with a degree in English. During the war he served overseas as a personnel officer. In 1946 Birney began his teaching career at the University of British Columbia where he founded the universities first creative writing program. Drawing on his wartime experiences Birney wrote the book Turvey which was a best seller in Canada and won him the Stephen Leacock Medal for Humour. Today it is for his poetry that Birney is mainly remembered. He twice won the Governor General's Award, Canada's top literary award and in 1970 he was made an Officer Of The Order Of Canada for his poetry.

At the end of the war in 1949 Birney broadcast a live radio program on CBC directly from Canada to England. During the program he read Bert's poem "The Heart Carry On" as part of the show. Birney tried on several occasions to get a book of Bert's work published and supported Gawsworth's efforts as well. In the end though none of that came to fruition and the prospect of getting a book of Bert's poems published seemed as remote as ever.

In July 1965 Bert's poem "Working Class was read out live on the CBC television program "Camera Canada" and that it seems was the last anyone would ever hear of Bertram Warr. By the 1960s even Aunt Mary must have thought that the chances of any book of Bert's poems being published were highly unlikely. Enter Len Gasparini. Len Gasparini was a Canadian poet, editor and publisher born in Windsor Ontario in 1941. Just how Gasparini became interested in Bertram Warr's poetry is not known, but he did and in spades. Gasparini was so impressed with Bert's work that he believed a book should finally be published and that he was the fellow to make it happen. Sometime in 1968 he contacted the family and together with Aunt Mary worked diligently over the next two years to get a book of Bert's work published. Even so the publishing of Bert's book "Acknowledgement To Life" very nearly didn't happen. There were problems with the publisher and some ruffled feathers between Earle Birney and Gasparini. Mary still wanted to have Birney involved in the project and Birney for his part was more than happy to have a part in the publishing of a book of Bert's work. Birney was enlisted to write the preface to the book. The problem was that Birney had very little faith that Gasparini was up to the job of carrying the project off properly. He was very unhappy with the selection of some of the poems that Gasparini wanted to include. Birney felt that some of the poems were not good enough or not sufficiently developed, being works in progress. He did not think these should be included. Birney was also very unhappy with Gasparini's initial introduction written for the book so much so that he threatened to withdraw his support for the project completely if Gasparini was allowed to stay involved. This set off alarm bells with the publishers, The Ryerson Press. They contacted Mary and informed her that if Birney pulled out there was a real danger that the project would be cancelled altogether. Mary however persevered and was determined to at last see a book of her brother's work published. Mary managed to get Gasparini to rewrite his introduction, addressing Birney's concerns and the selection of poems to be included was also worked out to everyone's satisfaction. With Mary in the role of peace maker things were patched up between Gasparini and Birney and eventually Birney agreed to contribute his preface to the book. By this time it was late 1969 and yet another hurdle had arisen. The Ryerson Press was about to be sold to McGraw Hill Publishing Company and there was a danger that if the book was not published before this sale that the project would be scuppered by the new publishers. Finally though all the T's were crossed and the I's were dotted and in 1970 "Acknowledgement to Life" was sent to

174

the presses and it was one of the last books published under the Ryerson Press banner. Mary's dedication and perseverance had paid off and Bert's legacy lives on. In his preface to the book Earl Birney wrote that - "Had Bert lived I think this book is evidence he could have been a leading poet of his generation."

Epilogue

Bert's life, like the lives of so many who are caught up in the struggles great and small of their times was cut brutally short by the cruel randomness of war. His is a story of remarkable accomplishments and even more so of potential unrealised. Bert's skill as a poet is recognised and greatly admired by all who read his work but much of it is just a glimpse of what might have been had he lived to hone his skills and master his art. Bert Warr only lived a short 25 years but he has left us a rich body of work. Much of Bert's writing stands on its own, complete and fully developed but also much of it is a glimpse of what he may have become. There are many of his poems which lack those finishing touches that a more experienced writer would have added. His legacy is as much about what he has left us as it is about what heights he may have attained had he lived and continued to master his art. As full and rich as his 25 years were his story is above all a story of vast potential unrealised, a life barely begun. Bert firmly believed that it was the duty of the modern poet to point the way to a better life for everyone and he tried to live his life by his beliefs not only through his poetry but through his every day actions. Through his work with The People's Convention, the various refugee organisations that he was involved in and his day to day dealings with people Bert practiced what he preached. The best of Bert's poems challenge us to take up the fight where he left off, to try to make ourselves higher and finer and to help people. But above all Bert challenges us to live like he himself did, keeping a warm heart and an open mind no matter how large the task before us is or how the odds are stacked against us to have the heart to carry on.

Appendix I

List Of Bertram Warr's Published Poems

Yet A Little Onwards

Introduction
War Widow
I Sit With Nothing In My Hands
Death Of An Elephant
Winter Stalks
Working Class
Discord
The Murder
Rejuvenation
From Atheism
The Deviator
Immaculate Conception
The End Of The World
To A Passionate Socialist
On A Child With A Wooden Leg

Acknowledgment To Life: The Collected Poems Of Bertram Warr
The Dead (For Bertram Warr) Patricia Ledward

Part 1 Yet A Little Onwards

Working Class
War Widow
The Deviator
On A Child With A Wooden Leg
Death Of An Elephant
The Murder
Winter Stalks
To A Passionate Socialist
Rejuvenation
I Sit With Nothing In My Hands

177

Acknowledgement To Life

<u>Appendix</u>

The Outcasts Of Society
An Unfinished Essay

Poems Of This War by Younger Poets

War Widow
Children In The Dusk
Poets In Time Of War (For Wilfred Owen)
Working Class

Poetry Quarterly Spring 1941

Tears Who Are Distant As Another's Reality

Contemporary Verse: A Canadian Quarterly October 1945

Winter Stalks
Death Of An Elephant
The Heart To Carry On
Stepney 1941

Appendix II

Bertram Warr Military Service

Service No. 1391138

Royal Air Force Volunteer Reserve

Background

Enlisted at Euston

Pre War Address: 84 Cloverlawn Avenue, Toronto, Ontario

Canadian

Training

No. 158 Squadron Conversion Flight

Service

Posted to No. 158 Squadron 4 Group Bomber Command at East Moor 24/9/42

Flew as Air Bomber to F/Lt. J.D. Cole on Operations to

15/10/42 – Cologne: 289 aircraft: 289 aircraft -109 Wellingtons, 74 Halifaxes, 62 Lancasters, 44 Stirlings. 18 aircraft lost - 6 Wellingtons, 5 Halifaxes, 5 Lancasters, 2 Stirlings. 6.2% of the force. This was not a successful raid. Winds made establishing their position and the marking of the target by the Pathfinders difficult. Also the Germans lit a large decoy fire away from the target which attracted most of the main force and received most of the bombing.

Aircraft: Halifax II W1157 NP-A
      Crew: Pilot: Pilot Officer (PO) J.D. Cole
            Nav:Sgt R.C. Stemp
            A/B: Sgt B.J. Warr
            WOP: Sgt A. Ward
            MUG: Sgt P. Harrison
            RG: Sgt L. G. H. Watts
            FE: Sgt R. Gowing

7/11/42 – Genoa: 175 aircraft - 85 Lancasters, 45 Halifaxes, 39 Stirlings, 6 Wellingtons. 6 aircraft lost - 4 Halifaxes, 1 Lancaster, 1 Wellngton. 3.4% of the force. Returning crews claimed a very successful and concentrated raid and this was confirmed by photographs.
    Aircraft: Halifax II BB209 NP-G
    Crew: Pilot: PO J.D. Cole
            Nav: Sgt R.C. Stemp
            A/B: Sgt B.J. Warr
            WOP: Sgt A. Ward
            MUG: Sgt W. A. Robinson
            RG: Sgt W. J. Hanks
            FE: Sgt R. Gowing

26/11/42 – Mining Operation: 30 aircraft minelaying off Lorient and St-Nazaire and in the Frisians Kattegat. No aircraft lost.
    Aircraft: Halifax II DT505 NP-H
    Crew: Pilot: PO J.D. Cole
            Nav: Sgt R.C. Stemp,
            A/B: Sgt B.J. Warr
            WOP: Sgt A. Ward
            MUG: Sgt W. A. Robinson
            RG: Sgt W. J. Hanks
            FE: Sgt R. Gowing

3/12/42 – Frankfurt: 112 aircraft - 48 Halifaxes, 27
Lancasters, 22 Stirlings, 15 Wellingtons, 6 aircraft lost - 3
Halifaxes, 1 each of the other types. 5.4% of the force.
Thick haze prevented the Pathfinders finding Frankfurt.
Most bombs fell in the country areas south-west of the city
    Aircraft: Halifax II DT505 NP-H
    Crew: Pilot: PO J.D. Cole
           Nav: Sgt R.C. Stemp
           A/B: Sgt B.J. Warr
           WOP: Sgt A. Ward
           MUG: Sgt W. A. Robinson
           RG: Sgt L.G.H. Wattss
           FE: Sgt R. Gowing

6/12/42 – Mannheim: 272 aircraft - 101 Lancasters, 65
Halifaxes, 57 Wellingtons, 49 Stirlings. 10 aircraft lost - 5
Wellingtons, 3 Halifaxes, 1 Lancaster, 1 Stirling. 3.7% of
the force. Target completely cloud covered and many crews
bombed on dead reckoning. Mannheim reported only 500 or
so incendiary bombs and some leaflets
    Aircraft: Halifax II W1217 NP-S
    Crew: Pilot: PO J.D. Cole
           Nav: Sgt R.C. Stemp
           A/B: Sgt B.J. Warr,
           WOP: Sgt A. Ward
           MUG: Sgt W. A. Robinson
           RG: Sgt C. G. Dawson
           FE: Sgt G Reynolds

8/12/42 – Mining Operation: 80 aircraft of 1, 3 and 4
Groups to the German and Danish coasts. 5 aircraft lost. 3
Stirlings, 1 Halifax, 1 Lancaster. 6% of the force.
    Aircraft: Halifax II W1257 NP-S
    Crew: Pilot: PO J.D. Cole
           Nav: Sgt R.C. Stemp
           A/B: Sgt B.J. Warr,
           WOP: Sgt A. Ward
           MUG: Sgt W. A. Robinson
           RG: Sgt C. G. Dawson
           FE: Sgt E. Heweston

11/12/42 – Turin: 82 aircraft of 1, 4 and 5 Groups and the Pathfinders. 48 Halifaxes, 20 Lancasters, 8 Stirlings 6 Wellingtons. 4 aircraft lost - 3 Halifaxes, 1 Stirling, 4.8% of the force. More than half the force turned back before crossing the Alps due to severe icing conditions. 28 crews claimed to have bombed Turin but the city reported only 3 high explosive bombs and a few incendiaries.

    Aircraft: Halifax II DT585 NP-L
    Crew: Pilot: PO J.D. Cole
          Nav: Sgt R.C. Stemp
          A/B: Sgt B.J. Warr,
          WOP: Sgt A. Ward
          MUG: Sgt W. A. Robinson
          RG: Sgt C.G. Dawson
          FE: Sgt R. Gowing

20/12/42 – Duisburg: 232 aircraft - 111 Lancasters, 56 Halifaxes, 39 Wellingtons, 26 Stirlings. 12 aircraft lost - 6 Lancasters, 4 Wellingtons, 2 Halifaxes, 5.2% of the force.Target area was clear and bombing force claimed much damage.

    Aircraft: Halifax II W1221 NP-M
    Crew: Pilot: PO J.D. Cole
          Nav: Sgt R.C. Stemp
          A/B: Sgt B.J. Warr
          WOP: Sgt A. Ward
          MUG: Sgt W. A. Robinson
          RG: Sgt C.G. Dawson
          FE: Sgt R. Gowing

14/1/43 – Lorient: 122 aircraft - 63 Halifaxes, 33 Wellingtons, 20 Stirling, 8 aircraft lost - 6 Lancasters. 2 Wellingtons lost, 4% of the force. This was the first of 8 raids carried out against this French port being used as a U-Boat base. The Pathfinder marking was accurate but later bombing by the main force was described as "wild."

Aircraft: Halifax II DT559 NP- D
        Crew: Pilot: PO J.D. Cole
            Nav: Sgt R.C. Stemp
            A/B: Sgt B.J. Warr,
            WOP: Sgt A. Ward
            MUG: Sgt W. A. Robinson
            RG: Sgt C.G. Dawson
            FE: Sgt R. Gowing

Detached to No. 1 AAS Manby for No. 59 Bombing
Leaders Course 17/1/43

Ceased detachment 1/2/43

7/2/43 – Lorient: 323 aircraft - 100 Wellingtons, 81
Halifaxes, 80 Lancasters, 62 Stirlings. 7 aircraft lost - 3
Lancasters, 2 Halifaxes, 2 Wellingtons. 2% of the force. The
Pathfinder marking plan worked well and two Main Force
waves produced a devastating attack.
        Aircraft: Halifax II DT635 NP-F
        Crew: Pilot: PO J.D. Cole
            Nav: Sgt R.C. Stemp
            A/B: Sgt B.J. Warr
            WOP: Sgt A. Ward
            MUG: Sgt W. A. Robinson
            RG: Sgt C.G. Dawson
            FE: Sgt R. Gowing

8/3/43 – Nuremberg: 335 aircraft -170 Lancasters, 103
Halifaxes, 62 Stirlings. 8 aircraft lost - 4 Stirlings, 2
Halifaxes, 2 Lancasters. 2.3% of the force. This distant
target was out of range of the target marking aid known as
OBOE
and would prove typical of raids to such distant targets.
There was no cloud
over the target but it was hazy and the Pathfinders had great
difficulty in

marking the target. The marking and bombing spread over 10 miles along the
line of the attack with more than half the bombs falling outside the city.
However Nuremberg reported that much damage was caused in the city.

     Aircraft: Halifax II DT635 NP-F
     Crew: Pilot: PO J.D. Cole
           Nav: Sgt R.C. Stemp
           A/B: Sgt B.J. Warr
           WOP: Sgt A. Ward
           MUG: Sgt W. A. Robinson
           RG: Sgt C.G. Dawson
           FE: Sgt R. Gowing

11/3/43 – Stuttgart: 314 aircraft - 152 Lancasters, 109 Halifaxes, 53 Stirlings. 11 aircraft lost - 6 Halifaxes, 3 Stirlings, 2 Lancasters. 3.5% of the force. This was not a successful raid. The Pathfinders reported accurate target marking but the Main Force was late arriving over the target. Also there was the reported use by the Germans of dummy target markers. Most of the bombing fell in open country but the suburbs of Vaihengen and Kaltental were hit.

     Aircraft: Halifax II DT635 NP-F
     Crew: Pilot: PO J.D. Cole
           Nav: Sgt R.C. Stemp
           A/B: Sgt B.J. Warr
           WOP: Sgt A. Ward
           MUG: Sgt W. A. Robinson
           RG: Sgt C.G. Dawson
           FE: Sgt R. Gowing

27/3/43 – Duisburg: 455 aircraft - 173 Wellingtons, 157 Lancasters, 114 Halifaxes, 9 Mosquitoes, 2 Stirlings. 6 aircraft lost - 3 Wellingtons, 1 Lancaster, 1 Halifax, 1 Mosquito. 1.3% of the force. This raid was a failure. It was a cloudy night and OBOE sky marking was lacking because 5 OBOE Mosquitos were forced to return early due to damaged aircraft, resulting in a widely scattered raid.

Aircraft: Halifax II DT635 NP-F
Crew: Pilot: PO J.D. Cole
        Nav: Sgt R.C. Stemp
        A/B: Sgt B.J. Warr
        WOP: Sgt A.Ward
        MUG: Sgt W. A. Robinson
        RG: Sgt C.G. Dawson,
        FE: Sgt R. Gowing

Flew as Air Bomber to W/Cdr T.R. Hope DFC on Operation to

29/03/43 - Berlin: 329 aircraft - 162 Lancasters, 103 Halifaxes, 64 stirlings. 21 aircraft lost - 11 Lancasters, 7 Halifaxes, 3 Stirlings. 6.4% of the force.
Wing Commander Hope's aircraft was damaged by flack and was forced to return to base early not having bombed the target.

Aircraft: Halifax II HR715 NP-A
Crew: Pilot: W/Cdr Hope
        Nav: Sgt R.C. Stemp
        A/B: Sgt B.J. Warr
        WOP: Sgt K. G. Cottrell
        MUG: Sgt W. J. Hanks
        RG: Sgt C. H. Garner
        FE: F/Lt V.G. Hope.

3/4/43 – Essen: 348 aircraft - 225 Lancasters, 113 Halifaxes, 10 Moquitoes. 21maircraft lost - 12 Halifaxes, 9 Lancasters. 6% of the force. Due to predicted poor weather conditions the Pathfinders planned a combination of sky marking and ground marking. However the weather over the target was clear and crews found the use of two types of marking confusing. The resultant bombing, however was accurate and a higher proportion of aircraft produced good bombing photographs than on an any previous successful raid on Essen.

186

Aircraft: Halifax II DT635 NP-F
Crew: Pilot: PO J.D. Cole
Nav: Sgt R.C. Stemp
A/B: Sgt B.J. Warr,
WOP: Sgt A. Ward
MUG: Sgt W. A. Robinson
RG: Sgt C.G. Dawson,
FE: Sgt R. Gowing

The aircraft was shot down near Pfalzdorf, north of Goch.
There were no survivors.
The crew are buried in Reinberg War Cemetary.

Decorations

None

Promotions

Sgt.

Appendix III

A Brief History of RAF 158 Squadron

No. 158 Squadron Royal Air Force was formed on 4 September 1918 at Upper Heyford in the county of Oxfordshire. The Squadron was scheduled to receive Sopwith Salamander aircraft but may not have received any. The squadron did not see any action before the First World War came to an end and was disbanded in November 1918. World war two began on September 01 1939 and the RAF began bomber operations on 03 September with an operation to bomb German naval vessels moored at Wilhelmshaven Naval Base. As the war progressed RAF bombing intensified and new squadrons, as well new bigger and better aircraft, entered service. A major construction campaign was being carried out to build many more and bigger airfields across the UK to support the fighter and bomber squadrons. One such squadron was 104 which was flying the Wellington two engine bomber affectionately known as the "Wimpy" named after the hamburger eating character from the Popeye cartoon. In October of 1940 a detachment from 104 Squadron was sent to Malta in October of 1941. the remaining home contingent of 104 Squadron based at RAF Driffield in the East Riding of Yorkshire was renumbered and 158 squadron was reborn.

158 was attached to No 4 Bomber Group (RAF) and was initially equipped with Vickers Wellington Mk. II aircraft. The squadron flew its first operation of the war on 14 February 1942. On that date 7, 158 squadron Wellingtons along with 60 aircraft from other squadrons raided Mannheim. On 01 June 1942 the squadron flew its last operation with Wellingtons when 6, 158 Wellingtons joined with hundreds of aircraft from other squadrons for a raid on

Essen. This was the second of the so called "thousand bomber raids" of the war.

In early June the squadron converted to the Handley Page Halifax Mk. II and was rebased at RAF East Moor in Yorkshire. 158 flew its first operation in Halifax aircraft on 25 June 1942 when 11 squadron Halifax aircraft joined in another thousand bomber raid, this time to Bremen. In November of 1942 the squadron was again moved, this time to RAF Rufforth. The squadron would call Rufforth home for a scant three months, In 1941, a suitable site for a bomber airfield was identified near the village of Lissett in East Yorkshire and construction of the infrastructure and runways was completed and ready for use in late 1942. Of all the Yorkshire airfields, Lissett was the closest to Germany and only two miles from the coast. Lissett was a typical wartime station with three intersecting runways with the main one running almost East/West. Accommodation for air and ground crews was in 'dispersed' buildings to the north and east. The first occupants at Lissett were Blenheims and Beufighters from RAF Catfoss. In February 1943, 158 Squadron arrived at RAF Station Lissett and was to remain there until the end the war. The first operation from Lissett was mounted on March 12, 1943, against Stuttgart, with the loss of one aircraft and all of the crew. Successive raids on Berlin later in the month cost the squadron two more aircraft and the lives of nine airmen. This was the beginning of a terrible spring and summer for the men of 158 Squadron. Many of the aircraft fell victim to flak or German night fighters, and a few struggled back to England before crashing short of an available runway.

In December of 1943 the squadron converted to the much improved Halifax MK III. 158 would fly the MK III for the rest of the war. Halifax Mk.VI. aircraft were brought on to the squadron in April 1945 and flew alongside the squadrons MK III aircraft on the last two operations that the squadron and the whole of No 4 Bomber group would fly during the war. After the cessation of hostilities in Europe, the Squadron was transferred to RAF Transport Command and rebased at RAF Stradishall in Suffolk. Here the squadron flew the Short Stirling in the air trooping role.

The end of the war against Japan led to the downsizing of the Royal Air Force and No.158 Squadron was disbanded on 1 January 1946.

158 squadron, like most other RAF Bomber Command squadrons was composed of three flights, A, B and C of 8 aircraft each. The squadron was commanded by a Wing Commander and each flight was commanded by a Squadron Leader. Crews were posted to one of the three flights, A, B or C and usually spent their entire time with the squadron in the same flight.

On the 7th of January 1944 the men and aircraft (Halifax IIIs) of 'C' flight were detached from the squadron and used to form the nucleus of a new squadron, number 640 based at RAF Leconfield in East Yorkshire.

Although the majority of 158 crew were British there were men from many other nations who served with the squadron. Canadian and Australian crewmen were by far the most numerous of non-British personnel in the squadron numbering 384 (380 RCAF, 4 RAF) and 163 men respectively, many more came from New Zealand and there were also men from the U.S.A, Rhodesia, South Africa, Ceylon, The West Indies, Jamaica and Poland in the squadron.

Appendix IV

Introduction to The Halifax Bomber

The Halifax was a four engine, long range heavy bomber developed by the Handley Page Aircraft Company. The Halifax first took to the skies on 25 October 1939 and the aircraft entered service with the RAF in November of 1940. By the end of 1943 every squadron of Number 4 Bomber Group, including 158 squadron, had been equipped with Halifax bombers. Halifax aircraft were also flown by Number 6 RCAF Group. A total of 6,116 Halifax bombers were built during the war. The type proved to be so versatile that it was used in a variety of roles besides that of bomber throughout the war. Halifax aircraft were used in mine laying, anti-submarine, reconnaissance and metrological roles operations as well as being used to carry cargo throughout the war. Halifaxes were also used to drop paratroops and special agents behind enemy lines for the SOE. Halifaxes were used to tow gliders and in fact the Halifax was the only aircraft the RAF had that was capable of towing the large Hamilcar gliders used in Operation Overload during the D-Day invasion.

The list of duties that the Halifax was capable of filling is impressive but its primary role was that of bomber, it was in this roll that 158 Squadron flew its Halifaxes. Although entering World War II flying Wellingtons and ending its existence flying Short Stirlings for transport command in 1946, RAF 158 Squadron will always be remembered as a Halifax squadron. The squadron flew all but its first 35 operations of the war in Halifax aircraft. Between 25 June 1942, when the first Halifax operation was flown by the squadron and 25 April when 158 flew its last operation of

191

the war, Halifax aircraft flew an incredible 4,175 individual sorties with 158 squadron to some of the most heavily protected targets in Germany and occupied Europe.

Based in Yorkshire in the heart of what was to become known as Halifax country, 158 Squadron flew three variants of the Halifax, Mark II, Mark III and Mark VI during the war. Mark II and Mark III three aircraft flew the bulk of operations for the squadron. The Mark VI did not come on to the squadron until April 1945 and these aircraft were only used on the last two operations the squadron flew during the war.

All marks of the Halifax used by 158 carried a crew of seven, pilot, navigator, bomb aimer, wireless operator, flight engineer and two gunners, mid upper and rear. These men trained and worked together many long hours ensuring they could operate in all conditions and under all situations as a closely knit team.

The Halifax MK II flew its first operation with 158 in June of 1942. MK II Halifaxes had a long range, were able to carry a heavy bomb load and could fly at a higher altitude than the Short Stirling which was the RAFs only other 4 engine bomber at this time. Halifax MK II aircraft carried a very heavy work load for the RAF during the early years of the war.

Mark II Halifaxes were very sturdy and strong aircraft able to sustain a considerable amount of damage and still maintain controlled flight. However the MK II's did have flaws, several of them serious. Fitted with 4 Rolls Royce Merlin engines the aircraft was under powered and this, coupled with trouble caused by its pointed Delta shaped twin rudders, led to the MK II gaining a reputation as a difficult aircraft to fly.

192

Perhaps the most serious flaw of the MK II Halifax was the pointed delta shaped twin rudder. This design made it difficult to keep the aircraft straight on take-off. It could also lead to the aircraft overbalancing at low speeds or when a prop was feathered and during tight turns. This last was especially true during the corkscrew manoeuvre the crews used to try to evade enemy fighter aircraft. This rudder overbalancing led to the aircraft entering a deadly spin from which it was nearly impossible to recover. These flaws were a major contributor to the high aircraft loss and casualty rates Halifax squadrons suffered during this part of the war.

Appendix V

Bert's Unpublished Essays About his conscientious objector Stance: Exact dates written unknown but the first essay must have been written sometime after June 1940 and the second sometime afterwards but before March 1942.

Essay One: Untitled

Until now I have had no conscious association with this war. I have gone on with my life, aware certainly of the war, subject to the restrictions and sacrifices of the new life we lead, but not accepting the struggle as mine, and hence conscious driven to lunge into it with that wholehearted fanaticism of complete giving which is my way.

In each of the crisis that have so far arisen, I have experienced periods of doubt and indecision. In September when Poland was invaded, when the Russians entered Finland, when Norway and Denmark fell to the Nazis, each of these examples of injustices almost drove me from my position of rationality by the feelings of horror, at the monstrous inhumanity of the Nazis and of an emotion stirred duty that was mine, to avenge these innocent victims and to throw all of me into the struggle to wipe out the evil of their suffering. The influence of the newspapers was strong and their work upon my imagination made difficult the maintenance of rational attitudes against the unreasoning emotional impulses to rush out as a crusader for the right. I do not condemn my emotions. Their case is strong enough, for Nazism is evil and its final abolition, for ethical reasons, is justifiable cause for war. I say ethical reasons, but in our decision we are guided by no ethics. Conquer or perish is the cry. It is a struggle for power between the intolerant old champion and the challenger, feeling his strength and ready at last to pit himself in the battle field, for the material prize. Germany is envious of England's position, and provoked war, so that our power may pass to her by conquest. But to assume that, because we have been led into evil, by a force whose aspirations irk him into a challenge of our superior position, that justice and the right are on our side, is falsehood. The position of the altruist, is therefore difficult. Conscious bidden, he goes out to defend the right, but in order to carry out his task he forced to ally himself with, and become the exploited instrument of, a power whose motives he must as a lover of justice abhor.

His position, together with that of his fellows in the army, is simply that of a misguided fool. And is this not one of the damndest (sp), blackest tragedies of the war. The army itself embodies the spirit of Nazism. Have we not the same blind surrender of the personality to the cause, the total absence of freedom of will, the the will disciplined to the dictates of the Books of Regulations. we may argue reasonably, that since such a system is proved of most efficiency in our own country in the fighting forces, a unit where the utmost cohesion is essential, then the same system, extended to the nation, should produce a similar efficiency in operation, and increased potentiality of each individual as part of the nation, united under a common discipline.

Thus then it must be considered that in the Totalitarian State we do see evidence of the workings of evolution. A sobering thought indeed.

Why does the British Government seek seek friendship with Russia. As champions of Self-Determination and Freedom, we are at war with Germany. She has killed, we say, innocent people, robbed them and expelled them from their homes into misery and horrible privation. Our fight is to restore to these hundreds of thousands of innocents, their rightful place in society; and to carry our fight until we have made for evermore impossible a recurrence of all the late years of hideousness.
And to Russia, the partner in the crime of Poland, we extend now the hand of friendship. Even after Poland, there came the murder of Finland and still he have no cause for friction with Russia. Our hands stretch forth to Russia in friendship

and in Russia, much more so even than in the Germany of Hitler, the blood purge has been employed to mould the nation into a unit. It is a fact that more people have been killed in Russia since the Third International assumed power, than have been killed in Germany since the coming of Hitler.

Second Essay: Why I Object

All life is a battle and we come into the world variously equipped for our fight. We are tough and cunning and selfish enough, most of us, to stand up boldly against the world. How eagerly we rush forward, in victory, to claim our bit of plunder, never forgetting though -- wise old campaigners that we are -- to keep a shrewd eye on our flank lest the fore rush in in our unguarded moment, to wrest from us those things which by conquest have become our rights. There are two kinds of men, each few in number, who fare badly in the battle - the virtuous man and the coward. The virtuous man is defeated by his principles; they lie heavily on his smiting arm and rot his armour; he is a dull fighter and easily succumbs to the alert enemy.

As for the coward, poor blessed shrinking creature, the blow that toughens us, that sends us roaring for vengeance, that rouses our anger, flattens him in his shivering defencelessness. Back he crawls, naked and beaten. His whole whole life is a retreat and we must tread upon him and try to forget him.

If it is such a fierce useless world, why cling to it so tenaciously? Is it worthwhile? Yes, the fight is sweet, and we want not to leave the field of battle. Against these impulses to duty. I have two weapons. One of them is fear. Of it I need say nothing. I have thought simply of suffering and horror and probable death, and its influence has been strong. The other, the dominant one, is reason. In periods of calm, I can look dispassionately at the lying presses, listen to the smoothing oil and large hypocrisies of the old men who rule, and consolidate my position with regard to what

196

they represent. I hate them for their insincerity and greed, and acknowledge with awe the immense inhumanity of their dealings with the people. I see then the division between the nation and its leader. The decent idealism of the mass, geared to sacrifice and effort for good, exhorted and whipped into new energies, contrasts itself with the desires of those men who seek only for selfish gain through those energies.

Appendix VI

Warr is Visited: From the March edition of Free Expression magazine

Warr is Visited - by himself

Warr was informed one evening by the lady of the house that an unusually courteous young man had that day called to see him and seemed disappointed to find him not at home. As no one ever visits Warr, and certainly none of his acquaintances either treat him with courtesy or experience disappoint through his absence from their company, the most courteous young man aroused his curiosity. Perhaps it was a worshipper who, having paid his shilling and read Warr's literary effort, was come to meet the flesh to express appreciation to the flesh and even to invite it to tea. But perhaps it was a hypocrite coming wreathed in smiles to steal Warr's typewriter for which the monthly instalments had ceased to be met quite half a year ago.

The young man telephoned the following day and requested that Warr remain at home that afternoon for an hour in order that he might have the privilege of an interview. Warr is indulgent, and sometimes the queerest people bob up. The young man came, courteously remarked "How cosy your room is. May I sit by the fire? I'll just remove my coat" , was solicitous about the cat on which he had walked, and began to chat about books - Nanking Road, The Rains Came, and what he thought about D H Lawrence, a volume of whose works he noticed in his rapid scrutiny of Warr's bookshelf. He was quite tall, quite slim, quite bald at the top front, an unimposing brow with shrewd vertical wrinkles between the brows, a beaky sort of nose with blackheads that ascended to, or descended from - it doesn't really matter - a pair of hard, hard, hard service grey eyes. After he had gone Warr was unable to remember whether or not the moustache existed. Certainly he would remember that Warr hadn't one. There he sat in Warr's more more comfortable chair (Il n'y en a que deaux) with his legs crossed, smiling and chatting and staring all the time very hard at Warr who dared to wonder who the devil was his visitor.

Your English plainclothes men are well disguised. In America one simply looks at the feet of a suspect to learn whether or not he is of the law. This young man would pass anywhere for a gentleman. His feet were medium and probably moved well to music. Hence it was a surprise to Warr when he displayed, with an apologetic smile, the little black C.I.D. folder with a quite recognisable photograph of himself inside it. Yes he had a moustache in the photograph, although not an ostentatious one. One concentrates more on photographs; they don't speak and distract the visual sense.

The young man had lost interest in D H Lawrence. Warr sat opposite him. trying to see the fire at least and waiting to learn why and what the young man though he had done. Of course he knew the police existed, and had tried many times without success to make policemen give way to him on the pavement by walking rapidly with a stern expression on his face. But they never do. Sometimes he used to sigh and wish for a teazle (Note a teazle is a tall, wild plant with leaves, flowers, and seed heads that are prickly, presumably Bert wanted to whack the constables with it.)

The representative sat for a minute, not speaking, looking at a sheet of paper that had come from his pocket. He handed this to Warr and said pleasantly: "I suppose you are curious about my visit. This will explain it. do you remember those words?" On the paper was typed a single line, 'I am a communist. Heil the revolution.' Warr thought at once of, 'A spectre is haunting Europe, the spectre of communism.' Equally majestically silly.

"Yerss" he answered because he did remember those words. Rather he remembered some of them, 'Heil the revolution'. This was a literal quotation from a letter he had written to America some time ago, in December he thought. 'I am a communist', however, was not his statement. It looked like something from a police report, standing up alone without the support of an adjective; not in the least as he himself would have worded such a declaration. He would have shouted, 'Hosannah, I'm a throbbing red" or something something just a little more becoming to an exhibitionist. But there it was, on Scotland Yard's own paper, factual and unelate (sp), 'ich bin communist'. But what stupidity it was not typed in German. It was English, 'I am communist.' It appeared to Warr that this statement was was the result of an attempt to paraphrase a sentence in his letter which was roughly this: 'I have joined the ranks of the dialectical materialists having read some of Karl Marx.'(Note: dialectical materialism is an approach for explaining the transition from capitalism to socialism. Derived from the writings of Karl Marx and Friedrich Engels.) Then followed the correctly quoted, 'Heil the revolution.'

Warr is unmalicious and tolerant, not by nature, twas grown in him. His mind dwelt on the vision of a weary civil servant, wife and little ones waiting at home with hot dinner of sprouts and carrots and oatmeal, scurrying to finish the last of work near end of day, and faced with a long quotation which must be typed into an official form. Could Warr find it in his heart to rebuke said civil servant for shortening his statement. Indeed it pleased Warr to feel that by cutting it down while preserving the kernel of sense, the creature was able to dash out of the office several moments before the rest of the army. But dreams about civil service are futile. Warr forgave on the instant, and only pointed out the paraphrasical 'inexactitude', to employ half the term attributed to some hack journalist. The young man looked surprised by Warr's denial of authorship, and wrote some words in his notebook. Then he began: "You know of course how careful we must be these days in tracking down and dealing with what are known as subversive influences in this country." His voice smiled charmingly, but his metallic eyes looked at Warr as though he were the personification of the subversive influences itself. He continued: "Your letter was read by the censor, and because of that statement was passed along to us. It is my job to visit the people who make such statements to learn something about them as well

200

as to ask them to explain. Now, would you care to tell me what you meant by it."

Warr tried only to explain the word 'revolution'. He said that he that he held the Marxism conception of history, and that the revolution which he had heiled in his letter was already kin progress and its result would be a better world. The young man seemed to consider this harmless enough. "After all" he said, "that is what we are fighting this war for, a better world. But I have read Marx - part of my job of course to learn about these people and their theories". (part of his job indeed). "But I can't say that IR agree with the Russian method of changing the world. Do you mean a revolution stirred up by foreign agitators, a bloody revolution?" The eyes looked at Warr again. Evidently the young man placed much importance in the answer to this question. Revolution that said please and was without blood he tolerated; revolution with a mess on the pavement, nicht gut, "'ere wat's awl this abaht?" Warr attempted circumspection and mumbled about means and ends and justice. Then the young man, after writing again in his note book, went on:
A\"Are you a member of the Communist Party of Great Britain, or of any other organisation financed by a foreign power?" Warr was not. "Do you read the Daily Worker?" Warr replied "Not anymore", and the eyes were active. "Have you read any of the others, besides Marx, I mean the big bugs like Harry Pollitt and Pritt?" He appeared not to notice Warr's 'no' to this question, but suddenly remarked in a tone of animation: "By the way Churchill was excellent in the House today. I have it here in the Evening News." He reached for his overcoat which lay on Warr's bed, and continued, "He is replying to a question by Gallacher, do you know of him? He is the Communist MP in the House." He read some wittily worded innuendo attributed to the man, and watched Warr closely in order to gauge the extent of his appreciation. "He's magnificent, don't you agree?" Warr said "Really a master rhetorician." This was apparently satisfactory.

201

Then particulars were taken. Identity card and military service registration what-is-called-a-certificate but is, in reality a cheap little buff card, were inspected and written about the the note book. How long had Warr been in England? Where had he lived, worked? The inevitable "What do you think of England?" with its inevitable reply. Had he any friends who visited him, and lastly, "To whom was this letter addressed?" Warr replied that it was written to a woman in New York. "Friend?" "Yes, a friend." "Is she an English girl?" Warr replied that the girl was an Austrian refugee, and was disturbed when the young man said, "Yes, I know she is. I've been looking through her record. There seems to be nothing wrong, although one never knows." Later in the evening Warr learned that Die Schwarz, a soul who inhabits his flat, had met the young man on his previous visit, and described him as "a very nice young man. I felt that I could tell him anything.' Apparently she had told him about the Austrian girl.

Then it was half-past six and the young man rose to go. "I have a chess game booked at seven-thirty" he said, "mustn't be late. Thank you so much Mr Warr, for your help. I hope I haven't inconvenienced you by asking you by asking you to remain at home for this interview. But I am sure you understand now the difficulties created by statements such as yours in that letter. So if, in the future you could confine yourself to - what shall I say - less provocative expression, why you would help us tremendously."

Still he smiled, held out his hand courteously, and threatened with his eyes. Then he put on his coat, and left Warr's room, this time not walking in the cat.

"I must pay my respects to the lady of the house," he said, "She seemed a charming person." Which he did, and then went away.

Bibliography

Altmark, German Supply ship,
https://en.wikipedia.org/wiki/German_tanker_Altmark, 10
Nov 2023, at 05:30

Battle Of The Atlantic,
https://en.wikipedia.org/wiki/Battle_of_the_Atlantic, 30
November at 06:00

Betty's Café Tea Rooms, York,
https://www.bettys.co.uk/timeline-1940s, 01 NOV 2023 at
07:03

Bigwin Inn, Historic Bigwin Island residences,
https://www.bigwinmcc1.ca/Bigwin-Island/Bigwin-
History.aspx#:~:text=Bigwin%20Inn%20opened%20its
%20doors,fireplaces%20and%20large%20open
%20verandas. 21 September 2023 at 05:12 (UTC)

Birney, Earle, https://en.wikipedia.org/wiki/Earle_Birney,
01 Nov 2023 at 06:00

Chorley W. R, In Brave Company, Salisbury 1990

Culture 360, https://culture360.asef.org/resources/czech-
pen-club/, 15 October 2023, at 05:54

Dieppe Raid, https://en.wikipedia.org/wiki/Dieppe_Raid, 23
January, at 06:00

Fraser, C.S., Canada's War Poet: The Writings Of Bertram
Warr, The Poetry review, London Nov/Dec 1950

Gawsworth J, Bertram Warr Obituary, Times Literary
Supplement, London, 07 August 1943

Gawsworth, John, Wikipedia,
www.ea.wikipedia.org/wiki/John Gawsworth, 23 March
2023, at 04:02 (UTC)

Graf Spee, German Pocket Battleship, https://en.wikipedia.org/wiki/ German_cruiser_Admiral_Graf_Spee, 10 Nov 2023 at 05:30

Hess, Rudolf https://en.wikipedia.org/wiki/Rudolf_Hess 27 November at 05:30

Lang, David, unpublished notes and letters

Middlebrook, M. and Everett, C., The Bomber Command War Diaries: An Operational Reference Book 1939- 1945, Leicester 1996

Owen, Wilfred, https://www.poetryfoundation.org/poets/wilfred-owen#:~:text=Owen%20wrote%20vivid%20and %20terrifying,poetry%20into%20the%20Modernist%20era. 26 November 2023 at 07:00

RAF Bomber Command Aircrew of WW II, https://en.wikipedia.org/wiki/RAF_Bomber_Command_airc rew_of_World_War_II, 20 Oct 2023, at 15:00 (UTC)

Rationing, Imperial War Museum, https://www.iwm.org.uk/history/what-you-need-to-know-about-rationing-in-the-second-world-war, 30 November 2023 06:00

Raynor, Patricia, unpublished notes and letters

S-Plan, Wikipedia, https://en.wikipedia.org/wiki/S-Plan, 01 Oct 2023 at 07:01

Streib, Werner, Wikipedia, https://en.wikipedia.org/wiki/Werner_Streib, 28 July 2023, at 13:22 (UTC).

Warr, Bertram., Acknowledgement To Life: The Collected
Poems Of Bertram Warr, Editor: Gasparini, L.,
Toronto/Winnipeg/Vancouver 1970

Warr, Bertram., Unpublished letters, notes and essays

Warr, Francis., Unpublished letters

Windsor Star,
https://windsorstar.remembering.ca/obituary/len-gasparini-
1086441860, Gasparini L, obituary, accessed 24 October
2023 at 05:000 UTC

About The Author

Neither his BSc from The Open University, U.K., nor his 30 years as a licenced aircraft engineer prepared Tony Frost to write a historical biography. But his lifelong passion as an amateur historian, long-term membership in the RAF 158 Squadron Association, and his service as an archivist and webmaster for Burt's RAF 158 Squadron made him uniquely qualified to tell the life story of the uncle he never met - Bertram Warr.

Tony Frost was born in Toronto Canada and moved to the U.K in 1988 after an 8-year stint in the Canadian Airforce. He has lived in the UK ever since. He worked in civil aviation, mostly at London's Heathrow Airport, until his retirement in 2016. He has recently moved from London to the quiet countryside of Suffolk to be near his two lovely daughters, Rhiannah and Esmeralda.

Introduction

On the night of April third 1943 the seven men of the bomber crew of Halifax F for Freddie of RAF's 158 squadron climbed aboard their aircraft for the last time. Wearing their bulky flying suites and carrying their parachute packs the men would have made their way along the narrow passageway to their crew positions. Part of the crew that night was a young Canadian, Bertram Warr. Bert was the crew's bomb aimer. Lying prone in his position in the nose it was the bomb aimer who directed the aircraft once it was over the target and it was the bomb aimer who released the bombs which would rain down on the city below.

Their target on this night was Essen in the heart of Germany's industrial Ruhr Valley. It was an area bristling with ack-ack anti aircraft batteries and Luftwaffe night fighters. This was the 14th sortie for Bert and his crew and it would be their last. They would be shot down and killed by a Luftwaffe fighter ace on the return leg of their flight.

Bertram Warr, a socialist and pacifist was one of the most promising poets of his generation. A man of whom Canadian poet Earle Birney would say "had he lived could have been one of the leading poets of his generation." How did a man of Bert's convictions and beliefs end up in the belly of an RAF bomber raining destruction down on the cities of Nazi Germany?

This is his story. It is the story of how this young man with plenty of enthusiasm and a budding talent for writing made his way from provincial Toronto Canada to the heart of the British literary world of London, to study and learn his art. It is also the story of how just as he was beginning to mature as a man and a poet he became caught up in the great events of his time and was killed and his voice was lost to us. Bert was only 25 when he was killed. His few dozen pieces of published work serve mainly to show us the potential, largely unrealised that he had.

1

Bertram Warr was my uncle. He was one of my mother's two older brothers, Frank being the other one. Both brothers were in the Airforce, Bert was in the RAF and Frank the RCAF. Both were killed within 6 months of each other in 1943. The family trauma of losing both brothers was so intense that even some 25 years plus after they were killed the subject of the brothers was almost taboo in my mother's family. Growing up in the 1960s and 70s we were never encouraged to talk or ask questions about Bert or Frank. I grew up knowing only the bare minimum about "the boys" as they were always called the few times they did come up in conversation. These conversations were always short and the subject would invariably be quickly changed especially if my grandparents were within ear shot.

My grandfather Bertram Howard Warr once said that a man dies twice when he loses a son and he lost three. For her part my grandmother took the loss of the boys perhaps the heaviest of all of the family. Years later when the organisers of the Remembrance Day parade in Toronto approached her to participate in this annual event which marched down Toronto's main north-south thoroughfare, Younge Street to the war memorial she flat out refused, coldly telling them "You killed my boys."

All this is a roundabout way of saying that while I was growing up I didn't know much about my two uncles who had died in the war. Reaching adulthood I didn't take much interest in them either. I was living very much in the now and they were very much of the then. That itself is a bit strange because I always did have a keen interest in history. Be that as it may by the time I took an interest in learning more about my two Airforce uncles it was almost too late. I say that because not only were Bert and Frank themselves dead but nearly everyone who had known them when they were alive was also dead. My research for this book had to rely almost exclusively on the letters that Bert and Frank sent home during their time in the Airforce. Luckily many, if not most of these were saved by my Aunt Mary.

2

Mary was devoted to the memories of her two brothers and although she didn't like to speak about the boys much to us she guarded their memories diligently. Mary kept all their letters and all of Bert's work published and unpublished that she could get hold of. It is primarily from these letters, notes and essays along with some articles published by poetry magazine editors and writers who admired Bert that I have drawn the material for this book.

Bert was strongly socialist and very much against being part of the military. This remained true even after he volunteered for duty in Bomber Command. I do not believe that Bert would have wanted to be remembered as a member of the military. He served and did his duty to help end the Nazi tyranny but he did so because it had to be done not because he wanted to. Bert wanted to be a poet and it is as a poet that he would have wished to be remembered. However, a great many, in fact most of Bert's letters that remain are from his time in the Airforce. He spent over 4 years away from home living in England, the last 20 months of that time in the RAF so that a large part of this book by necessity focuses on Bert's time in the RAF.

Of course a lot of my research led me through RAF material and to Bert's squadron, RAF 158. The members of RAF 158 Squadron Association's archive team proved an invaluable source for material. This was true not only for information about Bert but for information about his squadron and the RAF in general. They were so helpful that to give something back I ended up volunteering to be on their archive team and now I also run their website. In fact it is safe to say that if I had not become involved with Bert's RAF Squadron Association that I would not have written this book. That is a story for another time however.

While pouring over the letters sent by Bert to the family along with his notes, essays and poems I feel that I have in a small way gotten to know Bert as a person, at least as much as is possible by only reading letters and other material.

Bert lived in an era before social media of course so we don't have any tweets, blogs, snapchat postings etc and have to rely solely on hard copies of letters that have survived down through these last 80 years since his death in 1943. I have tried to present Bert as fully rounded human being and not as some idealised version of himself. This proved more challenging than may at first be apparent because to do that I had to rely almost exclusively on things that Bert himself wrote in his letters and notes. Most if not all of the letters written by other people to the family and of course all of the obituary material focuses on the positive aspects of Bert's personality and his immense potential as a writer. The one or two reviews of Bert's poetry that survive focus on his writing and how he was still maturing and learning as a poet but do not explore Bert's character. We learn very little about Bert the man from these articles. As for Bert's letters home they present us with the version of his life that he wanted to show his family. While they are a rich source of material they are perhaps not always as candid as letters to friends may have been. Things people tell their families are often quite different to what they would tell a best friend. None of Bert's letters to friends have survived but luckily we do have another very rich source of Bert's letters, those that he wrote to Mrs Nora Senjem. She seems to have saved all of Bert's letters and after his death she sent them to the family. Nora Senjem was a Hungarian refugee whom Bert had met shortly after he arrived in London. She was very involved in the world of the refugee artists and intellectuals whom had fled Austria and Hungary in an effort to escape the Nazis. Mrs Senjem had also taken Bert under her wing and over the years became very close to him. It seems that she was almost like a second mother to Bert. Bert's letters to Mrs Senjem are full of things that he did not write to the family about and even things that he did write to both are often written to Mrs Senjem with a very different slant to them. After Bert was killed, Frank met with Nora Senjem, and he sent word of these meetings home in letters. I have also drawn much material from Frank's letters home.

It was a great delight to have access to all the surviving letters that Frank wrote to the family. These cover the time from when he left home to head overseas with the RCAF in September of 1942 until his untimely and unlucky death in October 1943 six months after Bert died. Many thanks to Dave and Claire Lang for these letters. Frank and Bert, although both very close to the family and both exhibiting that fierce family loyalty that was a Warr family trait were very different at least judging them on the contents of their letters home. Bert was very reserved and very aloof from those around him. With very few exceptions he tells us nothing or next to nothing about the people in his life. This is true from his very first letter home, written from Bigwin Resort in May 1938 to the very last letter he ever wrote home from RAF Lissett with 158 shortly before his last flight.

Frank on the other hand, was very open in his letters and very informative about all his friends and acquaintances. Frank comes across as much more open and friendly than Bert. However this is misleading. Bert was indeed aloof and was often to be found sitting quietly in a corner smoking his pipe and sipping on his whiskey at social gatherings but he always was ready to lend a helping hand to anyone and everyone whom he felt needed it. Bert often even went to the extreme lengths of getting himself into debt so that he could offer money to someone who he thought was in more need than he was.

I hope that I have managed in this book to convey these traits of both the brothers. I have given Frank two whole chapters of his own as I believe that his story deserves to be told along with Bert's and not only that, Frank's story interweaves with Bert's. I feel that you cannot tell Bert's story without including Frank and of course, Bert's sister Mary as well. I have written about Mary in this book because not only were Bert and Mary very close but the publication of Bert's book "Acknowledge to Life" would not have happened without Mary's perseverance. Also We would not know what happened to Frank's aircraft with out

5

the dogged determination and some incredible detective work by Mary, but more about that in the chapters about Frank.

I hope that this book entertains and informs but most of all I hope that it is in some small way a worthy attempt to keep alive the memory of Bertram War and perhaps will introduce new readers to his poetry. I have deliberately not tried to analyse any of Bert's poems as I am in no way qualified to even attempt such a thing. I will leave that to the likes of people like Alan Gardener, John Gawsworth and Earle Birney who are eminently more qualified than me for such a task. My intention was to give the reader an insight into Bert the man and the events of his life while introducing the reader to Bert's poetry along the way. Above all though, I wanted to try to leave a fitting memorial to Bert, and Frank too. I believe that these two brave brothers deserve at least that much and more. I hope that the reader may think so too and that I have at least succeeded in some small way of keeping the memories of Bert and Frank alive in a way worthy of them.

Chapter 1: A Little Family History

Bertram James Warr was my mother's brother. Uncle Bert was born in Toronto Canada on December 7th 1917. His father, my grandfather, Bertram Howard Warr had come to Canada from Bristol England in 1903 and his mother, who was my grandmother, Mary Teresa Henneberry had come from Waterford Ireland in 1913.

My grandfather was born in 1883 in the Clifton suburb of Bristol known as Pill and his parents were Edward Warr and Myra Cook. They had 6 children of which Bertram Howard was the youngest. His father was a partner in the local firm of Withers and Warr: Farmers and Foragers and they seem to have been a comfortably well off late Victorian British middle class family. The 1891 census reveals that they had at least one servant the curiously named Minnie Cowmeadow. There were close ties between the Withers and Warr clans with at least one marriage between the two families. Bertram Howard's sister Emily married Richard Beard Withers. Emily and Richard had 8 children one of whom Joan, would later lodge at the same rooms as Bertram James in pre war London. Because Bertram Howard was the youngest son there was presumably no prospect of him going into the family business and without a university education or any formal training in a profession, his prospects in England were limited. He decided to take a gamble and roll the dice on a future in Canada. He had heard that there were great opportunities in Canada for hard working men. In 1903, aged 20, Bertram Howard set sail from Liverpool for Canada with his 24 year old brother George. He had to work hard all his life though to provide a home for his family. Money was never plentiful in the Warr household in Toronto, especially during the depression. My grandfather had various jobs throughout the depression years. At times he delivered ice to the neighbourhood families using a horse drawn wagon. He shovelled snow off neighbourhood driveways in winter and in the spring and summer offered his services as a gardener. He also worked as a caretaker in a local school.

Bertram Warr's mother, Mary Teresa Henneberry was born in Kilkenny Ireland on 26 September 1891 and grew up in the outskirts of nearby Waterford. Mary's parents were Walter Henneberry and Bridget Murphy. Mary Teresa was the third child born into a family of 8, 4 boys and 4 girls. At age 15 her mother sent Mary and her 20 year old sister Kate to work in a Quaker school in Waterford. The job was a live in position. The girls worked from 7 in the morning until 10 at night with only one or two afternoons off a week.

They began their day by going around the school and lighting all the fires in order to make sure the place was nice and warm for when the staff and students arrived. After that Mary would spend the greater part of her day in the kitchen washing dirty dishes from all the school meals. And this little person, she stood only 5ft 1in, spent most of the day standing in front of a sink full of water, soaking wet from the dish water running down the front of her apron.

Because Mary was only 15 she wasn't permitted to go out of the school grounds. On her afternoons off the only thing she could do to relax was lay down on her bed and rest. That was in between beatings she got from sister Kate. Kate being older was allowed off school grounds during the afternoons off and it seems that she expected Mary to clean her shoes for her so she could be ready for the off. If Mary was too tired or didn't get tKate's shoes cleaned fast enough in her own free time Kate, annoyed at having her free time delayed, would beat her little sister.

Mary and Kate's mother, Bridget would come to the school to collect the girl's wages which she then used to look after the other children of the family and run the house. The girls saw very little if any of their wages. Years later when questioned about how she felt about having all her money taken by her mother, Mary just shrugged her shoulders and said "Well, she needed it for the family."

It seems that Kate's belligerence was not restricted to her sister, she was always getting in to quarrels with the other staff. This got so bad that she had to leave the school. Although the school was happy with Mary and wanted her to stay she went back home with Kate.

Nell, one of their relatives in Wales, wrote that she was getting married and wanted Mary to take over her position in the house of a Mrs Lewis. Nell looked after the Lewis's child and was a sort of companion for Mrs Lewis. Mary agreed and at age 17 she crossed the Irish sea by boat and went to work in Wales. Nell and her husband met the boat at the dock and took her to the Lewises. Mary worked hard for Mr Lewis, who was a manager of a mine. He and his wife grew very fond of her and she them. But that life was far from ideal The only recreation that Mary had while with the Lewis's was taking their young son out to parks and for walks and her health was poor in Wales. Mary longed for a way out of the place. Reading in the local papers of the money to be made in Canada, Mary wrote to the British government in London and got permission to emigrate. She went home to Waterford to say goodbye to her family, they slipped two or three pounds into her hands for the trip and off she went to Dublin to board ship bound for Liverpool. Her mother went with her to see her off on the boat to Liverpool. From Liverpool she boarded a ship for Canada. Mary Henneberry was 22 years old in 1913 when she crossed the Atlantic on her own to start a new life in Canada. Mary set off on this new life into the unknown completely on her own, having no relatives nor any friends in Toronto. Some years later her brother Jim would emigrate to Toronto but by then Mary was married and had a family. Those first years in Toronto she was all on her own. Mary spent the rest of her life in Toronto, returning to her homeland only once or twice for short visits over the next 60+ years of her life.

Bertram Howard and Mary Teresa met in 1913 and married in 1915 and would have 7 children. Bertram James born

9

December 7 1917 was the second child the family had. Bert's older brother Frank, destined to meet his end as a navigator in an RCAF 424 Squadron Wellington bomber, had been born the year before in 1916. The boys had four younger sisters, Mary born 1919, Marjorie born 1920, Emily born 1924, and my mother, little Cecelia born 1931. There was a third boy, Richard. There is no record of when Richard was born. He was either born between Marjorie and Emily or Emily and Cecilia. Richard had serious health problems and died as a toddler. The only word Richard ever uttered was "mama" shortly before he died in his mother's arms.

The six Warr children grew up in a rented house in the St Claire area of Toronto. In the early 1940s they moved to another rented house in the area at 84 Cloverlawn Avenue just east of Dufferin Street. Bertram and Mary would live there until the 1970s when the landlord sold the house. Then, together with their daughter Mary, they bought a house in the Toronto suburb of Etobicoke. There they would end their days. Mary lived with them and looked after them and the house as they grew older. My grandad continued to work in his garden, which he took a lot of pride in. He hated winter because it meant that he couldn't work in his garden and would count the days until the spring thaw would again allow him to get out and get cracking in his flower beds.

In the early 1950s Mary had met Patrick Connolly and they had gone out for several years but Pat felt unable to commit to a relationship at the time because he had to care for his sick mother.. In the mid 1950s Mary broke off the relationship and moved to New York, where she worked for a time as a secretary at the United Nations. After Pat's mother passed, away Mary moved back to Toronto and resumed the relationship with Pat. Patrick James Connolly and Mary Myra Warr were married in 1958. They had plans to build a house and bought some vacant land with this in mind. There were no water or sewage services to this land, so they spent a great deal of time digging to look for water in order to sink a well. They never did find any, and the house was never built. Shortly after this Pat got sick with cancer.

For Mary a lifetime of caregiving was about to begin. Mary cared for Pat until he died in 1962. It was after this that Mary began caring for her parents full time. The owner of the house on Cloverlawn Avenue sold up, and the new owners were not interested in renting. 1964 Mary and her parents bought a house together on Prince Edward Drive in the Toronto suburb of Etobicoke in the west of the city.

That house was less than 2 Km from where her sister Emily and her family lived. Emily had married Victor Lang in 1951 and they moved in to a house on Lilibet Avenue which is south of Bloor Street and east of Islington Avenue in Etobicoke. Emily and Victor had three sons, Michael, Richard and David. In the house on Prince Edward Drive Mary cared for her ageing parents until their deaths. Grandpa, Bertram Howard Warr, died at the grand old age of 92 in 1976 and my grandma, Mary Warr died at the equally grand age of 89 on 14 July 1980. Mary then sold that house and moved to a house even closer to Emily and her family on Coney Avenue just east of Islington Avenue and south of Dundas Street.

In 1982 my mother, Cecelia had a massive stroke and underwent emergency surgery which saved her life. However she never fully recovered from her stroke and was severely disabled for the rest of her life. Mary again stepped in and brought her ailing sister home to live with her. Cecelia's two youngest children my sister Maureen Anne aged 18 and brother James Patrick aged 17 at the time also moved in with Mary. Jim was named for both his uncle Bertram James Warr and Mary's husband Pat. Mary cared for her sister until in 1986 when she finally succumbed to her illnesses and passed away. Maureen and Jim continued to live with Mary until she died from cancer aged 80 in the year 2000. On top of the stroke, Cecelia had been living with the lifetime effects of polio which she had contracted in the 1950s. After a long battle with that she recovered,

11

married and had four children of which I am the eldest. After me was born Mary Catherine and then Maureen and Jim. At the time of her stroke she and her husband, Harry had been divorced for over two years.

The three Warr sisters were very close their whole lives. Mary, Emily and Cecelia would gather with their children and later with their grandchildren and great grandchildren in either one of the two houses for get togethers for every birthday, anniversary, Christmas and Easter. Like her mother Emily was a devoted mother and her home was always full of love. Emily was not as strict with her three boys as her mother had been with her children. But, she must have found a pretty good balance because her boys between them produced two PhDs and a Masters degree and have lovely children and grandchildren of their own. Family get togethers were at Aunt Em's or at Aunt Mary's and were always occasions that we looked forward to weeks in advance. They were filled with great food, lively conversation, and always plenty of laughter. Mary and Emily loved to have the family over and Christmas was especially a time that everyone looked forward to. In later years we would usually spend Christmas day at Aunt Mary's. Dinner was of course the traditional turkey cooked to perfection with all the trimmings and plenty of veg. Boxing Day we spent at Aunt Em's and that day we usually had a glorious ham, again cooked to perfection with plenty of fresh veg to go along with it.

The fourth sister Marjory, married Ed Van Vlyman in 1948. Marjory was 28 when she married Ed. They had 8 children. They were not as close as the rest of the family simply because they lived thousands of miles away in Southern California. Ed was an aircraft engineer and worked for Avro Canada near Malton Airport (Now Toronto's Pearson International). When Prime Minister Diefenbaker cancelled the Arrow project and Avro closed its doors Ed was thrown out of work along with 50,000 others that the company had employed. Ed was offered a great opportunity working for a company involved in the design and manufacturing of the tyres and wheels for the Lunar Rover used on the Apollo moon landing program. This was at their plant in California. So Ed and Marjory sold their house in Toronto, bought a motor home and set off with their brood of 8 for California. Where they lived for the rest of their lives, heading north to visit the family in Toronto when they could.

Chapter 2: A Poet Growing Up

All six of the Warr children went to St Clare elementary school and all of the children were good academically. After school when homework was finished they were allowed to play with the neighbourhood kids. During the cold Toronto winters Bert and Frank played hockey in the streets near their home with the other boys of the neighbourhood who called the pair the Battling Warrs.

In the 1920s that part of Toronto was still fairly rural and there was a big field at the end of the Warr's street with an orchard in it. In the summer all the children would spend hours playing in the field and the orchard. No doubt the Warr's and their dog, would have spent many happy hours playing in those fields. There was always a family dog in the Warr household. Even years later when my grandparents were living with Aunt Mary they always had a dog and it was usually a springer Spaniel. Looking at family photos from the early 1940s the family dog, Skippy is often there front and centre. In what would become one of Aunt Mary's favourite photos, a uniformed Frank can be seen kneeling down tightly holding onto the beloved Skippy.

They were a very close knit family who looked out for each other. If trouble with neighbouring kids was brewing a favourite family saying was "My name is Warr and if you want to start one just keep it up." It was very much a case of if you took on one of the Warr children you took on the whole clan.

Granddad Warr worked during the day and relaxed in the evenings sitting in a big armchair in the living room smoking one of his pipes. I remember years later there was still a rack full of pipes beside that chair. Granddad would pick the pipe he wanted to smoke that evening from that rack. He was a devoted father, but left the day to day running of the house and the raising of the children to his wife, Mary. Mary was a caring and loving mother but she brooked no nonsense and was strict with the kids. That was probably true of most working class families of the time.

Mary was a devout Roman Catholic who went to mass as many as 3 times a week. The 6 children were often involved with all kinds of church activities. All the children were brought up as Catholic and all the sisters remained devoted to the faith their whole lives. Young Bert's declaration of agnosticism, at age 20, caused a lot of friction between Bert and his parents and was one of the factors in his decision to leave home. Granddad Warr was Church of England but he was not religious. He did support his wife in her beliefs and was happy to have the children raised as Catholics.

Although they were a loving family, at times there were fireworks. Emily Warr said that "My mother was Irish and my father was English, let the fight begin." I remember that whenever we visited my grandparents and Aunt Mary and there was an argument, usually between me and my sister Cathy, Aunt Mary would at some point interrupt with "Fight ya divils, I hate peace."

My earliest memories of my grandparent's house were of their house on Cloverlawn Avenue. That house had a big wooden front veranda that was covered by an overhang that was the floor of one of the second floor bedrooms, and which allowed you to sit out in all sorts of weather. Inside the front door was an umbrella stand which in true British fashion was always full of a variety of brollies. That hallway had a wooden floor which led back to the kitchen at the rear of the house. A door to the right just past the entrance led to a big front room in the corner of which stood my grandfather's big comfy chair and his pipe rack.

Bert loved smoking pipes too. In one of his letters home he speaks about finding a lovely old pipe in a second hand shop which after a thorough cleaning became one of his favourite smokes. After Bert joined the RAF he would often receive packages from home or from department stores back in Toronto. The most common items in these were cakes, chocolates and cigarettes but sometimes they would also include pipe tobacco. Bert would share out the cakes,

15

chocolates and cigarettes with his mates but he never shared his pipe tobacco. That he kept to himself. After Frank arrived in the UK Bert would quite often save the cigarettes from these packages or at least some of them for him because Frank hadn't yet developed a taste for British cigarettes. Neither Frank nor Bert liked British coffee which they said was made with chicory and had a very bitter taste. So if any of these packages ever contained coffee it was shared between the two of them. Frank never mentions smoking a pipe in any of his letters so I'm guessing he was not a pipe smoker, that would seem to have been Bert and Grandad Warr's vice exclusively.

After watching grandad Warr clean his pipes I would often go back out into the hallway and head to the kitchen which was at the back of the house. A door at the back of the kitchen led to a back porch and my grandfather's beloved garden. In one corner of the kitchen were grandma's birds. Grandma Warr always kept one or two budgies in a bird cage in the corner. One of the birds was always named Petie. I have no idea how many Peties there were down through the years, but there must have been a few. Back in the hallway, once you passed the door to the front room, but before reaching the kitchen was another door on the right which led to the dining room. We had many happy meals seated around the big dining room table. Before reaching that door however were the stairs which led up to the bedrooms and the bathroom. These memories of this house must have been very early because I remember always having to go for an afternoon nap and being made to lie down on grandma's huge bed which was covered by a very puffy down blanket that puffed up and surrounded you when you lay on it. Tired or not I never got any sleep and during these nap times and had to pretend to go to sleep for an hour so before being allowed to come back down stairs and join the rest of the family. I must have been very young at this time but Cathy must have also been there and equally she must have had to go for a nap in another one of the bedrooms. This would have been several years before Maureen or Jim were born.

16

Grandma was always knitting us woollen socks. we got knitted woollen socks from grandma Warr for every birthday and every Christmas from my earliest memories until she passed away in 1980. Knitting socks must have been a lifetime habit because in a letter home in the summer of 1943 Frank wrote "By the way mom I think I have enough woollen socks to last me a long time thanks to you."

In his delivery days and afterwards when he shovelled snow and worked in the springs and summers as a gardener to support the family my grandfather Bertram would write poems which from time to time were printed in the Toronto Star Daily newspaper. In some of his letters home from England in the early 1940s young Bert encouraged his father's writing and even suggested that he look into self-publishing. In 1950 my grandfather did just that and self-published a book titled "In Quest Of Beauty and which contains 50 of his favourite poems.

It seems that a talent for writing ran in the family and at school young Bert began to show signs of that talent. It was at De La Salle High School that Bert's teachers really began to be impressed with his writing ability and he was encouraged by teachers and especially family to develop that talent. After graduating from Del, Bert took journalism classes at the University of Toronto. By now though it was the 1930s and the depression had hit hard. Money was never plentiful in the Warr house. Frank, Bert and the two eldest sisters, Mary and Marjory and Emily too, once she was old enough, were counted on to help out by getting part time jobs when they could find work. I know that Mary being the oldest of the girls was the first to go out to work. She worked in The Old Mill Restaurant on Kipling Avenue and also worked at Simpsons department store on Yonge Street in downtown Toronto. Bert was very close to his sister Mary and she obviously idolised him. Bert's letters are full of support, guidance and much gentle teasing for his younger sister for whom he seems to have taken on the dual roles of hero, and mentor.

17

My grandfather Bertram Howard had of course grown up in England at the height of the British Empire's strength. He came from a middle class family and no doubt had typical British middle class ideas and views, Britannia Rules the Waves etc. At that time there was a strong belief held by many if not most of the British that they were superior to just about everyone else and their empire was proof of that. Bertram Warr would have been brought up in that atmosphere. When he emigrated to Toronto in 1903 he found himself in a city whose people were mostly British and who thought the same. Toronto and Canada were part of the British empire and that empire was the biggest and the best in the world. The British empire is long gone of course, the two world wars and the economic as well as political realities of the rights of people to self-determination have seen it off. However you still see even today an echo of those ideas of the superiority of the British nation and British people amongst some. At its worst it rears its ugly face in the skinheads and other far right violent neo-Nazi groups and at its gentlest and most benign it is on full display at the royal Albert Hall on the Last Night Of The Proms when the whole crowd sings along with such songs as "Land Of Hope and Glory."

in 1914 came the harsh reality and brutality of WW1 and following that the great depression. By that time, if he hadn't been before my grandfather had begun to believe in socialism and passed his ideas of social justice for the working class along to his children. Bert and Frank being the eldest were more involved and got exposed to these ideas earlier than the girls. However the girls became involved in charity work and social programs designed by the Catholic Church to help the local community through these rough times as soon as they were old enough. In his letters home from England Bert refers to Mary as a socialist like him. Bert fully supported Mary's position, and in his role of teacher and mentor often suggests books with socialist leanings which he thinks Mary should read. Mary worked for several organisations that supported the working

18

man. She was also very active in the Catholic Church and worked with, and ran at least one of their organisations that was set up to help the local families of the congregation. During the early part of the war Mary served on a war council and Bert wrote home in May 1940 about this new work. "No one told me that Mary Warr has a new job. What the heck is a socialist like her doing on a war council? The money is fine $18.00 per week. Her work on the forum is more worthwhile, but I suppose she has to make a living."

Mary maintained her socialist beliefs her whole life but often voted for the whomever she thought was the best candidate regardless of their political affiliation. Emily was very much the same in that regard, voting her conscience and the candidate rather than along strict party lines. For her part Marjory after she moved to California never did take out U.S. citizenship and so never had the opportunity to vote in elections. They were all devout Roman Catholics throughout their lives and that organisation tends to be very conservative however it maintains a very strong network of charities set up to help the poor and downtrodden. Mary never lost those ideas of social justice that she had learned from her parents and brothers in her youth and continued to support various charities throughout her life. When they got old enough Marjory and Emily went out to work as well. Little Cecelia was still only 16 by the time the war ended and times were better and she didn't have to go out to work.

As well as journalism classes Bert studied bookkeeping and worked in an office. The extra money coming into the house must have helped, but right from the start Bert chaffed at the tedium and dull routine of office work. Office work was not for Bert and he longed to be able to pursue his dream of becoming a poet. But he carried on studying and working to help out.

By the spring of 1938 at the age of 20, Bert had had enough of office work, left the bookkeepers and Toronto, and headed to the Muskoka region of Ontario's cottage country where he found work for the summer as a porter at The

Bigwin Inn resort on Lake Of Bays. By this time Bert was showing real signs of his talent for writing. Bert and his father were having major disagreements about writing and to top it off Bert had by this time announced to the family that he was now agnostic and did not want to be a practicing Catholic anymore. This announcement rocked his mother as she was so devout in her faith. She took a dim view of her second eldest rebelling against what she believed was the true faith and this caused even more friction between Bert and his parents. Even at this early age Bert was flirting with socialism and his poetry reflected his beliefs. He was a Modernist. Modernists in poetry believed that poems should be about social justice and help point the way to achieving a more just society for all members of that society, rich and poor, ruling class and working class alike. My grandad was more traditional in his views about poetry. He believed the duty of the poet was to point out the beauty of nature, love and the world around us. Bert and his father would have long, often very heated discussions about these two opposing views of poetry. Naturally this caused friction between Bert and his parents. In addition Bert was disillusioned with the staid and conservative attitudes of the Canadian Author Society. Without membership in this group though, getting published in Canada as a young poet was not easy. All of these things no doubt played a part in Bert's decision to escape to the countryside where he could take time to think about just where he wanted his life to go. Bert's adventure in Muskoka was as much about escaping from parental attitudes as it was about escaping to an exciting summer of work and play in the idyllic countryside of cottage country in Southern Ontario.

Bert was 20 years old when he left home to go to Muskoka. He had grown in to a fine young man of 5ft 10 inches tall and was of slim build. His sister Mary said that Bert had his mother's hazel eyes, a mop of chestnut hair and a keen wit. Earle Birney said of Bert that there is a fine sensitivity in his face and strength and calm and affection. Bert has also been described as a man with a stern face but with very kind eyes. The kind of eyes that have seen a lifetime of stories.

Suddenly with a sharp eyebrow raise comes a soft smile painted across his face which reveals his compassion and kindness. With slicked back hair and a dimple on the right side of his cheek he seems to capture the intense stare any young man/soldier would hope to portray.

In the years to come this callow youth with a huge potential and the drive to carry it off would grow into a fine intellectual and maturing poet. Bert arrived in England in 1939 still living his grand adventure begun in Muskoka, and he spent the next few years learning, writing and developing his ideas of social justice. By the time Bert arrived in England he had the beginnings of the socialist ideas which he would continue to develop through his contacts with the literary and intellectual scene of London and the refugees whom he knew and helped. Alongside this he still had many of the ideas of the typical provincial lad from Toronto that Britain and the British were the best. These ideas though were not deeply held and seemingly were a veneer that he threw off as he matured. In Halifax he told us of the grocer who gave him credit and didn't want payment until after Bert had found work in England. He hastened to add "and him a jew." An early letter of Bert's from England also relates the following - "I accidentally stepped into a protest by 10,000 (or so it seemed) communists all screaming out we demand arms for Spain. There were about 1,500 police to handle them and quite a bit of pushing and wrestling. They seemed to be mostly bespectacled Jews. There was hardly an Englishman among them." Interestingly this is the only mention in any of Bert's letters of the Spanish civil war which was a cause celebre of many serious socialist of the time.

A second passage from another letter home from Bert's early days in England, which unfortunately survives as only a fragment dovetails nicely with this. This fragment helps illustrate that Bert was at this time still feeling the excitement of living his dream and not yet settling down to the business of the hard work that making that dream would entail. The second excerpt is about the IRA bombing

21

campaign known as the S-Plan. Bert doesn't refer to it as that but that is what it is known as to us. Bert, dismissively refers to the bombers as "an organised gang of tramps from the north of Ireland." He wrote that they were doing their best to blow London to smithereens. His interest seems to be mainly that they have blown up tube stations and power stations close to Shepard's Bush. He then goes on to say the police are guarding Parliament, Buckingham Palace and other important buildings. Then the letter cuts off because the last pages are missing, but again there is no hint in what does survive of any opinion pro or coin about the bombing campaign.

Bert's derisive dismissal of what was a major undertaking by the IRA (300 explosions/acts of sabotage, 10 deaths, 96 injuries between the start of the campaign in 1939 and it's end in 1940) at once acts to allay any fears the family back home may have, but also shows no interest in the social justice/injustice of the ideas behind the campaign.

Both of these statements show that at this time Bert held a very broad stereotyped view typical of many British people and people of British descent of the Jewish people. Bert also exhibited a typical attitude to women at this time namely, male chauvinism. Writing about a concert that he attended early in the war he says that the performance was spoiled because there were too many women in the orchestra. It is tempting to extend these views we have of Bert to include the British view of everyone who was not British being inferior, but the evidence is not there for this and that is probably not fair to Bert. Because in the long run we know that Bert was not like that. He was a kind, helpful and, above all else, tolerant person ready to help anyone and everyone whom he thought he could. We know that both of these statements are misleading, both Phil Pinkus and Phil Sketchler were Jewish and Bert greatly respected and admired Pinkus. And of course Bert continually supported and encouraged his sisters and Patricia Ledward, to get educated and be as active and positive in the community as possible. Bert worked hard to help all the refugees, men and women that he could. Many of his friends and the people he socialised with, especially the Austrian and Hungarian refugees that he met at Mrs Senjem's dinner parties were of course Jewish. I believe that those statements were nothing more than the residual thoughts of attitudes that he encountered growing up in Toronto in the 1930s where the idea of Rule Britannia was so prominent. Once exposed to the reality of empire and the people in it through his years in London Bert's true nature of social equality for everyone regardless of religion, race or sex came through.

While we cannot perhaps consider Bert to have been a man of action he certainly did not hesitate to act once he had made up his mind about something. He didn't hesitate to travel to England to live his dream. He wasted no time hanging around home after returning to Toronto from Bigwin. It was a short five days before setting out for Halifax and then on to England. He wanted to be a writer and saw that his best chance would be to go study in England so he did. Similarly once he had decided that being a conscientious objector would mean sitting on the sidelines working on a farm or going to a prison and effectively not accomplishing anything for the duration of the war he acted and decided to fight his fight not the fight that the corrupt politicians and ruling class wanted. It may be only a matter of semantics but it is an important point that Bert stuck to his beliefs and went off to war on his own terms. He spent the early war years defining himself as a socialist and eventually a conscientious objector, however Bert was uneasy with this status. He looked around and, yes he saw the corruption of the British leadership and was loathe to fight for them when he believed they were mainly interested in maintaining the status quo of the British Empire remaining a world power and stuffing their pockets with war profits to boot. He also saw the great suffering that the bombings were causing the people of London. The very working class people that he was determined to help and the idea of going off to a work farm or prison as he would have had to have done had he maintained his status as a conscientious objector, was not something that he felt could do. He needed to make a stand and so he decided to join the military when called up and fight for the cause he believed in, namely to help the people. This eventually led him of course to volunteer for aircrew duty in the RAFVR.

He also had leadership qualities as evidenced by 158 Squadron sending him on a Bomb Leaders course in preparation for taking over the duties of Bomb Leader for the squadron. Bert's leadership was not the razzle dazzle follow me sort. By all accounts he was a very quiet, thoughtful person keeping to himself in most social settings but he must have been looked at as a leader within his crew, someone you could rely upon to help out whenever needed and to make the right decisions under pressure when it mattered most. Otherwise he would not have been sent on the Bomb Aimers course.

Chapter 3: Bigwin Inn, Big Dreams

The Bigwin Inn Resort was on Bigwin Island in Lake of Bays about 250Km north of Toronto in Muskoka, the heart of Ontario's cottage country. The resort was built in 1915 by local Hunstville businessman C. W. Shaw. Shaw's resort did a roaring business. By mid 1930s it had gained an international reputation and had become the resort of choice in the area for socialites, politicians and even royalty. Among many others, Clark Gable and Carol Lombard visited as did Earnest Hemingway and H.G. Wells. Princess Juliana of The Netherlands once came to the island for a stay and the Rockefellers were regularly seen about the place too. Big bands such as The Duke Ellington Band and The Count Basie Band often played in the inn's Octagonal restaurant which doubled as the dance hall. Shaw would often get permission from the band leader to sit in with the band and play his trumpet. I can't help but wondering if Shaw was any good or not. Did he play quietly in the background or did he blast it out? In any event the big bands seemed to have survived Shaw's jamming with them. They carried on and they came back to the resort year after year, so he couldn't have disrupted things too much.

In mid May of 1938 the big arrival at Bigwin Inn was Bertram Warr. To get to the resort Bert would probably have hitch-hiked from Toronto 235 km to the south. Then he would have taken the big old wooden ferry across from the mainland to the island, docking at the resort's private dock. Bert worked at the resort all through the spring and summer of 1938. When he first arrived from the crowded, dirty, city in May he was ill and was taking medication. The fresh air and good food that he got at the resort soon had him feeling much better. By summer's end he was the picture of health. Work at the resort was often hard, particularly before the resort opened for the season. When Bert first arrived he was told that he would be a porter for the season, that is if he was kept on. Whether or not he was kept on depended on how hard he worked before the resort opened. His employment also depended on the whims of Shaw, who was picky about who he kept around the place and who he let go. Usually though he kept the hard workers but if he took a dislike to someone, hard worker or not he wouldn't hesitate to get rid of them. In the weeks before the resort opened Bert worked as an odd job man. That meant doing anything and everything that needed doing to help Shaw meet his opening day deadline of mid-June. This meant that Bert was up at 6 AM every morning and often worked until 7 at night. At 7 all the workers stopped for the day and headed off to have dinner and a good night's sleep ready for the next day's 6 AM reveille. It didn't take Bert long to figure out Shaw's penchant for getting rid of slackers or anyone he took a dislike to. So Bert kept his head down and worked hard, doing everything that was asked of him.

He must have been a good worker because a couple of weeks before the resort opened his boss told him that he was sure to be kept on for the season. According to Bert, Shaw was a tough old bird who fired staff at the drop of a hat. Bert writes that most of the staff were scared stiff of "Old Weevil as they call Shaw. He takes delight in firing people." Once when Shaw was in a bad mood he ran into one long serving bellboy and fired the fellow simply because the lad had been there for 4 seasons and "Old Weevil" was tired of seeing him around the place. Bert wrote though that "He doesn't bother me but he does think I'm too saucy when I answer him."

For his first 3 weeks work, paid pro-rated at the end of the month, Bert received the princely sum of $20.19 cents. Although a full months pay would not have amounted to much more, only $25. Not surprisingly Bert was usually broke and he was looking forward to the tips he hoped he would get once there were actually guests at the resort.

Partway through the season he wrote home that an ice cream seller had opened up at the hotel. In the sweltering heat of a Muskoka summer, cold, fresh ice cream was too much to resist. Bert told the folks at home that now he really would be broke after buying ice creams every day.

Bert seems to have always been short of money and getting in debt by borrowing a little cash from the other lads. This trait would be something that he would carry with him all the way to England and right up to his death. Mrs Senjem, Bert's Hungarian refugee friend, tried to get him to save money. She did manage to get him to open a bank account but there was never much money in it. At the time of his death his bank account held £5. She never did manage to get him to be more careful with his money and Bert would be constantly in debt his whole time in England.

Bert continued to work hard doing odd jobs before the resort opened for the season. Once he was tasked with getting rid of a family of mice that had nested in a linen drawer of one of the resort's out buildings. The mice were frightening the waitresses and kitchen staff. Bert wrote that it "was mice work if you can get it." That thought sums up Bert's attitude to his whole Bigwin experience. Once the resort opened Bert began his work as a porter, which according to him was the best job at the place. "I'm my own boss and tips are good. We have almost as good a time as the guests. We go swimming, use sailboats and launches and go canoeing on the lake. We pay 15 cents an hour to rent a canoe, that's half what the guests pay."

His only complaints about the place were having to put up with the swarms of mosquitoes and black flies which were everywhere. Typical of the Muskoka region and actually most of rural southern Ontario in general, Bigwin Island suffered from plagues of these flying pests. Bert wrote home tongue in cheek that he was losing weight in spite of being well fed because the black flies take a pound of flesh each time they bite. Swarms of mosquitoes and black flies have always been a plague in cottage country in southern Ontario.

Bert also wasn't thrilled with having to wash his clothes in the sink in his room. This was only a temporary inconvenience though because once the resort opened the laundry opened as well. Bert complained that " I have to

27

look respectable every day and wear a clean shirt, just as bad as at the office." That was pretty much the only similarity between working in the dull, stuffy office in Toronto and working in the idyllic rural setting of the resort. Bert was having the time of his life at the resort and seems to have looked at the whole thing as one long working holiday that was as much an adventure as it was a job.

The day of the hotel opening rapidly approached. The first guests that season were a convention of the Lyons Club. Before the Lyons Club arrived Bert was confirmed in his porter's job and fitted for a uniform. he wrote that "We look like admirals of the fleet." Bert was to work as an outdoor porter. That entailed taking tickets at the cinema, acting as doorman at conventions and looking after the beds and rooms of 50 of the staff. He was also always on call for any other jobs that might pop up and needed doing.

The lifeblood of the resort seems to have been conventions. When there was a convention all the rooms were full. Conventions were usually rowdy affairs with the booze flowing freely and the place jumping. Very often, in between conventions most of the rooms were empty and there was very little going on. During these down times Shaw, always looking for ways to save a penny, would lay off most of the waitresses in the restaurant. Upwards of 50 of them would continue to get room and board but no pay until the next convention arrived and they were rehired.

There were no newspapers at the resort so Bert got the family to send him the Star Weekly magazine which helped him keep up with the goings on back home in Toronto. The family would continue to send Bert the Star Weekly for the rest of his life. When he was in England he looked forward to getting these weekly magazines very much. During some of his lonelier times in London they were a very welcome link to familiar places and times. He would often head over to the Canadian High Commission at Canada House in Trafalgar Square where he could read the Star Weekly, The

28

Globe and Mail and other Canadian newspapers and magazines from all around the country.

Most of the time work at the resort was routine but occasionally something out of ordinary would happen. Once an old lady died at hotel and Bert was horrified to see how the staff managed moving the body. They wanted to ensure that guests in the restaurant were none the wiser so "They lugged her out the back door and across the golf course to one of the freight docks. A launch took her to the mainland from there." For a young lad of 20 seeing a dead body in the hotel where he worked must have been a bit of a shock to say the least. Bert can't have seen too many dead bodies before except at funerals. Death at resorts and hotels, while not usually a common occurrence, is not unknown. I'm sure the long term staff were well practiced at moving corpses and getting them to the mainland with the minimum of fuss and without attracting the attention of the guests at the resort.

In July a fellow Bert knew in Toronto named John Francis Sweeney wrote him a letter asking if Bert could put in a word with the bosses about getting him a job. Against his better judgement Bert agreed. There were several fellows getting fired by "Old Weevil " Shaw so Bert wrote home that "There might be an opening for the big lug. I hated to recommend the big palooka but he might be alright. I sent him a telegram so he might be here by Monday" Even at this young age Bert was helping out people when he could even when his better judgement warned him against it. Bert appears to think that this Sweeney fellow was pretty lazy and in all likelihood would let him down. Sure enough Sweeney did just that. "Sweeney arrived Sunday. Instead of getting up early Monday to go to work he slept in. The lazy hulk. He worked Tuesday helping the plumber and complained loud and long about feeling tired. He is on night work now (Wednesday night) washing floors and is going to return to the city on Sunday. What a dope for me to recommend to the boss." In spite of Sweeney letting him down Bert would continue for the rest of his life to help everyone that he could. This was especially true once he got to England and floods of refugees fleeing from the Nazis were pouring in to London.

In spite of Sweeney letting him down and making him look bad to the bosses Bert's position at Bigwin remained secure because he was a hard worker who was willing to do whatever was asked of him, and in a cheery manner. He worked hard and enjoyed his time off too. On days off there were plenty of trips to the nearest big town, Huntsville, 23KM from Bigwin. The lads and most likely some of the girls too would go to Huntsville for meals out and to go to the movies. They usually hitch-hiked to town after crossing from the island to the mainland on the steamer. One time they did rent a car, but that ended badly when they managed to run out of gas on the way back. They had to walk in the rain to the nearest gas station to get a bucket of fuel. Bert wrote that it wasn't too bad because it was only 2 miles.

Once Bert hitch hiked to the small town of Baysville 10 KM away where his sister Mary was spending time on vacation. Mary had taken a job in Toronto with a real estate firm where she was making $13 per week. Impressed, Bert wrote that "Now that is money!" It was double what he was making at Bigwin but then Mary wasn't having the adventure that Bert was plus she was stuck in an office in the city, one of Bert's worst nightmares. I think that in spite of Mary's riches and his debts Bert was much happier in Bigwin than he was in an office. He was having the time of his life and making a little money too.

Before the resort opened a boat load of about 80 new waitresses arrived one day and like most 20 year old lads Bert seems to have had his eye on one or two of them. But he never writes of them again in his letters to his parents. So whether or not Bert had a summer romance on Bigwin will forever remain a mystery. Although Bert had a girlfriend named Hazel back in Toronto he doesn't seem to have been very close to her. He only mentions Hazel once in a letter home in mid-summer and at that all he wrote was that he really should write to her soon. Hazel or HK as Bert calls her in his letters rarely gets a mention but occasionally he does write in his letters home from England that he must write to HK. We learn next to nothing about Hazel other than she seems to have been an actress on the stage and a singer as well. But that is much more than we ever learn about any other girl in Bert's life apart from Patricia Ledward. Bert met Patricia on one of his university courses in London and it is an open question as to whether or not there was a romance between the two. It seems that besides HK and Patricia Ledward Bert did have a few other girlfriends. In one of her letters to Mary after Bert had died, Nora Senjem wrote that "Bert had lent his typewriter to one of his girlfriends." But in his letters home Bert never mentions any of them.

In spite of his agnostic beliefs Bert wrote to his parents that everyone went to the Catholic church by boat to attend masses. In a later letter though, he wrote that there was only one other lad on the island who was a catholic and who went to the church. I wonder how often Bert actually went to mass considering his beliefs. Bert may have been trying to ease his deeply religious mother's mind by writing to her about going to church. After all, he never wrote anything indicating how frequently he made the trip across the lake to the little church. If so, it was a tactic that he would use again in England once the war had started and he was serving on active duty in the RAFVR (Royal Air Force Volunteer Reserve). He never did tell his family that he was flying on active duty. Instead he led them to believe that he was working in a non-combat roll.

Bert's time at Bigwin was most notable for two reasons. First, it was at Bigwin that Bert was to meet a friend who would change his life forever. When he first arrived at the resort Bert bunked in a shack with several others lads and took his meals in the kitchen. But once he was taken on for the season he was moved to a room in the Caddy House at the golf course where there were only two to a room. Bert's roommate in his Caddy House room was a fellow named

31

Phil Pinkus. Pinkus, also from Toronto, had spent time travelling in the U.S.A. and, like Bert, also wanted to be a writer. The two lads had a common goal and that seems to have been a basis at least initially for their friendship. Pinkus had the idea that he wanted to go to England and it seems that right away Bert was intrigued. Pinkus was using his time at Bigwin to earn enough money to buy a ticket on an ocean liner and head to England where he planned on joining the RAF. Pinkus wanted to do a basic 4 year tour in the RAF which he said paid very well. He planned on using the money he hoped he would be able to save from his pay to pay for journalism classes at university. Bert had absolutely no desire to join any military organisation but the idea of going to England where he could learn about writing in one of London's world class universities and try his luck in its vibrant literary scene must have been too tempting to resist. He would be free of family religious pressures and the stifling restrictions of the Canadian Authors Association.

The other notable thing about Bert's time at Bigwin is that it seems to have been a golden summer for Bert, his last golden time. One last carefree period as an adolescent before he actually did go to England and settle into the business of becoming a serious writer. Bert's letters home from this time are very light and full of the joys of that summer. He talks about canoeing and swimming on the lake and hitch-hiking or borrowing cars to go Huntsville with the lads for nights out. In one letter near the end of summer Bert writes to the family that "This is no place to come to read or study. It's too noisy, I haven't been able to really concentrate all summer." I suspect though that Bert's lack of concentration all that summer was due to something else. Perhaps on some level he knew that he was turning a corner at Bigwin. At Bigwin he was free from the tedium of office work, the demands of study, and family religious pressures over his agnosticism. Also he was not butting heads with his father over their conflicting ideas about poetry. Perhaps he knew that at the end of the summer, whether or not he went to England it would be back to those and other just as difficult realities.

How difficult would it have been on the huge expanse of the resort or in fact the whole island for that matter, for Bert to have found a quiet corner somewhere to read and study? Surely if his heart had really been in it and he had the right mind set he would have found somewhere quiet that he could study for an hour or two most days. I think that perhaps Bert was not ready to study that summer and was more than happy to have one last golden summer of fun before getting serious about life and writing.

Bert and Pinkus continued to dream of heading to England after the season at Bigwin was over in September. All through that summer the two boys must have spent many evenings in their room at the Caddy House talking about and planning their big journey long after lights out. In September when the summer season and their jobs at Bigwin were ending, Bert and Pinkus decided to put their plans in operation. Bert arrived home in Toronto on September 14th full of his plans for travel to England and no doubt excited and eager to be on the road. Because Bert was back at home there are naturally enough no letters from the time just before he left for England. His sister Mary's diary is strangely empty for the 5 days that Bert was at home and if Bert had a diary it is now long lost to us. There can be no doubt though that Bert was excited and itching to get on the road and start living his dream. For Bert's Family it was another matter. The lone forlorn entry in Mary's diary 5 days later on September 19th, the day Bert left the family home for the last time simply and sadly reads "Bert Left." Little could Mary or any of the rest of the family Bert was leaving behind, have known that, that was the last time any of them would ever see him.

Chapter 4: On The Road

Bert and Pinkus started off with enthusiasm and high hopes but not much else. The pair had very little money and planned to hitchhike the entire 1100 miles (1770Km) to Nova Scotia, they didn't arrive in Halifax until October 9th, nearly a month after setting out from Toronto on September 19th. Whatever adventures they had along the way are lost to us now. Bert doesn't seem to have written any letters during the trip to Halifax. If he did none of them have survived. The first we hear from him is a letter that he wrote October 10th the day after he and Pinkus arrived in Halifax. Bert wrote that they had stopped briefly in St John New Brunswick where they had hoped to be able to board a ship to England. There weren't any ships in port at St John that were headed to England so they decided to push on to Halifax as they didn't much like St John anyway.

Bert's trip to Halifax is a bit confusing. Did he hitch-hike with Pinkus to Montreal where Pinkus then stowed away on a ship to St John? We know that Pinkus stowed away on a ship in Montreal from a newspaper article about him written when he was in the RAF and stationed in India. Did Bert stow away as well or did he hitch-hike to St John on his own where the two then met up again? Or did the two lads start out from Toronto separately and meet up in St John from where they then proceeded to hitch-hike together to Halifax? We know that Bert and Pinkus definitely arrived in Halifax together from the letter Bert wrote home on Oct 10th. "Arrived in Halifax Sunday afternoon (09 Oct '38). We have located in a housekeeping room in the residential part of the city."

Pinkus met a fellow named Phil Sketchler who was stowing away on the same boat from Montreal as Pinkus. Pinkus and Sketchler must have arrived in St John together. Did Sketchler also go with the lads from St John to Halifax or did he set off on his own arriving in the Nova Scotian capital separately? Sketchler, had similar plans to Pinkus. He wanted to go to England where he planned to join the

34

British army and spend his life as a career military man. It seems that when they got to Halifax Sketchler did not share the room with Bert and Pinkus but went his own way as Bert doesn't mention him again until after Sketchler has arrived in England.

In any event the lads arrived in Halifax that October where they found plenty of ships bound for England. Now though the two were nearly flat broke and didn't have the money the tickets for the trip cost. They spent no more than a day looking for accommodation because they arrived on the Sunday and by Monday they were settled in their housekeeping room. Most places they looked at were asking for the princely sum of $6 per week for a room which was out of their price range. They finally found an affordable place. Initially the landlady wanted $5 a week but the boys talked her down to $3. The room's furnishings were basic but the place was clean and had a kitchen with everything they needed to make and eat meals apart from the food, that they would have to supply themselves. A kindly Jewish fellow who ran the local grocery offered to let them have groceries on credit. Amazingly he was willing to wait for payment until the boys were in England and had found work there.

In the wider world at the end of September Britain, France, Germany and Italy signed the Munich Agreement. This agreement which amounted to a complete betrayal of the Czech people by Britain and France called for Germany to annex a portion of the Czech Republic called the Sudetenland. Hitler's excuse for this land grab was that there were 3 million ethnic Germans living in Sudetenland. This agreement was signed 30 September. That same day arriving back in London British Prime Minister Neville Chamberlain claimed the agreement meant "Peace for our time." Of course this was complete nonsense because all it did was appease Hitler and feed his desire for more and more expansion. Chamberlain was so desperate to avoid war that in spite of all of Hitler's double dealings he took Hitler's word that he would make no further demands for territory in Europe. In fact less than a year later the Munich agreement and the idea of peace for our time was shown to be a complete mockery because the Germans invaded Poland. This of course led to declarations of war against Germany by both Britain and France and marked the beginning of World War II. Winston Churchill who at the time the Munich Agreement was signed was not in the government was one of the few people to be opposed appeasing Hitler. He called the Munich Agreement an unmitigated disaster. Churchill said of Chamberlain "You were given the choice between war and dishonour. You chose dishonour and you will have war." Chamberlain's naivete in following this path of appeasement was playing directly in to Hitler's hands. The more concessions Hitler could wring out of the British and the French without the use of military force the stronger his hand got.

Bert and Pinkus had more immediate things to worry about than the annexing by Germany of some unknown part of a little known country in far off Eastern Europe. Winter was coming and it was starting to get cold in Halifax, especially at night. One of their main worries was just trying to stay warm at night. Their rooms may have been comfortable but they were cold. The houses in Halifax seem to have been largely timber framed and very badly insulated. In December Bert wrote that before going to bed he and Pinkus put on all their clothes including their shoes and gloves. Then they climbed into their beds pulled up their covers and were quite warm. That whole passage in Bert's letter seems to sum up to me Bert's attitude to this whole time. He was continuing his last golden summer of youth and going on a big adventure to England to top it off. There is a sense of youthful excitement and the awareness of what an exciting experience the whole thing was in spite of their trouble finding a ship to carry them to England on the cheap.

As far as Bert was concerned the sooner they could find passage the better. He didn't think much of Halifax and wrote that "The more I see of these other cities the more I appreciate Toronto. Halifax is a very dead city. The best thing about the place is the weather. St John and Halifax are both poor and dirty. Halifax is swarming with children most of whom are unwashed. The houses are all wooden and look like they haven't seen any paint since they were built. They are nice and clean on the inside though. The people just don't seem to care about the outside but Maritmers* are very friendly and eager to help whenever they can."

Pinkus found work but Bert doesn't say doing what. He does say though that Pinkus was not paid any money for working and that he was given meals as payment instead. That form of payment seems to have been fairly common for those dark days of the great depression. Bert took on more than one job where payment was not in cash but in the form of food. In fact Bert's first job in Halifax was washing dishes in the kitchen of a local restaurant for which initially he wasn't being paid either. He too was getting free food instead of cash. That situation must have changed though because Bert wrote that when the restaurant wasn't busy he was laid off and so he didn't get paid. Bert's money had to pay the rent on the room and the lads daily expenses then anything left over presumably was put aside and earmarked for buying the tickets for their passage. Whatever the case, with Pinkus being paid in food and Bert possibly still being at least partially paid in food, cash was in short supply. They were not saving enough for their tickets and were still stuck in Halifax.

*Maritimers are what Canadians call the folks who live in the East coast provinces of New Brunswick, Nova Scotia and Prince Edward Island.

They carried on working all through November and by the time early December rolled around it looked likely that they would be spending Christmas in Halifax still trying to find a way to cross the ocean. Bert was hoping to start seasonal work over the busy Christmas shopping period in Eatons. Eatons ran a big Canada wide chain of department stores and at the time were one of the biggest retailers in the

37

country. Bert says jobs were plentiful even if money for doing the jobs was not. He started working in the Carlton Hotel and that did pay a wage, however meagre. By a happy coincidence the dietician at the hotel had worked with Bert that summer at Bigwin and Bert perhaps feeling a little lonely or homesick or both wrote "So I'm practically among family."

They carried on in these jobs for some weeks and Bert spent his 21st birthday on December 7th still stuck in Halifax. For his birthday the family sent him a card with money in it. The mail must have been a lot a safer in those days because they regularly sent money back and forth in letters and it would seem they sent relatively large sums. The family sending Bert cash through the post continued even after Bert was in England and the money always seems to have arrived safe and sound. In any event the money came in very handy because Bert, broke as usual went out and bought all the family Christmas presents with it and posted it back that way. That was typical of Bert. He was always generous and not in the least bit selfish. He would give until he had nothing more to give and then he would borrow money and end up giving that away as well to someone whom he thought had a greater need for it than he did. He was generous to a fault and under present circumstances when he and Pinkus were desperately trying to save enough money to buy tickets for their passage he would have been better off being a bit more selfish. I'm sure that the family wold rather he had spent his birthday money on himself or put it aside with the rest of the money that he was saving for the ticket for his passage instead of using it to buy them Christmas presents.

Bert and Pinkus tried everything by hook and by crook to get passage on an England bound ship. They went to see the shipping master at Halifax harbour and "pestered him every day." Someone told them of a man in the Norwegian embassy who seemed to be able to get people over to Europe and they went to see him to see if he could help. Bert even went to St Mary's Basilica, the Roman Catholic

Cathedral in Halifax and enlisted the help of a priest. This priest gave Bert the names of a couple of people from the congregation who were in the shipping business. But none of that came to anything and they remained stuck in Halifax.

At one point they were pinning their hopes on a specific ship out of Boston which was arriving soon with 500 head of cattle in its holds. The lads were hoping that the cargo company would hire local men to go on the crossing to look after the cattle. That was a cheaper option than brining in experienced cow hands from Montreal as they sometimes did instead. That hope seems to have fizzled out because Bert only wrote about this in one letter and never mentions it again.

Phil Sketchler fed up with trying to save enough money to book a ticket on a liner decided to try stowing away. After all it had worked for him in Montreal so why not Halifax as well? Somehow he managed it and arrived in Liverpool where he was promptly arrested and detained by the authorities. He was put on trial and remarkably despite not even having a passport he was allowed to stay. He promptly joined the British Army Medical Corps, which of course had been his plan all along. He sent several letters to Bert trying to convince him to join up too. Bert's attitude to the military had not changed though, he wanted no part of it. Bert could be quite short with those he thought deserved it and he thought Sketchler a fool for joining the army and wrote "What a dope he turned out to be." It wasn't the fact that Sketchler had joined up that made Bert think him a fool. After all Pinkus wanted to join the RAF and Bert didn't think he was a fool. However Pinkus had plans to use the military as a means to an end to save the money he would need to take classes in journalism, which was his real ambition. For Phil Sketchler joining the military was the extent of his ambition. Bert thought Sketchler a fool because joining the military was the extent of his ambition. Sketchler seemed content to have joined the military and was more than happy to make a career toiling away as a junior NCO with no further ambition than perhaps one day reaching the lofty heights of sergeant or Warrant Officer. To Bert who hated the very idea of the military even then, such a career was unthinkable, not to mention extremely limited in its ambition and anyone who wanted that sort of life was a "dope."

Bert and Pinkus had been in Halifax since October 9th and it was now mid-December and they were no closer to getting to England than the day they arrived. With the news that Sketchler sent back the wheels began turning. Bert and Pinkus weren't saving much money so why not try their luck stowing away too? After all it had worked for Sketchler and it had worked for Pinkus out of Montreal. What did they have to lose?

With that in their minds, on December 23rd 1938 Bert and Pinkus made their way to Halifax harbour. They planned on stowing away on a cargo ship named the Beaverdale but members of her crew warned the boys off and told them they had no hope of getting aboard. Determined and undeterred they made their way to the Cunard Liner passenger ship Ausonia. Ausonia was scheduled to leave port that day, Christmas Eve. They snuck onboard her, found an empty passenger cabin where they stowed their bags and spent the night in this cabin undetected. At noon on Christmas Eve the ship set off. Bert and Pinkus were on their way to England at last. But it was not to be. After sailing about ten miles they were discovered and Bert wrote "We were politely asked to leave."

They were put aboard the pilot boat which was still alongside the liner. After two hours of pitching up and down on the waves they were then put aboard a Norwegian freighter which was sailing to Halifax. Back in Halifax harbour the lads were put ashore, disappointed and slightly seasick but undefeated. Was it the optimism of youth or dogged determination? It was now dinner time and options for sailing that day were fast running out. They didn't give up though, and were determined to try again. After a wash

40

and a shave, in of all places a local post office, Bert and
Pinkus headed straight back to the harbour. There they
boarded their third ship, the Canadian Pacific passenger
liner Montrose. They repeated the strategy they had used
when they had boarded the Ausonia and stowed their bags
in an unused stateroom. This time though instead of staying
put they mingled with the fair paying passengers in the
liner's lounges.

The Montrose set off at midnight on Christmas Eve.
Perhaps not quite as convinced of his agnosticism as he
would have people believe Bert went to midnight Mass.
Was he just seeing Christmas in or did he also say a prayer
or two that he and Pinkus would be successful this time and
finally make it to England? After all, he was already at mass
so why not? Of course another possibility is that he didn't
go to mass at all but merely wrote to his parents that he did,
trying to ease his mother's mind. He could just as well have
stayed in his cabin or gone to a passenger lounge to
welcome Christmas in with Pinkus and the rest of the
passengers, who must have been in a festive mood and
having a high time of it. Whatever the case, Bert and Pinkus
must have been holding their breathes and keeping their
fingers crossed as the ship left the dock. Would it be a case
of third time lucky? This time they made it past the pilot
boat and were headed out to sea. After they were out on the
open seas they left the passenger lounges and the ship's
chapel behind and spent a restful night in their cabin. On
Christmas morning Bert opened his cards from home and
opened his lone Christmas present, a shaving kit. This was a
gift from the housekeeper at the Carlton Hotel in Halifax
where Bert had worked. Cards and present finished with
they then left their cabin and presented themselves to the
captain. Maybe the captain was just a nice fellow or maybe
he was full of the Christmas spirit because as Bert wrote,
the captain "wished us a Merry Christmas, complimented
us on the neat way we had worked it and then sent us down
to dinner." The lads were allowed to stay on board and were
set to work earning their crossing as stewards. Bert was
thoroughly enjoying his great adventure "We have scrubbed

41

and polished our way across the Atlantic, brass, floors, stairs and decks galore, however it was fun." They were given one of the unused cabins to themselves and supplied with clean clothes and linen. Bert, possibly not believing all of this good luck wrote "To top it off we were forced to accept afternoon tea every day - some treatment for stowaways!"

Chapter 5: London: It's A Wonderful Joint

Bert and Pinkus worked hard during the crossing which
took about a week. Every day they would scrub decks,
polish brass and take on whatever task the crew set for them
with an unbridled enthusiasm. It was a one big adventure
and they were enjoying it fully. The Montrose docked in
Liverpool on new years day 1939. Bert wrote that they
expected to be shipped right back to Canada but possibly
because they had worked so hard during the crossing their
friend the captain again came to the rescue. Once they had
docked the local company lawyers along with the harbour
customs officials and the captain sat in the captain's office
on the ship. As the two lads stood before this array of
officialdom they expected the worst and thought they would
be trooped off to the next ship heading back to Canada,
turfed out on their ears. However the captain put in a good
word for the them with the officials and to Burt and Pinkus'
amazement agreed to let them stay. The company lawyers
and the immigration men wished the pair good luck and
shook their hands as they went ashore.

They spent that night in a local hotel and wasted little time,
setting off for London the next day. Of course as they had
almost no money they planned to hitchhike. They managed
to pick up a lift from a truck which took them the whole
way. They arrived in London in the dead of night but that
didn't stop the lorrie driver from taking the lads on a tour of
the capital before he dropped them at a rooming house at 6
in the morning. London, even in the dead of night must
have been an almost overwhelming site for two boys from
the back waters of provincial Toronto in the 1930s.

They stayed at those rooms for several days if not weeks.
Pinkus only stayed until he enlisted in the RAF. After
which he was sent for six months training in Ayrshire in
Scotland. Bert wrote home that Pinkus tried dozens of times
to get him to enlist in the RAF as well but Bert's attitude to
the military had not changed, he wanted no part of being in
uniform. Bert seems to have respected Pinkus'es decision

though and thought well of him. This was in stark contrast to his feelings about Phil Sketchley whom we know Bert thought was a dope. I think that this was probably because Pinkus was using the RAF as a means to an end not an end in itself whereas for Sketchley his ambitions seem to have only extended to enlistment and to enlist and have a career as a lowly enlisted man. Pinkus wanted to stay in the RAF for 4 years saving as much of his pay as possible, a figure which Bert puts at roughly $1500 CDN (roughly $28,000 CDN in 2023) for the four years. Pinkus planned using those savings to pay for journalism classes leading to him becoming a writer. It is obvious to see how Bert would respect that career ambition if not the method of getting there and how he thought the worst of Sketchley's lack of ambition. Pinkus and Bert stayed in touch over the next few years and on one occasion Pinkus even came to London on leave to visit Bert, but he soon disappears from our story and Bert stops mentioning him in letters home. I don't even know if he survived the war. The last we hear of him, Pinkus is serving as a navigator on RAF aircraft in the Punjab in India in 1942 and that information comes from a newspaper clipping that Aunt Mary had saved.

Bert's initial impressions of London were that "It's a wonderful joint – it would take years to see it all but it rains all the time, the houses are cold and the people drink tea all the time." He was thoroughly enjoying himself and found work right away. London was emerging from the depression and Bert says the help wanted sections of the papers were full of several columns of ads every evening. He was working within 3 days of arriving in London. He had found work washing dishes at a Lyons Corner House cafeteria in the heart of Piccadilly. The job paid 38 shillings and 6 pence a week. That's about £1.90. He found accommodation in Tubman Street in Shepards Bush and that set him back 10 shillings a week but included having his laundry done, leaving him 28 shillings and 6 pence to get by on. The job was meant to be a stop gap just to get some money coming in until he could find something else. He was applying for other work straight away and was hoping to get on at a publisher's soon. In the event though Bert was to work at Lyons for several months and be thoroughly fed up with washing dishes by the time he did find other work. Lyons was half an hour travel from the rooms in Tadmore Street and Bert worked from noon until as late as 10 PM some days. He worked when the restaurant was busy and was given the day off without pay when things were slow.

Lyons Corner House Café in Piccadilly was somewhat of an institution for locals. My wife Tracy's family has deep roots in East End London that extend far back in to the city's past. She tells me that for her grandparents and other family members during the tough years of the depression a trip to the café in Piccadilly was a special treat. It's nice to think that perhaps one day while Bert was busy washing dishes in the kitchen out front Tracy's grandparents were enjoying a cup of Lyon's special mix tea. If Bert happened to do any bussing that day perhaps they could have even had a chance meeting. Perhaps Bert passed by their table or maybe they were sitting near the kitchen and caught a glimpse of him arms deep in soapy water. The odds are against such a meeting but you never know.

At some point between the last week of April and the middle of June Bert left Lyon's and took a job working as a bookkeeper at an Oyster company in Billingsgate Fish Market. He went to work in the London offices of The Whitstable Oyster Fishery Company which is still in business today. By the time he had that job he was taking three classes a week at Birkbeck College University of London in Bloomsbury Camden. At Birkbeck Bert took classes in journalism and literature. He was working hard learning his craft and honing his writing skills and developing his philosophy.

As well as changing jobs and starting school Bert also changed addresses. He moved from the Shepherds Bush rooms at Tadmore Street to 181 Sutherland Avenue in Maida Vale a few blocks west of Regents Park. It's not known how long Bert stayed at the rooms in Sutherland

Avenue. His landlady there, Mrs Bush sold those rooms and moved to new rooms at Lanark Mansions and Bert moved with her.

His old landlady at the Tadmore Street rooms whom he had once thought so kindly of came in for some withering criticism. Across the envelope of one of his letters from home she had written "Please Mr Warr give your family your new address. I can't keep forwarding your mail." A reasonable request one would have thought. However Bert thought otherwise and angrily wrote the family calling her " a disagreeable old wretch." Bert could be quite short and cutting with those he thought deserved it and he didn't often mince his words.

Although far from home Bert wasn't entirely alone and cut off. His cousin Joan Withers from Bristol was lodging at the same rooming house as he was. Joan was the daughter of his father's sister Emily Isobel and her husband Richard Withers. Richard was a member of the family the Warr's were in the forage and hay business with. She was born 02 February 1918, only a couple of months younger than Bert, and she was only 20 when she came to live in London. Just when Joan started lodging at the same address as Bert isn't clear but a good guess is that it was when he was at Mrs Burns rooms in Sutherland Avenue. It was definitely by April of 39 because Bert wrote home on April 21 that he, Joan and Rashbrook went to Hampstead Heath together. Rashbrook was Alfred Rashbrook known to one and all as "Tiny." Joan and Tiny were married in the afternoon of Saturday 16th of September 1940. The ceremony took place in between air raid warnings. The reception was held at a restaurant in London but Bert doesn't say where. The wedding and meal were both a huge success. There were 14 people at the reception meal. Their aunt Queen and Joan's brother Roy both came up from Bristol along with some other unnamed relatives and Rashbrook's family came down from Gloucester for the celebration as well. Presumably Joan and Tiny then left for a honeymoon but again Bert's letters don't say one way or the other.

46

The Withers seemed to have been very well off because Bert tongue in cheek wrote home 18 Febraury 1940 that "Joan Withers has returned to London after being away for two weeks. Only her spring holiday of course and quite exclusive of her summer ones." Bert, Joan and Tiny had many days out together exploring and enjoying the parks and countryside around London. After Tiny and Joan were married Rashbrook enlisted in the army and was eventually posted to a base near Maidenhead in Kent.It was the early days of the war and most young men were enlisting ion one branch of the military or another. In early June Joan left London and went to live in Maidenhead near Rashbrook's base so that she could be near him. That letter written on 6 June 1941 is the last time Bert mentions Joan or Tiny in any of his surviving letters. I do know that Joan and Tiny had two children but I don't know any other details about them. By that time Bert was only a few weeks away from enlisting himself and from the time he enlists his letters are mainly concerned with his training and leave etc. Bert also spent time with his Aunt Emily Isobel who was known as Queen. She came to London several times usually staying in Joan's rooms and had Bert down to her house in Pill, Bristol for Christmases and other holidays. Aunt Queen never married and lived alone in her cottage in the countryside near Bristol, close to the rest of the family. On her visits to London Bert and Joan kept her busy going to concerts and plays and visiting galleries etc. She seems to have loved her visits but was always happy at the end of her short two week breaks to be returning to the tranquil life that she enjoyed in the countryside.

In a sense, once Pinkus left for the RAF Bert was alone. He was still very much enjoying living his dream but he was not yet taking any courses and was working at a menial job where the prospects and social contacts were limited. True, his cousin Joan Withers was living in the same flats as Bert but really, she was a stranger. There is no mention of her in any of the surviving letters grandpa Warr got from his relatives back home so she was as much a stranger to Bert

47

and the family as she is to us all these years later. We have no photographs of her either. In his letters home Bert for his part does nothing to to enlighten the family as to what Joan was like. He includes no descriptions of what she looks like nor any of what her personality was like. Instead he tells us of what Joan and Tiny were doing from time to time especially if it involved him. He talks about trips to the countryside that he took with Joan and Tiny and dinner parties and breakfasts that they shared, but he gives us nothing more.

This is true of Bert's letters in general. There is an aloofness and an almost cold reporting style to his letter writing to his family. From what he says we do get the sense that he cared deeply for the family but there is a distance too. Affection does come through sometimes in his letters when he writes to his sisters especially Cecelia, the youngest but even then there also seems to be a coolness, a lack of ability to express deep feeling.

After Pinkus left, Bert was alone, a stranger in a strange land. His one concrete link with home had been Pinkus. Now he was on his own in the great city. He was still having a great adventure but the loneliness of his life was also weighing on him from time to time. Where Bert's letters let us down in this regard we can still get a very good sense of what Bert was feeling by turning to his poetry. He wrote several poems in his early days in London that express his feelings in ways that he was unable to in his letters home. He had a sensitive soul, the soul of a poet and the best way that we can now get to know him is through his poetry

The opening lines of the poem "In The Dark" written around this time give us a glimpse of how Bert was feeling.

> *Many months ago in this city,*
> *Ears closed to me like faces folding,*
> *And I, as blood dashed from sudden wound,*
> *Appealed without a sound.*

We really get a sense of Bert's feelings of isolation and loneliness from these lines. The last line is especially telling I think. "I ... appealed without a sound." That would seem to seem to sum up Bert's social life in a nutshell. Mrs Nora Senjem who had known Bert almost since he first arrived in England as related in a letter Frank wrote to the family after Bert was killed, and after he had visited her tells us "I should like to collect all the details that I have of Bert, unfortunately this is very little, our mutual friends know less about him than I do. Everybody without exception liked him and appreciated him for his very decent and sweet nature. He was always very quiet in society and spoke very little." Bert it seems was as closed a book around his London acquaintances as he was in his letters home. The family were still sending the Star Weekly magazine to Bert on a regular basis and this was a very welcome link to Toronto and the family. He loved reading about the Toronto Maple Leafs his favourite ice hockey team in the NHL and the colour comics also seem to have been a favourite. Joan and Tiny also seemed to have loved those comics as did the landlady's young son. Bert wrote that on a Sunday morning the landlady would serve her lodgers their breakfasts in bed. After having eaten a hearty full English breakfast, traditionally consisting of fried eggs, bacon, english sausage, fried tomatoes and often blood pudding, he would relax and read the Star Weekly and the comics, while still in bed. Bert would send the comics in to Joan's room where she and Tiny were laying in bed also and they too would read the comics before sending them on to the landlady's young lad. Bert was certainly still enjoying living and studying in England but he was also at times at least feeling home sick and lonely. This really isn't surprising as in early 1939 Bert was not yet 21 years old. He was pretty much on his own, living thousands of miles away from home, in a place that although familiar was still strange. One time Bert went for a walk through Hyde Park which is one of the biggest and nicest parks in London a city noted for its parks. Bert ever eager to fly the flag of home and perhaps also feeling homesick wrote that "It's a nice treat to walk through

49

Hyde Park these days. It's not a bad place but High Park in Toronto has it beat by miles."

In contrast the letters that Frank sent home after he arrived in England in early 1943 are very warm and full of information about the people in his life. He talks openly and often of his friends and the family back home really engaging with their questions and answering them in terms we would expect in the letters from a loving son and brother to the folks back home. Getting to know Frank and Bert is of course impossible but through his letters it seems at least possible to catch more than a glimpse of who Frank was as a person more so than we get from from Bert's letters. Bert's letters and essays etc, tell us very little about Bert the man, focusing instead on Bert the intellectual. This is especially true of his essays. It is from Bert's poetry that we must try to catch glimpses of his feelings and who he was as a person.

Mrs Burns, Bert and Joan's landlady at Tadmark Street found herself struggling financially and was forced to sell up or abandon her flats there and move to a smaller holding at Lanark Mansions in Maida Vale, just around the corner from the EMI studios, which were to become famous as the recording studios the Beatles used for most of the 1960s. Bert and Joan moved with Mrs Burns to Lanark mansions. Mrs Burns was to remain Bert's landlady for the remainder of his short life. He stayed at her rooms every time he came to London after he joined the RAF too. They had a friendly relationship just as with Mrs Senjem, Mrs Burns seems to have taken Bert under her wing and been a bit of a mother hen to him. She would bring him breakfast in bed when he slept late on days off work and she looked after him when he had colds, which he seemed to have perpetually before he joined the RAF. For their part Bert and Joan when they had lunches, teas or dinners would often invite Mrs Burns to join them. It wasn't all smooth sailing though as at one point Bert and Joan staged a mini revolution when Mrs Burns announced that she would have to raise the rent. Bert and Joan were both outraged and refused to pay. This was during the blitz when there were plenty of empty apartment building buildings full of empty flats. Mrs Burns told them it was necessary because of the rising cost of gas and electricity. To which they both howled that that was not their problem. They must have gotten this issue resolved though because they both continued to live at Lanark Mansions and relations with Mrs Burns suffered no long-term damage because she continued to look after Burt and they still included her in their dinners

Bert continued to take his classes at Birkbeck all throughout that summer. One of the courses that he took was a literature course given by the well-respected poet Gwendolyn Murphy of whom Robert Graves was to write to Bert "I'm glad that you went to her class. She is no fool and humble and willing to learn from those who know."

It was at one of these courses, very probably Gwendolyn Murphy's, that Bert was to meet Patricia Ledward. Patricia, daughter of renowned sculpture Gilbert Ledward was a fellow student and would become a noted author, broadcaster, editor and a minor poet. The pair became became close friends for a time and also may have worked together for Favil Press the publishing company responsible for the "Resurgam" Younger Poets series an edition of which was published with 14 of Bert's poems in it. Bert and Patricia both had broadsheets published in that series by Favil Press in 1941. Bert never explicitly says so in his letters home but it is very probable that he and Patricia were more than just friends. In one letter home during the war he does say that Patricia is "chasing" him but that he has managed escape. He did not want to commit to any relationship during the uncertainty caused by the war. Who knows what would have been for Bert and Patricia had Bert lived through the war?

As that summer of 1939 rolled along, the last summer of peace before the second world war, there were increasing numbers of refugees fleeing the Nazi persecutions and terrors making their way to London. Bert volunteered to help at least one of these organisations. Between his university connections and the connections he made amongst the refugees he soon found himself involved in London's world of art and culture. Bert spent many evenings at the home of his good friend Mrs Senjem. Mrs Senjem herself was a refugee. She had fled with her daughter from Hungary leaving behind her husband and her son. She would often have dinner parties and other gatherings of artists and intellectuals. It was at this time that Bert really began to become serious about his social beliefs. Bert's last youthful adventure wasn't ending but it was changing as Bert himself was changing. Bert was beginning believe it was not enough to hold Modernist views and to write Modernist poetry but it was also important to put those beliefs and views into practice. He was learning and beginning to become a serious thinker and writer. Much of Bert's ideology was picked up at college and he was no doubt also learning much more at Mrs Senjem's gatherings from the artists and other deep thinkers who attended. However a lot of what Bert was learning and writing about he was developing by looking inside and examining his own emotions, ideas and feelings. This introspection revealed a young man who cared deeply about the injustice and suffering of the downtrodden and working classes who had suffered so much under the years of the great depression. Bert was outraged by what he saw and looking around at the extreme wealth and seeming indifference of the ruling and upper classes of England was determined to use his poetry to try to help bring about at least some easing of the pain and suffering and a levelling of the playing field.

By mid-May of 1939 Bert had left Lyons Corner House and had begun the more agreeable work as a bookkeeper at the Whitstable Oyster Company. Although as we know Bert was not a fan of office work it was a step up from washing dishes and besides he finished work most days by noon which gave him plenty of time in the afternoons for writing and studying for his courses. Time which it seems that he used diligently. Bert's output of poems and essay from this time is the most prolific of his short life. Most of Bert's surviving poems and all but one or two of his work that was published during his lifetime date from the period between when he began taking university courses in London in the summer of 1939 and his very early RAF days in the summer of 1941.

Chapter 6: And War Begins

Unfortunately no letter's of Bert's have survived from the time between June and November 1939. So we don't know what his thoughts or actions were during the time directly leading up to and the start of the war in early September. What we can be sure of though is that Bert continued taking classes at university and pursued his writing and involvement with refugees groups and socialist organisations.

On September 01 Poland was invaded by Germany. Germany's stated reason for the invasion was to bring the German ethnic population of Poland and the free city of Danzig into the Reich but its real reason for the invasion was territorial expansion, a desire to dominate Europe and to become a real world empire. In a surprise move the USSR which had entered into a secret agreement with Nazi Germany attacked the Poles from the east. On the third of September Britain and France both having guaranteed that they would support Polish independence, delivered ultimatums to the German government demanding that the invasion be halted. The deadlines for these ultimatums passed with no comment from Germany, nor any cessation of the invasion, therefore both Britain and France declared war on Germany. In the following few days many other nations including, Australia, Canada and New Zealand quickly followed suite, declaring war on Germany themselves. The Second World War had begun and for the second time in less than 25 years the world found itself at war. At this point however these declarations of war by France and Britain were empty in themselves as the two nations could do very little to help the Polish. The Nazi invasion raced ahead and by the third week of September it was obvious that Poland could no longer resist the invaders as large sections of her country had already fallen to German troops. Poland formally surrendered on Sept 27 was divided between the Germans and the Soviets and was to be occupied by both of these for the next 5 plus years of the war.

All we know of Bert at this time was that he had thrown himself into his studies and his poetry. Raised as a Roman Catholic he had become sceptical and as we know had declared that he was agnostic and now he also considered himself to be a socialist, however he still wanted to see the principles of the New Testament taken seriously. He believed that it was the duty of the socialist poet to hold a mirror up to society showing it all of its failings and flaws, pointing the way to a better world, making men higher and finer and above all to help people keep a warm heart and open mind. Bert's honesty and humility also led him to reflect that "it is not so much the urge to create for art's sake which motivates me but rather the desire for success and honours … my desire is to become impervious to economic success."

Bert's idealism pushed him to try to write for all the right reasons, namely his beliefs. But being human he also couldn't help feel pride and satisfaction when he had work published and was recognised as an up-and-coming writer with great potential. Of course he also needed to eat and pay the rent and he wanted to be in a position to be able to support himself through his writing instead of having to work at office jobs. On the one hand he wanted to write for purely idealistic reasons and on the other hand he wanted to make enough money to write for a living. Most of all though Bert wanted his writing to matter. He wanted to make a difference through his poems and essays, to inspire people to action and to work for a better world. Poems such as his Working Class were meant to not only make people think but to move them to strive to make things better.

Bert's beliefs led him to a socialist outlook that the end of the war would usher in a new age, sweeping away all the dictators, profiteers and gangsters that he believed were running things not only in Germany but in the U.K and Russia as well. This idea of a sweeping change to usher in a new kinder gentler age to borrow a phrase from George W Bush, was something that a lot of socialists and communists

of the time believed. Real change though rarely if ever
sweeps in overnight. Human progress is slow and real deep
and meaningful change takes time, decades if not hundreds
and even thousands of years. We have become used to
technological changes occurring at an ever faster pace but
people can't change that fast and there is no way that our
social and moral norms can keep pace with it. Certainly in
the early 1940s technological change was not occurring as
fast as it does now but the war effort definitely saw the
beginning of this technological revolution.

Bert's idea of sweeping social changes after the war were
idealistic and unrealistic but his beliefs that "we are fighting
the war for the wrong reasons" was not entirely wrong.
Britain not only declared war on Germany because of its
moral obligation to safeguard the rights of the much
smaller and weaker Poland against a much bigger and more
powerful aggressor but also to safeguard its position on the
world stage. Germany's real reason for the invasion was
territorial expansion and acquisition of resources. Britain as
well as wanting to help maintain Poland's independence,
was interested in maintaining her position as a leading
power in the world and ensuring that her empire remained
strong and intact. In many ways Britain's part in the defeat
of the Axis in WW2 was a Pyrrhic victory. Germany, Italy
and Japan were ultimately defeated, regaining freedom for
the many millions of peoples throughout the world who had
been subjugated and enslaved by these powers but
everything or almost everything else that Britain was
fighting for she lost. He empire was broken up and she had
piled up so much debt fighting the war that her status as a
world power was greatly eroded. The end of the war
ushered in an era of social justice and social awakening
although not on the scale that Bert would have hoped for
but at least enough so that countries such as India, Rhodesia
and others were in a position to gain independence and self-
government. The era of great empires and colonialism was
ending and there was a growing realisation that the people
of the so called third world had the same abilities and rights
as the hitherto thought to be superior peoples of Western

Europe and America. Many people believe that the decay and erosion of Britain's empire actually began at the end of WW1 being caused by the heavy debt that she incurred fighting that war. That is probably true but one thing for sure is that the process was completed by the cost in money, resources and manpower of WW2.

However this was not evident in 1940 and the U.K. government continued to carry out their strategies for fighting the Nazis who were trying to muscle in on her place as a world power both economically and in terms of actual lands under her direct control. The Nazis however were not only trying to build an empire they were carrying out a program of extermination and enslavement of any and all whom they deemed racially inferior. The allies opposition to the axis was very much from the moral high ground more so than any desire to maintain the status quo.

In the winter of 1940 Bert's socialist ideas were becoming more entrenched and more formed and he began thinking of himself as a conscientious objector. In February he wrote that "The war goes merrily along. The politicians plead to the people to make sacrifices while they go on like a lot of Al Capones. This is just another big business racket and however just the cause these ghouls are only interested in filling their pockets." Bert may be correct in his assessment of the motives of the ruling classes and businessmen but the U.K. government and its people were also keenly aware of the atrocities being committed by the SS in the cities of Poland and there was a very real sense of moral outrage and a feeling that the war was being fought against a truly evil regime.

It was at this time that Bert became involved with a socialist publication titled "Free Expression." During the early stages of the war this group either came into existence or tried greatly to expand their very limited influence. They believed that the freedom of the individual was paramount and they were against all restrictions of personal freedom. They were especially opposed to the restrictions brought about by the Emergency Powers Act passed just before the outbreak of WWII. The Emergency Powers Act gave the U.K. Government special powers to take almost any action necessary to carry out the war successfully. In practice this meant that these powers controlled many aspects of everyday life during the war – including blackouts and food rationing.

Bert also became involved with the socialist/communist gathering called "The People's Convention." The People's Convention was a conference that was proposed by the Communist Party of Great Britain in 1940–1941. Its organisers attempted to convince the Labour Party and trade union members that the government was only for the rich and was dominated by those whose appeasement of Hitler had "caused" the Second World War, were opposed to the Soviet Union, and who were profiteering from the war. The conventions literature never explicitly came out and stated that the convention was communist backed but all the same it was pretty obvious that it was. Bert tried to attend a meeting of the convention in Manchester. As usual he had no money so he had to try to hitch -hike to the meeting. He couldn't get timely rides and had to give up and return to London and never did attend any of the groups meetings. Bert was socialist but he never was a communist. He thought that Stalin was just as evil as Hitler and he was just as opposed to Stain's regime as he was to Nazi Germany. Bert was equally convinced that members of the current U.K. government and others of the ruling class and big business were profiteering from the war. He believed that they needed to be stopped from making fortunes from the toils and misery of the common man.

Bert was more convinced than ever of the untrustworthiness of the press and its role as little more than a propaganda agent for the government. After all it's not for nothing that they say the first casualty of war is the truth. All of the warring nations used the press to put out propaganda to greater and lesser extents. Bert believed though that the British press in particular was a tool of the ruling class used to keep the workers down. When "Yet A Little Onwards", Bert's broadsheet of 14 poems, was published in 1941 the press got his personal details wrong, which of course did nothing to change his mind about them. The press clipping reads " Mr Bertram Warr, a 23 year old Canadian wrote the third and latest pamphlet. He calls it "Yes, A Little Onwards." (Note they even got the name of the broadsheet wrong substituting the word Yes for the word Yet) Mr Warr came to this country three years ago. His first job was as a dishwasher in a restaurant. He is now a member of an ambulance unit in London.

Bert makes no mention of the typo but he very strongly objects to the reporter writing that he served in an ambulance unit. "It is a horrid lie that I am serving in an ambulance unit. I intended to but was flung out the door wherever I applied."

These feelings about the press did not lessen and by the autumn of 1940 in the heat of the Blitz, Bert was still commenting in letters home about how the press, especially the American press were greatly exaggerating the destruction being caused by the German bombs in London.

In spite of this mistrust of the press Bert made frequent trips to Canada House, then the Canadian High Commission, now the Canadian Embassy located in Trafalgar Square London, to read the Canadian newspapers. Apart from letters from home this was the best way catch up with the news of what was happening back home. Bert's visits to Canada House to read the papers also allowed him to catch up with news about his beloved Toronto Maple Leafs. In the early months of Bert's arrival in England he quite often writes home about how the Leafs are doing in the league and in the playoffs but as he becomes more politically aware and active his interest in sport seems to vanish. Or maybe it was just that the war made caring about hockey and the Leafs a very low priority. Certainly as Bert developed his socialist ideas and as his feelings of being a conscientious objector on political grounds grow we hear no more about the Leafs. Bert's time was taken up by more important things than sports and boyhood teams and dreams. His political ideas, his writing and of course the war were the focus of his life now. The last we read about the Leafs in Bert's letters is in a letter that Bert wrote home about a BBC broadcast on the 9th of April. The BBC had broadcast a recording of the NHL playoff hockey game between the Toronto Maple Leafs and the New York Rangers. The broadcast was especially for Canadian troops already stationed in Britain. The match featured the iconic Foster Hewitt calling the play by play. Bert wrote that it was like old times hearing Foster call out his "he shoots he scores" catch phrase. It must have been a bittersweet experience for Bert sitting alone in his room listening to a voice so deeply connected to home and family. This is the last time that Bert mentions hockey or the Leafs in any of his surviving letters. Life for Bert was becoming to serious for such things as sports. The Maple Leafs were part of his old, last exciting youthful adventure which he was now leaving behind for the serious literary intellectual that he was becoming.

By March Bert's feelings had grown even stronger and he declared he was "now a socialist and against the war as it is for capitalist profits only. " And in somewhat dramatic fashion he declared " I should prefer to shoot Chamberlain and company as there is not one public figure in whom I have the slightest trust." Censorship could not have been in effect at this time or at least not very effectively yet because that is the sort of statement, tongue in cheek though it was, that would elicit a rasing of eyebrows in official circles and probably occasion a visit from the plain clothes boys. In fact Bert does get a visit from one of these fellows at a later date in connection with another letter but more about that later. He continues in the same letter "Am officially opposed on political grounds, so will not fight. The ruling class here is rotten but I thought it worthwhile using their army in my personal fight against the horrible huns! But I have made up my mind that killing Germans was a silly way to solve the problem. I am the only unit of the British Empire which is officially not at war."

Bert laid out his thoughts and feelings about the war in two unpublished essays. They were both written in the early months of the war when Bert was still wrestling with his conscience as to what role he would play, if any in the conflict. The first was probably written before he had decided not to go back home. It is very short and is untitled. In it Bert lays out his feelings about the war.

He declares that from an intellectual point of view he is against fighting in the war because "we are not guided by ethics." He believes the war is a struggle for power between "the old intolerant champion," England and the challenger, the Nazis. He admits though that his emotions, ironically spurred on by the very press and newspapers that he so mistrusts would lead him through an "unreasoning impulse to rush out as a crusader for right. I do not condemn my emotions. Their case is strong enough. Nazism is evil and its final abolition for ethical reasons is justifiable cause for the war." He resists these impulses to action though and maintains his intellectual position as a conscientious objector. Bert was perplexed by the British governments attitude towards the Soviet Union. "Why does the British government seek friendship with Russia? To Russia the partner in crime of Poland we extend the hand of friendship. Even after Poland, there came the crime of Finland and still we have no cause for friction with Russia. In Russia much more so even than in the Germany of Hitler, the blood purge has been employed to mould the nation into a unit. It is a fact that more people have been killed in Russia since the Third International assumed power, than have been killed in Germany since the coming of Hitler." This essay was written before Hitler launched Operation Barbarossa, the invasion of Soviet Russia on the 22 June 1941 so Bert's confusion is certainly understandable. On the one hand Britain is putting itself forward as a champion of virtue and democracy and on the other hand the British government is maintaining relations with one of the worst regimes in the

61

world from the point of view of human rights. Bert declares "the position of the altruist, is therefore difficult. Conscious bidden he goes out to defend the right, but in order to carry out his task he is forced to ally himself with, and become the exploited instrument of a power whose motives he must as a lover of justice abhor. His position, together with the that of his fellows in the army, is simply that of a misguided fool. And is this not one of the damndest (sp) blackest tragedies of the war."

He carries on with a sobering thought that may very well be true of all military organisations past present and future. "The army itself embodies the spirit of Nazism. Have we not the same blind surrender of freedom of will, the will disciplined to the dictates of the Books of Regulations." He then extends this reasoning to embody the ruling of the state. "We may argue reasonably, that since such a system is proved of most efficiency in our own country in the fighting forces, a unit where the utmost cohesion is essential, then the same system, extended to the nation, should produce a similar efficiency in operation, and increased potentiality of each individual as part of the nation under a common discipline. Thus it must be considered whether or not in the Totalitarian State we do see evidence of the workings of evolution." Bert finishes this line of thinking with a thought that I think most of us can heartily agree with. He declares this "A sobering thought indeed."

The second essay was written sometime later, after Bert had taken his initial stand as a conscientious objector. This essay titled "Why I Object" begins with an explanation by Bert as to why he is in general against war and ends with his attempts to explain why he is specifically against taking direct action in this war. This essay expands on the ideas developed in the first essay. In it Bert works through the idea that all life is a struggle and not just during wartime but all the time. He believes that two kinds of people fare badly in this struggle especially during wartime, the virtuous man and the coward. He admits to being afraid of going to war and dying but he knows that this is not his overriding reason

62

for not going to war. We know that he did not lack for courage and he knew it too. His reasons for not going to war are more aligned to those of the virtuous; his belief in the corrupt nature of the ruling class and the government. He says that " I can look dispassionately at the lying presses, listen to the smoothing oil and large hypocrisies of the old men who rule, and consolidate my position with regard to what they represent. I hate them for their insincerity and greed, and acknowledge with awe the immense inhumanity of their dealings with the people. I see then the division between the nation and its leaders."

He carries on somewhat naively about the virtues of the masses "The decent idealism of the mass, geared to sacrifice and effort for good, exhorted and whipped into new energies contrasts itself with the desires of those men who seek only for selfish gain through their energies." As we well know there are more than enough people in the masses who along the lines of the business elite and the ruling classes equally act with only thoughts of selfish gain. Bert was still only 23 at this time and he was still to learn the harsh reality that greed and acting in self-interest are not the exclusive properties of those with high social status and financial security, however that may be, at this time Bert was deeply affected by his beliefs and acted in good faith to follow them by declaring himself a socialist and a conscientious objector. I get the feeling with both essays that they were written perhaps as much to work through and clarify his thoughts and feelings to himself as they were to any potential reader. This may be especially true as neither of these essays was ever published.

Note: In order that the reader may get as full a picture as possible and decide for themselves, as much as they can, about, Bert's motivations for becoming a conscientious objector transcripts of both of these unpublished essays can be found in Appendix VII. However when reading these one must bear in mind that the fullest picture that we can obtain of Bert's stance must include his comments from his surviving letters. For that the reader will be limited to my

interpretations of these as the letters are far to numerous too
reprint in full here.

Chapter 7 Bert Begins to be Noticed

That winter of 1940 was the calm before the storm. The U.K. was at war with Germany but there was not yet a lot of action involving British forces. That doesn't mean however that there wasn't a lot going on. In November in a blatant bid at expansion the USSR invaded Finland in what became known as the winter war. The Fins fought valiantly but ultimately fruitlessly as they were hopelessly outnumbered. After inflicting many heavy defeats on the huge but badly organised Soviet forces Finland was forced to surrender on 13 March 1940.

In January of 1940 the UK government introduced rationing of food. Bert wrote that "everyone has a ration book which consists of little tickets torn off by the by the person from whom we buy the rationed goods. Thus when you buy a meal in a restaurant the cashier takes one ticket from your ration book." Disillusioned by the leadership though he was, Bert was still very patriotic in his way and willing to do his bit to defeat the evil of the Nazis. Bert's description of rationing continues " A very good system. O well it's all for good old liberty and democracy, I suppose, I hope I hope I hope." Not entirely convinced that the best interests of liberty and democracy were being served by the leadership in another letter he wrote that people were "Starving for butter. Grocers can't get supplies from big business. It's a racket, one of many."

Rationing was introduced as a direct result of shortages caused by the what came to be known as the Battle Of The Atlantic. The United Kingdom required more than a million tons of imported food and other materials per week to survive. The Battle of the Atlantic pitted the German U-Boats, surface ships and Luftwaffe aircraft against the heavily protected conveys of Allied shipping. The North Atlantic conveys were protected by war ships and aircraft of Britain, Canada and the U.S.A. The Battle Of The Atlantic ran from virtually the start of the war in September 1939 until the defeat of the Nazis in May 1945 making it the longest continuous campaign of the entire war. At the height of the battle in June of 1942 the Germans were sinking upwards of 124 allied merchant vessels per month. This total gradually decreased as the Allied navies and airforces gained the upper hand and by June of 1943 the germans were sinking only an average of 4 ships per month and losing a large number of U-Boats to the improved naval escort system. The Canadian navy became specialist at U-Boat tracking and sinking using their large number of Corvette anti submarine ships which were extremely effective at finding and sinking the German U-Boats. By the end of the war Canada had the 4th largest navy in the world and most of its ships were specialised for use against submarines.

During the Blitz and the winter of 1940 Bert continued to take classes at university and he continued to write poetry. By now the literary world was starting to notice him. He had several poems printed in the Poetry Quarterly and two of his poems, "War Widow" and "The Heart To Carry On" were included in the anthology "Poems Of The Forces" that noted poet Henry Treece was publishing.

In September of 1940 a broadsheet of 14 of Bert's poems was printed and sold for one shilling, which was about 5 pence. He wasn't about to get rich but he was being noticed. His publisher sent several of his poems to the noted writer Robert Graves. Graves was impressed and wrote to Bert saying " It was a great pleasure in times like these to know that there was another poet about. As you must be aware it is always a small number. So to find your poems was a great pleasure. I shall tell the other poets about them." Graves wanted to bring Bert into his literary circle and suggested that Bert get in touch with a friend of Grave's, Alan Hodge who worked in Whitehall and with whom Graves worked on books.

Graves finishes his second and last letter to Bert with the sentence "Please send me poems whenever." However Bert never contacted Graves again and he wrote home that he lost the contact details of Grave"s friend Alan Hodge. So even though he had wanted to could not contact him. Clearly this is not true because Hodge's contact details are included in Grave's second letter the original of which still exists amongst Bert's papers. Mary Connolly said that Bert did not keep in contact with Graves because Bert wanted to maintain independence from any group. This explanation doesn't ring entirely true either. I think there is another reason that Bert didn't carry on his correspondence with Graves. One of Bert's literary heroes was the World War I poet Wilfred Owen. Graves knew Owen personally and in his second letter to Bert Graves spoke poorly of Owen and said that "if he had lived I would have had to break off my friendship with him just as I did with Siegfried Sassoon."

For Graves to write disparagingly about Wilfred Owen and Sassoon as well, was probably just too much for Bert to take and more than enough for Bert to not want to have anything more to do with him. Owen was one of Bert's most cherished poetry heroes. He also thought very highly of Sassoon. In one of his university notebooks Bert wrote that "Owen and Sassoon were the two great poets produced by the war."

In a letter home dated 25 April 1941 Bert, ever mindful of mentoring his sister Mary wrote "Has Mary read Wilfred Owen Yet. He is miles above Rupert Brooke. Tell her to compare an anthology of the last war with this one. The poets last time were not at all socially knowing. They groped about not understanding the place of war in history. This time they know but I must admit it doesn't make them write very good stuff."

This quote is interesting for a number of points. first of all it would seem that one of the things that Bert admired most about Owen was that his poetry was helping to shape and evolve poetry into the modernist style. Owen was a poet whose graphic descriptions of the horrors of war did much to help advance poetry into the modernist style that Bert was a disciple of. Wilfred Owen was one of the best British

poets of the first world war. He was a lieutenant in the
Lancashire Fusiliers and served in France from december
1916 until his death. He was killed in November 1918 just
one week before the armistice. Most of his poems were
published posthumously and his reputation grew steadily
after the Great war.

The second thing that stands out about this excerpt is that
Bert thought that although many modern poets may be
themselves adherents of the modernist style most of them
were not very good. That is a sentiment shared by Robert
Graves when he writes to Bert that it was a pleasure finding
out that there is another poet about and that at any given
time there are not that many truly good poets about.

Bert's poem "Poets In Time Of War" is a poem that Bert
dedicated to Wilfred Owen and its inclusion by Bert's editor
among the poems that he sent to Robert Graves and Graves
response to its inclusion is what led Bert to turn his back on
Robert Graves.

Poets In Time Of War
(In Memory Of Wilfred Owen)

Poets, who in time of war
Divide in visionary horror
Soul's dream from body's missions
Knowing a holier connections
Than the will to destruction
Compelling the boy in arms to kill his broither

All who tell the grave story
Of love, the sad esentialiality
Of pain, whom no bitterness
Bars from life's true lovliness
Whose words are a tenderness
Of hands, caressing maimed humanity

Spirits who dream and move onward
Leaving to us your dreams gathered
And resounding forever in the air-
O, believe us this bodily despair
Stuns not our spirits, for there,
Serenely, our visionary heritage has flowered

In any event, whatever the reason, Bert did not maintain
contact with Robert Graves and his circle. Bert seemed
determined to go his own way and remain true to his
principles and his conscience.

He carried on taking courses at university and working with
the various refugee and socialist organisations that he was
involved with. Even as the Blitz carried on night after night
as the Luftwaffe tried desperately to destroy the RAF and
pave the way for the German invasion of England. In a
letter home dated 16 Sept 1940 Bert wrote that "For the last
four nights the anti-aircraft guns have fired almost the
whole night through. It is one continual roar of guns
mingled with the duller boom of bombs as as they fall."

He carries on as if that wasn't really anything out of the
ordinary and adds the description of of his cousin Joan's
wedding as mentioned above. "Joan and Tiny were married
on Saturday (Saturday 14th September 1940) in between air
raid alarms. It was a successful wedding. Aunt Queen and
Roy, Joan's brother, came up from Bristol, and Rashbrook's
parents from ColchesterAfter the ceremony we all tripped to
a restaurant where a meal had been ordered for the whole
fourteen of us. It was good, chicken etc. Have just heard a
bomb come whistling down some distance away, but it must
have been either a dud or a time bomb because it did not
explode. The noise gives me a headache. It starts every
night at about eight and ends about four in the morning."
Bert ever ready to avoid the dull office routine of work
finishes with "We do our sleeping when we can, go to work
hours late in the morning and leave early, which is good."

Through the air raids of the blitz Bert continued his work at
the oystery although at times this was a challenge. In the

building where he worked all the glass in the windows was blown out by a bomb that had blown up very close to the building. Bert had to work bundled up in his winter coat and hunkered down against the cold and rain pouring as the wind whipped them in through the broken windows, picking bits of glass out of the ledgers.

Life and work carried on in spite of the Luftwaffe raids. "They just began to repair the place today. Numbers of buildings in the vicinity were destroyed, it looks like war torn Spain. There is not much night life as everyone goes home early to sleep. Which is what I shall try to do now if the guns will stop for a few minutes. When I got back here to the flat in the afternoon of Monday the area was roped off as the police believed a time bomb had landed nearby. Everyone was evacuated and I went to a school for the night." In the true spirit of the Blitz Bert finishes this letter with the plucky fighting spirit we associate with this time. "Don't worry again as it is not half as bad as the American papers portray it. We just adapt ourselves to the new inconveniences." And perhaps more to reassure his family than anything else he finishes "No one is very upset and I am well and functioning."

On November 19 1939 Bert wrote home that "This week we must all register with a grocer for rationing of butter and bacon (which is eaten here in vast quantities and cannot be bought at a butcher store only at a grocers)." Everyone had to register for rationing at this time in spite of rationing not officially beginning until January 1940. In reality rationing doesn't seem to actually have come into effect, at least not for meat, until March. In a letter home dated March 10 1940 Bert wrote "Tomorrow rationing begins here. We are allowed 1/10 worth of meat in a week. That is enough for me as I only have Sunday dinner in the flat here and the rest of the time I eat bacon or sausages or something. Sausages are not rationed yet so we can eat all we want." He carries on in another letter written during the heart of the London Blitz "Starting tomorrow, the butter ration becomes 1/2 lb. instead of the meagre four ounces which has had to satisfy us until now. So many people are using margarine instead at 16 or 20 cents per lb that butter which sells at 35 cents per lb has been ignored and large stocks have accumulated." Somewhat humorously he adds "The margarine is not bad if eaten quickly so that you haven't time to taste it."

As the German attacks on the supply convoys began to bite, availability of meat has gone downhill drastically from Bert's initial optimistic report in March. "The meat situation is horrible. Instead of butcher's windows being crammed with great juicy looking roasts and steaks and chops, you see only plates of bilious looking insides of cows, old hunks of stewing meat, and a few scrawny looking chickens. Fowl are not rationed and turkey can be bought at about thirty cents a lb. Yesterday for dinner I splurged 40 cents on roast mutton and suet pudding. There was lots of it but that was the only point in its favour. All the taste had been boiled out of the meat, I suppose in the process of making it less leathery." The Germans were determined to starve Britain out and deny the British the supplies necessary to carry on the war. Using a combination of U-boats, aircraft and surface vessels the Germans kept a constant pressure on the convoys attempting to cross the Atlantic from Canada and the U.S. For their part their allies were just as determined to get the convoys through and adopted better and more effective tactics for convoy escorts. But in those dark days of the early 1940s the convoy losses were huge.

Rationing and constant nightly bombing along with the stress of worrying about the impending German invasion of Britain began to sap the spirit of Londoners. However demoralising as the meat rationing situation had become all was not bad on the rationing front. Bert wrote that "Oranges are very cheap here. Big ones cost only about 20 cents a dozen so occasionally I purchase one orange. "

In fact fruit and veg were never rationed but there were shortages of these especially anything that had to be shipped in from overseas. The government introduced a scheme designed to encourage people to grow their own vegetables wherever possible. The scheme became known as "Dig For Victory." Even so at the height of war and during the hardest times there were often long queues outside grocery stores as people lined up to try to collect their weekly rations. Often a person, usually a housewife, but occasionally a single man such as Bert would get to the front of the line after a long time spent queuing only to find out that the item they were lining up for had just run out, frustratingly leaving them to have to turn around and go home to try again tomorrow.

Under the rationing system each household had to register with only one grocer and could use their tickets in this shop only. When purchasing a rationed item along with the money the person had to give the grocer a ticket from the book. The same system was used in restaurants although it was not necessary to register with a particular restaurant so you could still eat where ever you wished on that score.

Germany relied heavily on Swedish iron ore for manufacturing the vast war machine that their armed forces ran on. In a bid to secure a safe trade route for this the Germans invaded Norway and Denmark on April 09. The British and French sent troops to Norway but they were really only token forces and the Norwegians were forced to surrender on June 10. The victory meant that the Germans had secured this much needed rich source of Swedish iron and a relatively safe route to bring these supplies into the Reich.

On the ninth of May the Germans launched their long anticipated attack and invaded France through the neutral countries of Holland and Belgium. The speed and organisation of the attack caught the French completely unprepared and their armies and those of the British were quickly overwhelmed and defeated. The British forces retreated to the coast near the port of Dunkirk were in one of the most daring operations of the war they were evacuated to the safety of home. Between the 26th of May and the 4th of June 336,000 British and allied troops were evacuated from the port and the beaches of Dunkirk and across the channel to the safety of England where they lived to fight another day.

On the 12th of May Bert writes that they all now have to carry gas masks wherever they go.
After Dunkirk the people of England, including Bert expected the Germans to invade at any time and sooner rather than later. Hitler did indeed plan to invade Britain and was building up an invasion force and the ships to carry it across the channel. Hitler's planned invasion of Britain was codenamed Operation Sea lion. Before he could put Sea lion into operation though Hitler wanted to have mastery of the skies over the channel and the U.K. itself. With that goal the Luftwaffe launched their bombing campaign that would rage throughout the summer and would go down in history known as the Battle Of Britain. Initially the Luftwaffe concentrated their attacks against RAF airfields, aircraft factories and radar stations. The Luftwaffe came very close to achieving their goal when they switched from primarily trying to cripple the RAF to terror bombing of British civilians. This switch in tactics was one of the luckiest things that occurred for the British in this early part of the war. The change in targets was designed by Hitler to cause wide spread disruption, confusion and chaos in London leading to a mass evacuation of the British capital. Hitler hoped that in this way he could force the British to agree to an armistice, ending British participation in the war and therefore eliminating the need to invade the island. This change in tactics proved to be a huge blunder and gave the RAF a much needed respite and allowing them to recover. In fact this change in Luftwaffe targets ended any hope that the Germans would attain the air supremacy over British skies and now neither the forced armistice that Hitler preferred over invasion nor invasion itself were realistic goals. In truth the ideas of a forced armistice was never realistic in any event. The British had no intention of entertaining any such thing at any time. By Oct 1940 Operation Sea Lion was postponed indefinitely. Churchill never seriously worried about the Germans actually

invading. He believed that a cross channel seaborne invasion of Britain by the Germans was always beyond their capability to carry out successfully. Churchill was happy to have the people believe that invasion could come at anytime believing that it kept them on their toes and in a high state of readiness for whatever was actually to come. Of course the people didn't know this however and all through the summer months they waited anxiously and more than a little nervelessly for the invasion.

Writing home Bert, somewhat tongue in cheek but with a note of the seriousness and worry about the future that everyone in Britain was feeling at the time, that he was now taking a course at college in German in order to be able to welcome Hitler properly when he arrives. It seems though that as worried as the people were about being invaded that the picture we have been handed down of the feelings of the time are correct and that for the most part people did indeed keep calm and carry on. Bert writes that every Tuesday he goes to the Globe Theatre where Alec Guinness or some other celebrity holds a poetry reading. He also went to Swanley with Mrs Senjem and her daughter for a day out. Mrs Senjem was also living in the flats at Lanark Mansions and that is how he met her and her daughter, they were neighbours. It may have been primarily through Mrs Senjem and her connections to the refugees that Bert got involved with that group of intellectuals and artists that were so influential on him.

As the summer wore on the invasion which always seemed imminent never happened. The Luftwaffe never were able to gain the air superiority over the RAF that Hitler deemed necessary before the invasion could take place. Without absolute control of the skies the invasion forces in the barges would be sitting ducks to the RAF fighter and bombers.

Giving up on his planned forced armistice with or invasion of Britain, Hitler let the Luftwaffe change its tactics and in September the Luftwaffe began bombing London and the

other big cities of Britain in the terror bombing campaign
that became known as the Blitz. Of course the people of
Britain didn't know of the postponement of the invasion.
Bert wrote on 9th of September that they expected the
invasion tomorrow. As much as he disliked and mistrusted
the government his patriotism and desire to see the evil of
Nazism defeated prompted him to close that letter with the
desperate "We expect to be invaded tomorrow, doubt if it
will succeed, I hope, I hope, I hope."

The invasion never happened and by October Hitler put
Operation Sea Lion on hold indefinitely. Hitler now planned
on beating the Soviets first before turning and dealing with
Britain. He wanted to deal with bolshevism which he hated
almost as much as he hated the jews. He planned on
invading the USSR in the spring of 1941 and had his
generals make plans accordingly. He would turn and deal
with Britain once the USSR was beaten and annexed to the
Reich. Hitler and his generals had convinced themselves
that they could inflict total defeat on the Soviets quickly and
decisively. They had a total disdain for the ability of the
read Army who they believed to be badly trained, badly
equipped and led by generals even worse. And of course the
Germans believed themselves racially superior to the
Russians and therefore able to walk over their sub human
inferior troops. That idea was of course nonsense. That
would be a lesson the Nazis would soon learn and suffer
much in the learning of it.

The Germans were well aware of the fate of Napoleon's
Grand Armee outside Moscow but they decided the same
fate wouldn't happen to them if they were clever and could
envelope and destroy Russia's armies close to the frontiers.
Of course no such thing happened. The Germans did inflict
heavy defeats on the Soviet forces, took hundreds of
thousands of prisoners and were able to push their invasion
forward to Moscow. The Soviets two things in
overwhelming abundance, a huge population and vast
amounts of land. So of course in the end the same fate
awaited the Germans as awaits any army foolish enough to

fight a land war in Asia and they were ultimately utterly defeated. In spite of the Germans racial superiority they were ultimately soundly beaten by the sub human forces from Asia. Proving once and for all that ideas of one race being superior to another are pure nonsense. Of course this is a lesson still being learned today over and over again from Rwanda and South Africa with Apartheid to the USA with racial segregation to Palestine where the conflicts between the Israelis and Palestinians still rage and many, many other places around our world.

Bertram Warr: This is the photo that Bert had professionally
taken in London shortly before he was killed

Bert and Frank late 1930s

Frank Warr: Rare colour photo of Frank. Date unknown but he looks very young

Bert and Frank: Circa 1920s

Bert looking cool in sunglasses and braces.

Frank and Al Hymus with unknown girl skiing. Frank was very sporty. He skied, played golf, tennis and many other sports.

Frank in a row boat looking somewhat uncomfortable in suite and tie

Aunt Queen circa 1920s. Aunt Queen was Bert's father's
sister. She lived in the district of Pill on Bristol and had Bert
down to her house for holidays. She also used to often visit
Joan and Bert in their flats at Lanark Mansions in Maida
Vale London.

Bert's sister, my Aunt Mary: Mary was devoted to Bert and worked diligently to get a book of his poetry published. Acknowledgement to Life was published in 1970 ensuring that Bert's legacy lives on. The date this photo was taken is unknown but it was probably taken in the late 1940s or the early 1950s

Frank and the Warr "Glamour Girls" as he teasingly referred to his three eldest sisters. L-R Marjory, Frank, Emily and Mary. The date of this photo is unknown but must be sometime in late winter of 1942 because there is snow on the ground Frank has been in the RCAF long enough to have earned his sergeants stripes, which are clearly visible in the photo.

Frank and his mother Mary Teresa Warr winter of 1942
during Frank's aircrew training at Malton airport. Frank
would ship out for over seas a few months later in
September and was killed on Oct 02 1943 flying his one and
only op as a navigator in a wellington with RCAF 424
squadron out of North Africa.

Frank training for aircrew Malton airport. L-R Willy
Wilson, "General Grant" and Frank. General Grant was
Frank's best friend in the airforce and the two shipped out
together for duty overseas.

Frank his childhood friend Al Hymus. Hymus grew up with
both Bert and Frank. He joined the army and was in
England at the same time that Frank was. There two spent
an almost comical amount of time trying to meet up. They
finally managed a visit during the August bank holiday
weekend of 1943 when they were able to spend a couple of
days together palling around. It was to be the last time they
would see each other.

Halifax MKII with 158 Squadron's designation of NP and the call sign of N for November. This was the type of aircraft that Bert flew all of his combat operations in. Note the rudder with the pointed leading edge. This is what caused the aircraft to go into uncontrollable rolls when the pilot went hard over rudder often resulting in fatal crashes.

Halifax Bomb Aimer position: As the aircraft approached the target the bomb aimer lay prone looking out through the perspex nose cone through his bomb aiming scope. He would direct the pilot to the target via radio intercom and once over the target give the signal to drop the bombs. At this point an automatic camera would fire off taking a photo of where the bombs landed. Until the camera had flashed the aircraft had to remain flying straight and true over the target and this presented the ack-ack and night fighters with a plum target.

The wreckage of Bert's Halifax DT635 NP-F. The aircraft was shot down by Major Werner Strieb flying a Messerschmidt BF109 for his third kill of the night April 03 1943. On crashing the aircraft broke in two at its mid section. The front of the aircraft hit the ground so hard that identification of the three bodies in the nose was not possible.

So violent was the crash of Bert's aircraft that the pilot Dennis Cole was thrown clear of the aircraft and through the roof of this neighbouring barn where his body was found still strapped into his seat.

A page from Bert Bert's flight logbook late March 1943
listing 6 training flights and 3 combat flights flown. Note
the combat missions are shown in red and were flown to
targets in Nurnberg, Stuttgart and Berlin.

Grandma Warr and my mom, Cecilia (Babs) on the Queen
Mary in 1948 on their way to England for a holiday and to
meet with John Gawsworth about his progress or rather lack
of, in getting a book of Bert's poems published.

Grandma Warr in mourning for Bert and Frank, "her boys"

Bertram Howard Warr, my grandpa, circa 1950s with
Skippy the family dog

The 158 Squadron memorial on the edge of the old runway
at the site of RAF Lissett Yorkshire

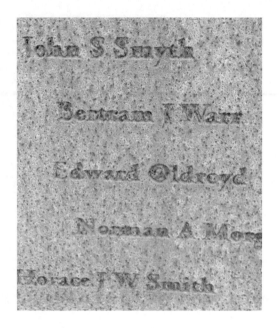

Closeup view of Bert's name on the 158 Memorial at Lissett
Yorkshire. 158 Squadron lost 851 men during the course of
the war which of course is 158 backwards.

Chapter 8: Bert Takes A Stand

On May 10th Neville Chamberlain resigned and was replaced as Prime Minister by Winston Churchill. In a letter home Bert related the change in PM "the old wolf Chamberlain has crawled halfway out the door at last. He is still cluttering up the place though as leader of the Conservative party. Churchill is held in good repute by the man in street chiefly because he makes fighting speeches like Hitler. I am trying to discover some other reason for his fame." Churchill did indeed make rousing inspiring speeches. On his first address to parliament after becoming P.M. he made his famous blood and sweat speech.

"I have nothing to offer but blood, toil, tears, and sweat. You ask, what is our policy? I will say: It is to wage war, by sea, land and air, with all our might and with all the strength that God can give us; to wage war against a monstrous tyranny, never surpassed in the dark and lamentable catalogue of human crime. That is our policy. You ask, what is our aim? I can answer in one word: Victory. Victory at all costs—Victory in spite of all terror— Victory, however long and hard the road may be, for without victory there is no survival."

Several days later Churchill made another of his famous rousing speeches remembered now mostly for these lines.

"We shall fight on the beaches, we shall fight on the landing grounds, we shall fight in the fields and in the streets, we shall fight in the hills; we shall never surrender."

Churchill made this speech on June 10th once it became obvious that the battle for France was lost and just 8 days before the French signed the armistice with the Nazis. Rousing stuff indeed. And while Churchill may also to have been one of the Al Capone's that Bert so loathed, the lines from his speech to parliament "a monstrous tyranny never surpassed in the dark and lamentable catalogue of human crime" show that Churchill was equally aware of, and felt

the moral responsibility to defeat the Nazis that Bert
believed was the only valid reason for war.

All through these tense summer months of 1940, Bert
wrestled with his conscience. Initially he decided to go back
home to Canada. His first thought was to try to get back
home, acting as a chaperon to children who were to be
evacuated from the U.K. to Canada ahead of the invasion.
As the summer wore on however and the invasion didn't
happen this plan was never enacted. Many children from
wealthy families were evacuated but that was paid for by
their families and there was never any general overseas
evacuation of children from less affluent families. A plan to
evacuate as many children as possible from cities was
carried out. These evacuations were to villages and farms
within the U.K. however and not for any locations overseas.

By August the bombings of London began and what became
known as the London Blitz had begun. The Blitz had a very
profound effect on Bert. As he witnessed more and more of
the suffering caused by the bombing, Bert's compassion and
his ideas of social justice led him to change his mind about
going back to Canada. At the end of October 1940 he wrote
"I feel I should stay here now and help the people who are
suffering under the bombing. It would be unfair to leave just
now when I can be of use in a difficult time." This must
have been a very difficult time for Bert as he wrestled with
his conscience. On the one hand he was completely against
joining the military and fighting for the corrupt ruling class
of Britain. But Bert was desperate to do his bit to help end
the Nazi evil, especially the terror bombing of the Blitz
which was causing so much suffering among the working
class of the country. Bert's solution was a compromise. He
would try and join the Red Cross or a London Ambulance
crew. That way he would be helping the war cause but he
would not be fighting for the corrupt government and he
wouldn't have to join a military unit.

We don't know how Bert celebrated his 23rd birthday on
Dec 07 1941. The Japanese marked the occasion by

bombing the American fleet at Pearl Harbour, sinking 4 battleships and damaging 4 others. All the battleships were later raised and returned to service apart from the USS Arizona. The attack also damaged or sank three cruisers and three destroyers. 180 American aircraft were also destroyed. 2,403 Americans were killed and a further 1,178 were wounded. President Franklin Roosevelt, in his address to the American people the next day said the day would live in infamy. The British and the Americans both declared war on Japan on December 8th. The British declared war because the Japanese had also attacked the British colonies in Malaysia and Singapore. Germany and Italy declared war on the US on December 11th, bringing the US into the war in Europe, which of course ultimately ensured the defeat of the Axis powers. The US probably would have been drawn into the European war in any event, but this rash act by Italy and Germany ensured it happened sooner rather than later thereby sowing the seeds of their own destruction by awakening the sleeping giant that of the U.S. industrial might. The U.S. had already been sending a lot of military aid to England through the lend lease program but now they would gear the majority industrial output and huge population to fighting and winning the war. For Hitler and the Axis powers it was only a matter of time. The only possible way that they could now win would be to win the race to build the atomic bomb, but Germany was hopelessly behind in that race. Hitler put more stock in the rockets of the V1 and V2 programs and jet aircraft than he did in building an atomic bomb. The V weapons and jets could of course make a difference but they were not game winners. That dubious distinction would be left to the atomic weapons; a single one which could destroy an entire city.

Still convinced that fighting for the bunch of Al Capones in the British government would be wrong Bert tried to carry out his plan to try to join the Red Cross or an ambulance crew. Fate had other plans for Bert though. When he attempted to join ambulance crews in London he wrote " I was flung out the door wherever I applied." This was because he was physically fit and of military age.

95

Bert was still determined to help and when he was notified in mid-January 1941 that we has to be conscripted for military duty he decided to accept this fate and go and fight. Bert's conscientious objector stand was very complicated. His pacifism was not based around the idea of the sanctity of life it was very much more a political stance. He believed very strongly that the Nazis were evil and had to be stopped. What Bert objected to was that the people in charge in the United Kingdom were not fighting the Nazis based around any ethical or moral reasons for stopping the them. They were fighting purely for capitalism and the continuation of empire which would maintain the status quo. The rich and the ruling class would continue to get richer and continue to rule on the backs of the working class man who was having to bear the brunt of the fighting and yet not receiving any benefit. Bert wanted to see an end to this. So he decided that he wouldn't fight for the politicians and ruling class. He would fight to help end the suffering of the common folk and to help bring about the social changes he believed were necessary and now thought could only be achieved through winning the war. In his essay about the war as we know, Bert wrote that the monstrous inhumanity of the Nazis stirred in him a feeling that it was his duty to help to avenge the innocent. However he had been resisting the impulse to rush out as a crusader for the repressed. " I do not condemn my emotions, their case is strong enough, Nazism is evil and its final abolition is justifiable cause for the war. But we are not fighting for any ethical reasons. We fight to maintain the status of the UK as a dominant economic and political power against the challenger who would usurp this position. Justice and right are not on our side because although the cause is just the motives of our rulers are corrupt."

Furthermore Bert continued to struggle with the idea of Russia as an ally. We know that he believed that Stalin was even more evil than Hitler and he had a real problem with the UK allying itself with him in the fight. The Russian front was essential to the defeat of Nazism. Hitler could not tolerate the communist state to his east and for him the essential struggle was not just against Britain and the western allies but was an ideological struggle between fascism and communism and his ideas of world domination by the German Reich. Politically Churchill and the west took the view of the USSR that the enemy of my enemy is my friend and were more than happy to see the USSR face the brunt of the attack while they prepared for the opening of the second front and the liberation of Western Europe. The U.K. and the U.S.A. did everything they could to keep the Soviet Union supplied with food, and weapons through convoys. It looked very much, especially in the early days of Hitler's invasion of Russia, that the Soviet armies would collapse in utter defeat and Hitler would make short work of his invasion leaving him free to turn his full attention once again to England. U.K. and U.S. support for the Soviets was essential for the war effort.

All these ideas and thoughts played through Bert's mind that whole winter of 1940-41. They ultimately led him to decide that when the time came and he was called up, he would opt to volunteer for duty as air crew in RAF Bomber command rather than take the conscientious objector route and go to jail or a work farm. all the men who flew in RAF bombers were volunteers. Bert's conviction that the people were worth fighting for and it was the people that he would go to war for is expressed in his poetry. He wrote several poems about the suffering that the blitz brought to the people of London. "Stenpney 1941" being the best example of his thoughts and observations of all that was happening to the people of the East End at the time and "War Widow" about the terrible effects of war on those left behind by the fighting man as he went off to die in battle.

I believe that in his heart Bert had wanted to join the fight all along but that he had resisted because of his position as a socialist and his opposition to the corrupt ruling classes which led him to declare that he was a conscientious objector. It seems to me that it is almost with relief that Bert finds that he can join the fight by declaring that he will fight for the common folk, to help end their suffering and not

97

fight for the Al Capones who make up the government and the ruling class. On the one hand he wanted to be a person who followed his intellect and didn't let his emotions rule him, but equally he was raring to enter the fray and do his bit to end the evil of Nazism. After all he had already publicly and emphatically declared himself a conscientious objector. At this point it would have been the easy road to accept a prison sentence or being assigned to work on a farm or down a mine for the duration. By making this decision Bert was able to follow his heart and not his head and enlist and join the fight without losing face. He still deplored the idea of actually joining the military. The idea of joining any military organisation was something that he had long resisted, but he was now willing and able to rise above these thoughts and enter the battle. Of course this is just my opinion, however it is an opinion reached after extensive study of all of Bert's surviving letters, notes and essays.

At about the time Bert was making up his mind to stand and fight a curious article that he had written was published in the March 1941 edition of the Free Expression magazine. Bert wrote the article on 12 February 1941. So presumably the visit from the government agent had taken place sometime in December 1940 or January 1941. Free Expression was the voice of a group who were interested in complete freedom of the individual and seem to have come into existence primarily to oppose the introduction of the Emergency Services Act. We don't know how Bert became involved with them but it is a good bet that it was through The People's Convention which he continued to be associated with. Bert writes about a visit he had from a plain clothes agent of the government's security services. At that time the man would probably have been in the Secret Service which was the forerunner of MI5. Bert gets the visit because of a letter he had written to America in which he had declared himself somewhat left of left and containing certain phrases that were flagged by the censor as indicating that Bert was a potential danger to security.

In the article titled - Warr is Visited - Bert relates that he was visited by a British plainclothesman from the C.I.D. (Criminal Investigation Department, a unit which investigates serious or potentially serious crimes) at his flat one afternoon. During the war the UK had about 10,000 censors who routinely read civilian mail looking for anything that could aid the enemy or that was a potential or actual security risk. The article is written somewhat tongue in cheek about a serious event that could have had very serious consequences for Bert had the agent been more officious and not seen that Bert posed no security threat whatsoever. The fellow read from a note book two statements attributed to Bert from his letter. " I am a communist" and "Heil the revolution." Either of those would have raised a red flag with the censors. The article continues with Bert's somewhat startled reply "Yers" having immediately remembered having written in the letter "A spectre is haunting Europe, the spectre of communism." Bert called both statements equally majestically silly and admitted to the agent that yes he had written heil the revolution but not written "I am a communist" which statement Bert attributes possibly to an overzealous police report.

The agent looked surprised, wrote in his notebook and matter of factly stated " You know of course how careful we must be these days in tracking down and dealing with what are known as subversive influences in this country. Bert wrote that "His voice smiled charmingly but his metallic eyes looked at Warr as though he were the personification of the subversive influences itself."

The interview continues and the agent tells Bert that it's his job to investigate by visiting anyone who makes such statements and then, putting Bert squarely under the gun asks him if would care to explain what he meant by them. Bert, perhaps scrambling a little at this point related that he held with the Marxism conception of history, and that the revolution to which he had "heiled" was already in progress, and its result would be a better world. The agent seemed

99

satisfied, with this because he replied "After all that is what we are fighting for, a better world. but I have read Marx-part of my job. I can't say that I agree with the Russian way of changing the world. Do you mean a revolution stirred up by foreign agitators, a bloody revolution?"

"The eyes looked at Bert again. Evidently the young man placed much importance in the answer to this question." Bert in his typically humorously, yet to the point and adroit, way wrote "revolution that said please and was without blood he tolerated; revolution with a mess on the pavement, nicht gut, "'ere, wat's awl this abaht? Warr attempting circumspection mumbled about means and ends and justice."

Next the agent, keeping the pressure up homes in for the kill, and bluntly asks if Bert is is a member of the communist party of Britain or of any other organisation financed by a foreign power?" To which Bert answers a truthful "No."

Wrapping things up and taking note of Bert's identity and military service cards, the agent asks where Bert lived and worked and how long he had been living in England and oh, by the way what did Bert think about Churchill's performance in the house that day? The agent rather ominously tells Bert that they have an eye too, on the young Austrian refugee lady in America to whom Bert had written the letter in the first place. "There seems to be nothing wrong but you never know." Ending the interview here the agent shakes Bert's hand and rushes off to play a chess match that he had booked at his club, leaving Bert with plenty to think and worry about. Bert had to worry about himself and his Austrian friend in the U.S. who through his careless words he may have dropped into big trouble. That must have been the end of the affair because Bert never mentions another visit from this agent nor any of his colleagues and of course Bert does enlist and does go off to fight. It would be anther 4 months before Bert was actually called up and enlisted in the RAF.

100

Note: For a full reproduction of this interesting article please see appendix 6.

A couple of months later, in May 1941 one of the more bizarre incidents of the war took place. On May 10 1941 deputy Fuhrer Rudolf Hess flew in a specially prepared Messerschmidt BF110 from Germany to Scotland. He managed to evade several pursuing Spitfires and crashed his aircraft in a farmer's field south of Glasgow. He told the farmer who found him still struggling to get out of his parachute that he had a message for the Duke Of Hamilton. Hess was apparently worried about Germany having to fight a two front war once Operation Barbarossa, the invasion of the USSR, was launched and he saw his flight and attempt at negotiation with the British as a way to prevent this. Hess claimed that he had a message from Hitler and that Hitler wanted to reach out to the British and make peace. None of this was true. Hitler, through the German press called Hess a madman who was deluded and deranged and that Hess had acted entirely on his own initiative with no prior knowledge by Hitler of his intentions. The British authorities of course investigated the claims that Hess was making. Once it became obvious that he carried no authority to negotiate, he was imprisoned as a POW. Hess was initially taken to Buchanan Castle which was near where is aircraft had crash landed and later to the Tower of London. He remained at the Tower Of London until he attempted suicide by jumping over a railing to the pavement below. Hess wasn't successful in his suicide attempt merely breaking a femur. On 26 June 1942 after a 12 week convalescence he was moved to Maindiff Court Hospital near Abergavenny in Monmouthshire Wales. He remained at Maindiff until the end of the war after which he was transferred to Nuremberg where the top Nazis were being tried for war crimes. Hess was convicted at Nuremberg of crimes against peace and conspiracy with other German leaders to commit crimes. He was sentenced to life in prison and spent the rest of his life in Spandau prison, the allied military prison in Berlin. He died by suicide at the age of 93 on 17 August 1987 while still in Spandau.

Bert wrote about the Hess incident in his letter home dated 14 May 1941. "As you are probably aware Rudolph Hess, the Nazi has come here. Nothing much is known of his reasons for deserting Hitler, but it seems that he has run out on the rest of the gang. Some people say he has seen the error of his ways and has experienced a sudden conversion to the way of god. It must have been a sudden conversion because, for three weeks ago, in a speech at some celebration he mouthed the fiercest threats and heaped abuse on England. One of his choice remarks was to the effect that England has had only a taste of what the Nazis intend doing to her in the aerial war. He planned the assassination of Dolfuss, some of the jewish pogroms, is responsible for the horrible Dachau concentration camp and throughout his career has been an ardent Hitlerite. He seems to have friends here among the higher ups of the titled world, who when he arrived here began to plead for him. I suppose they will plead for Hitler also when the time comes, but I doubt that their pleas will avail them any good. Feeling is much too strong this time. There will be no more castles at Doorn."

Castles at Doorn is a reference to the manor house in the Netherlands where Kaiser Wilhelm II lived in exile after the first world war. Bert who was never one to miss an opportunity to make his feelings about the corrupt nature of the ruling classes of Britain must have been delighted when it became known that several members of the nobility where willing to plead for Hess a man who was as evil as any in Hitler's gang.

May 1941 was a busy month for the war, not only did it see the Rudolph Hess incident, but this was also when the German battleship Bismarck was sunk. On 23 May, the Bismarck and heavy cruiser Prince Eugen sailed for the Atlantic, planning to attack allied shipping. The British sent the battleships HMS Hood and Prince of Wales in pursuit along with several cruisers. The British ships intercepted the two German ships in the straits of Denmark, which is between Iceland and Greenland and immediately engaged them. During the battle the Hood was sunk and the Bismark took damage to her fuel supply lines. Because of this damage, Bismarck made for France where her captain was hoping to get her repaired. The Prince Of Wales broke off the attack and the British lost contact with the Bismarck and Prince Eugen. On 26 May the Bismarck and Prince Eugen were spotted by an RAF Catalina of RAF Coastal command making for the Atlantic. By this time the RN aircraft carrier Ark Royal had joined the pursuit. Ark Royal launched 15 Swordfish aircraft and these attacked the Bismarck, damaging her steering so that now she could only sail in a large circle. By this time there were several more Royal Navy ships and two Polish ships pursuing the Bismarck. Her crew were unable to make any repairs to her steering and the writing was on the wall. It was only a matter of time now. The commander of the Bismarck, Admiral Lütjens sent a message to the German command base "Ship unmanoeuvrable. We will fight to the last shell. Long live the Fuhrer." Lütjens didn't have long to wait, the Royal Navy ships King George V, Rodney, Dorsetshire and Norfolk located the Bismarck and attacked. Together they scored some 400 hits on Bismarck sinking her on the morning of 27 May. The Bismarck had been sunk without ever having attacked let alone sunk any allied shipping. The sinking of the Bismarck and the Hood effectively marked the end of the age of the battleship. This was now the age of the aircraft carrier.

In early 1941, whilst waiting to be called up, Bert worked as a fire watcher during air raids. For the most part, this work was a walk in the park. Bert was assigned to lead a crew who were watching over an area centred around a hotel. Night after night during air raids they would guard their charges. On nights when there were no raids they would find empty rooms in the hotel and get some well-deserved sleep. Bert couldn't believe his luck, getting paid to sleep. What could be better?

His crew did have a few adventures though. Once, he had to extinguish an incendiary bomb by dumping a bag of sand on it and Bert says it just petered out. Granted not the most exciting event of the war but during this duty he did have at least a couple of incidents which were more exciting than that. One time during a raid, while watching a huge fire in the distance, a Luftwaffe bomber started circling overhead and dropped two bombs very close to where Bert and his friends were standing. They all had to throw themselves to the ground. Ever calm and cool under fire Bert's biggest concern over that incident seems to have been that he tore his trousers and got a scraped knee.

On another night, whilst on duty with an old cockney fellow Bert notes that there were a number of bombs dropped very close to them. They sounded like a rushing express train as they fell. Bert was impressed by the calmness of this old fellow who didn't move throughout. So Bert didn't move either, thinking the fellow a typical Tommy, cool under fire. The next day Bert mentioned the old boy to a colleague. The fellow replied that - "Yes old George is a good enough bloke, a pity though he's stone deaf!"

Chapter 9: To The Aerodrome: RAF Training

The last few weeks before he was called up Bert more or less just cooled his heels. He quit work at the oystery on the 26th of July but continued working with the People's Convention and he continued his job fire watching during the nights. He wrote home that "since May 10th, the date of the last blitz there has been no serious raid. I am able to sleep nights now. It is a very pleasant way to make money, eating supper and sleeping at a hotel and being paid £3.10 a week."
And that is how Bert spent the last few days of life as a civilian that he would ever enjoy. He enlisted in the RAF at Euston in London on Monday 4th of August 1941.

The next year was a whirlwind of training for him. His first two weeks of training were at or near Euston and he returned every evening at 6PM after training had finished for the day to sleep at his flat at Lanark Mansions. Bert's flat was only a five minute walk from the training centre. On August 7th he wrote "Have been working for the king since Monday. The new state is satisfactory, most of the day being spent in one's own pursuits. For two weeks I shall be here during which time I shall be equipped and undergo numerous inoculations." Although far from happy with being in the military, Bert was resigned to the path he had chosen.

After his initial trining, Bert was sent to Scarborough for aircrew training and then on to Scotland for actual flight training. Once he got used to the military routine he seemed to, if not enjoy his life in the military, at least be more comfortable with it. It wasn't until he was sent to Scotland that his moral plummeted. He found that in his free time he couldn't concentrate enough to write any poetry and he didn't write anything from the time of his enlistment in August 1941 until the spring of 1942. Bert's letters home from his training days and his days with the squadron also do not mention his increasing despair concerning what he was being tasked to do and his falling morale, his increasing

105

stress and his belief that he would not survive the war. Because he didn't tell his family that he was on active duty he couldn't write to them about all these misgivings and problems,. So there was no way the family could offer support, comforting words or any other help to Bert coping with these problems. Bert was of course very independent, but it must have been very difficult coping with these problems on his own when he had cut off his family who up until this time had been one of, if not his main support network.

Bert's letters home from the time he enlisted until his death continued to be full of questions about the family, the general goings on in the Warr household and to thank the family for the birthday, Christmas and other packages that they sent. Like all other wartime packages sent overseas by families, friends and organisations such as patriotic shop keepers, to sons, brothers and husbands the packages were full of cakes and other goodies thought to be in short supply in the barracks. Like most other fellows who received packages, Bert generously shared his care packages out with the other fellows of his unit. He routinely shared out everything except pipe tobacco, that special treat he kept for himself.

In his letters home Bert almost never mentions the name of any of the fellows that he is training with. Even later on, when he is serving at an active squadron we never learn the names of the men closest to him, namely the crew mates that he flew with. This is not surprising because he did not tell his family that he was flying let alone that he was flying combat missions. Of course they knew that he was in Bomber Command and posted to an active unit but just what he did there Bert never made clear. In one letter in answer to a question from the family, he even feigns surprise that they don't know what his job is. However he evades the question and doesn't tell them. He did this to spare them the nightly worry that all families with men on combat duty in the RAF faced. Is he flying tonight, did he make it back to base safely?

While this saved his parents the daily worry of wondering if Bert was safe, it was a false security. The grief it caused them when they got the telegram informing them he was listed as missing was far worse than if Bert had told his parents that he was flying operational missions from the beginning. When they did get the dreaded telegram, at one stroke they not only found out not only was he flying in combat, but that he was now missing. His aircraft having failed to return to base from his latest combat operation. It wasn't until after Bert was listed as missing that the family learned from Frank that Bert was in fact a bomb aimer and had been flying regular combat missions for months.

Most of the detailed descriptions of Bert's flying he wrote in letters to his ""Hungarian friend" Mrs Nora Senjem. Nora Senjem had fled Hungary from Nazi persecution with her daughter leaving behind her husband and young son. At her flat in London she hosted many social events and parties attended by many of the writers, musicians and artists of London's wartime refugee community. Bert was a regular attendee at these events. He and Mrs Senjem became very close. In fact she seems to have been viewed by him as a sort of mother figure and she seems to have had a similar view of Bert. She was very supportive and protective of Bert. When Bert wanted to have his portrait taken it was to Mrs Senjem that he turned for the name of a good photographer. In fact he even wrote to her asking that she buy him some underwear, "Jockey is the brand that I use," which she then posted to him at his base. When Bert returned to London on leave he usually stayed at his old flat at Lanark Mansions in Maida Vale but he spent a lot of time at Mrs Senjem's flat attending her dinner parties and other get togethers. She was a very important person in his life, this seems to be especially true of the time after he enlisted.

The weeks before he was called up were filled with worry that the long awaited German invasion of England was imminent. As late as June of 1941 it seems that the British public were still expecting the Germans to invade England at some point. In a letter home on June 19 1941 Bert wrote that although everyone still expected that the Germans would invade England it looked like that would have to wait until they had dealt with the USSR. By this time it was an open secret that Hitler intended to turn on his Russian ally and invade the Soviet Union. This seems to have been clear to everyone except for Joseph Stalin. Against all the evidence he seems to have been unwilling or unable to believe that Germany would betray him and attack the Soviet Union. Bert fully expected Germany to not only invade Russia but to beat them fairly quickly and then turn to deal with Britain. In fact that is exactly what Hitler himself thought too. It seems that everyone believed in the invincibility, or near invincibility of the German war machine.

They wouldn't have too wait long to see that theory put to the test because on 22 June 1941 Hitler's armies invaded the USSR. They launched a surprise attack and, using the Blitzkrieg tactics that had worked so well against the low countries, France and Britain the year before, quickly made huge gains of territory and defeated the Soviet forces wherever they encountered them, killing and capturing tens of thousands of Russian soldiers. The Nazis expected the invasion to be over quickly and the Soviets to surrender. The Soviets, in spite of being defeated in almost every battle did not surrender and as they retreated adopted a policy of scorched earth. As they retreated, the Soviet armies burnt or destroyed crops, farm and factory machinery and everything and anything else that might aid the enemy. A steady stream of refugees followed the retreating Soviet soldiers deeper into the country and away form the advancing Germans. Many millions did not escape though and this harsh policy was particularly hard on them, condemning them to a winter of hardship and the prospect of starvation during the extremes of a Soviet winter. As the Nazi armies advanced their supply lines got longer and longer and moving supplies and reinforcements to the front lines became more and more of an issue as the invasion progressed. The hoped for quick defeat of the Soviets did not happen and it soon became evident that this invasion would not be over anytime soon. Hitler and his generals continued to believe that the next push or the one after that would result in the Soviets surrendering and that the war would be over before winter. The Germans and their allies the Fins, Romanians and Hungarians took Kiev and surrounded and laid siege to Leningrad. They pushed on to Moscow. They were certain that when they took Moscow Soviet resistance to the invasion would collapse and the war in the east would be over. Stalin had other ideas though and had no intention of ever surrendering to the hated Nazis. He arranged for virtually all of his armaments factories to be dismantled and moved further to the east, far from any threat from the invaders.

Also at this time the British, who were aiding the Soviets were starting to get supplies in to the ports of Archangel in the far north of the Soviet Union. The Soviets were manufacturing thousands of tanks, planes, artillery pieces and small arms each month and the convoy supplies send by the British and Americans were a major reason that Soviet war production was able to accomplish this. The new Soviet T34 tanks were better than any tanks the Germans had and the only weapons the Nazis had that could knock one of those beasts out of action were their big 88MM anti-aircraft guns and there were not many of them. In fact because of the swiftness of their advances and the fierceness of the fighting the German panzer divisions were exhausted by early September and were dangerously depleted and badly in need of rest, resupply and refitting. Hitler was in no mood to halt the advance though and ordered the army to push on to Moscow as soon as Kiev was taken and secure. He was sure that this would end the war in the east and he would have secured the oil, rubber and other vital supplies that he needed in the Caucusus.

In a letter home dated 27 June 1941 Bert says that he has one month left before being called up. He continued his fire watching job at night and was planning a week's holiday the second week of July. Evidently the man in the street in

109

Britain had been completely shielded from the reality of just
how weak Britain's military situation was because Bert
wonders why England doesn't invade France and open a
second front. He quite rightly feels that such a move would
be ideal now that the bulk of the German army is in Russia.
What he doesn't seem to know is that the British were in no
shape at this time to send any troops to France. It would
have been a suicide mission and any force they did send
would have been quickly defeated. Britain had its hands full
with fighting Rommel's Afrika corps in North Africa and
trying to keep him out of Tobruk. Rommel since his arrival
in North Africa had won a series of stunning victories
against the British forces there. So audacious was Rommel,
and so stunning were his victories that he gained the
reputation as the best general in the war on either side and
earned him the nickname "The Desert Fox."

Ever willing to think the worst of the corrupt British
government Bert thought " There is something phony about
the whole thing. An opportunity like this and they (the
British) remain on the defensive." Bert thought the British
should invade France right away. He also thought it was
"pathetic and amusing to see the British capitalist
government wrestling with the formality of their attitude
towards the much hated Bolsheviks of Russia." In a speech
broadcast to the British people over the radio the day after
Hitler's armies launched their attack on the USSR, Churchill
says that he fully expects the Russian people to resist the
best that they can but that he expects the Germans to deal
them a crushing defeat and then to turn once again to
thoughts of invading England. But that in the meantime
Britain must do everything it can to support Russia in spite
of the fact that their form of government goes against the
principles of a free democracy. Churchill's overriding
concern was stopping Hitler. In his speech he says "Hitler is
a monster of wickedness, insatiable in his lust for blood and
plunder. ... The Nazi regime is indistinguishable from the
worst features of Communism. It is devoid of all theme and
principle except appetite and racial domination. It excels in
all forms of human wickedness, in the efficiency of its

cruelty and ferocious aggression. No one has been a more consistent opponent of Communism than I have for the last twenty-five years. I will unsay no words that I've spoken about it. But all this fades away before the spectacle which is now unfolding." Churchill thereby makes it plain that the British will support the Soviet Union any way it can to stop the common enemy and do everything they can to stamp out the evil of the Nazi regime.

In Bert's letter home of the 7th August we get a rare glimpse of a tender moment between Bert and my mom, his youngest sister Cecelia, who would have been nearly ten by this time "Thanks for the letter and beautiful drawing from Cecelia Genevieve Agnes Warr (the sister of you know who). I have shown C's bit of art to our cat which is sitting on the bed now, but I am afraid the animal does not like it, as a most unhappy expression remained upon its face during the length of the inspection."

After the initial first two weeks of being kitted out and undergoing all the necessary medical examinations and inoculations and he had completed the basic six weeks of basic military training Bert was sent Scarborough on the Yorkshire coast. Here he began his aircrew training. Scarborough and environs is a beautiful area. Bert wrote that "I am sitting in a park, on a height overlooking the sea immediately below, writing this with my gas mask case as a table. It is warm and the sun is shining in a cloudless sky."

When he got to that unit his daily life would change drastically. Bert initially found the physical demands of training very difficult but he stuck with it and gradually his strength and endurance improved. He wrote that "from 6 in the morning until late in the evening we are in motion, school, drill and study and there is much else to occupy me, boots, buttons and sewing have become supreme in importance." So demanding did Bert find his training that during his free time in the evenings he didn't have either the will or the energy to write anything. He spent what free time he did have relaxing by listening to the radio or going to concerts.

It seems that, all in all Bert enjoyed his time at Scarborough, although he found some of the classes he had to take tedious. This was especially true of military law of which he wrote - "the quantity is exceeded only by the absurdity."

Although he was finding it too difficult to write any poetry with the heavy training workload he was under, he did stay active in the literary world, giving lectures and teaching classes in some of the local Scarborough schools when time allowed.

One incident during Bert's time in Scarborough stands out. One day, while carrying out drill on a local road in in the town a Luftwaffe Junkers 88 appeared overhead. All the men of the unit dove for cover in the hedges lining the road as the German started his bomb run. They needn't have worried though because the fellow had poor aim and dropped his bomb harmlessly in the harbour. Bert's unit stayed put under cover in the hedges though because they thought that maybe the German would return to machine gun them but luckily a couple of Spitfires appeared overhead and drove him off.

In December of 1941 Bert was posted to West Freugh near Stranraer on the west coast of Scotland. Initially he found he liked the place and was thrilled to be starting flight training as a Navigator, but by the end of his 7 months in West Freugh he hated the place and couldn't wait to get back to civilisation, leaving behind the flies, the rivers of mud and the crowded barracks life.

Flight training was another matter though. After his first flight actually navigating an aircraft he wrote of the exhilaration that he felt and that he now knew "How thrilled Columbus was when he sighted the Americas. I experienced this thrill when we broke through a mass of clouds to see below the town for which we had set course. The disorder in the plane is enormous. Visualise a small area crowded with awesome pieces of metal, knobs instruments etc and Bert in the midst. A tremendous roaring of engines dulling my mind, attempting to read maps, converse with the pilot, find my pencil, which has rolled away again and last of all admire the view and all of this simultaneously!"

Bert seems to have had a cool indifference to personal safety during all this writing that "when we are coming in to land I think how interesting if we crash, doubtless I should die, that's all. I am not nervous." No doubt it was at least in part this calm coolness which would help him become a stalwart member of his bombers crew and mark him out for advancement once he was at an active squadron flying combat operations.

Chapter 10: Active Duty

During all these long months of training, although Bert had found that he was unable to do much writing, he was still in demand. Several anthologies of poems were published at this time which included some of his poems. These included a volume edited by his good friend Patricia Ledward, titled - Poems of This War. Four of Bert's poems were included in that anthology - War Widow, There Are Children In The Dusk, Poets In Time of War (Bert's tribute to Wilfred Owen) and Working Class which is now Bert's best known work.

By the summer of 1942 Bert had more than had enough of the mud and barracks life at West Fraugh and his spirits were very low. On leave in London he wrote "How pleased I am to be away from that awful hole in Scotland. The conditions are disgraceful and the food is terrible." Also at about this time his training as a navigator stopped and he was switched to training for a new position the RAF was introducing for its heavy bombers, the bomb aimer, and his spirits sank even lower. Bert said of this new work that "Some of the work is interesting but a large part is hideous to me and the most onerous of duties."

Bomb aimers had the responsibility of directing the aircraft the last few miles of the flight to the target and then pushing the button to actually release the bombs which would rain down death and destruction on the city below. At this stage of the war RAF bomb aiming was, in a word terrible. Because of the heavy losses they incurred carrying out daylight raids the RAF had stopped daylight raids all together and now only flew at night. The reason for this was that the RAF bombers were basically sitting ducks for the ack-ack and Luftwaffe fighters when they mounted daylight raids. The guns carried by RAF bombers were very ineffective against the armour of the German fighters. Unlike the American bombers which were armed with heavy 0.50 calibre machine guns, the RAF bombers were armed with much lighter 0.303 machine guns and in Wellingtons and Halifaxes only two of those giuns at that.

This was so that they could save weight in both ammunition for the guns, and for guns themselves, meaning they could carry a higher bomb load. By contrast not only did the American B17 carry heavier guns but it had 17 of them. The Americans did not bomb at night. They only bombed during the day when their crews could actually find and see the their targets. Of course this meant that the enemy could see them as well. But they believed that all the extra guns and the tight formations that their bombers flew more than made up for this.

Bombing only at night gave the poorly defended RAF bombers a better chance of survival because the German ground defences and fighters naturally found it more difficult to find and attack aircraft in the dark. It also made the job of the bomber crews more difficult. Not only was it far more difficult to even locate the target in the darkened, blacked out skies over occupied Europe but once they did find what they hoped was the right city, actually locating and hitting the target was literally a hit and miss exercise. As the time went on, improved tactics such as the introduction of the pathfinder squadrons and the introduction of targeting aids such as GEE greatly improved this. GEE was a radio navigation system which improved accuracy down to a few hundred metres at up to a range of 350 miles from the source of Gee signals. In spite of these improvements bombing at night was never an exact science. This lack of accuracy was the main reason that the RAF introduced area bombing which ultimately led to the very controversial fire bombings of cities such as Dresden. All that was still in the future though, but it is easy to see why the pacifist Bert was not thrilled to have his trade, changed from navigating, which he loved to bomb dropping which he hated. Also in these early days the bomb aimer often had to man a gun in the nose of the aircraft close to his bombing station. So Bert would have had to learn to fire this gun. These nose guns were never very effective though mainly because German fighters rarely, if ever attacked from the front plus the gun was still the small calibre and ineffectual 0.303 gun. The Luftwaffe preferred to attack from behind the bomber or, better yet, to come up from below their target, attacking the bombers at their weakest spots. Bert would have hated firing this gun, however he had made his decision to do his bit to help the war effort and he carried on no matter the personal cost.

Although Bert hated the life and came to hate his training at West Fraugh even more, it was here that he began to emerge from the mental fog that he had been in. His writers block began to clear and he began writing poetry again. It was also at this time that he met fellow poet John Gawsworth and I can't help but believe that the two events are related. When Bert had enlisted his life changed dramatically. He had been living the life of a budding intellectual, taking university courses, working for various poetry and Socialist magazines and at Mrs Senjem's dinners and parties, surrounded by talented artists and writers. For Bert those must have been intellectually exciting and stimulating times. Then suddenly he lost all that and he and he was thrown into the dull, repetitious world of military training with its tedious discipline, rules and regulations. No doubt the thrill and challenge of flight training alleviated a great deal of this tedium but that was of course not on the same plain as his previous life from an artistic point of view. It is not surprising that someone of Bert's sensitivity struggled to not only cope with this new life but to try to carry on writing at anywhere near the levels he had been attaining prior to enlisting. At his first meeting Gawsworth Bert did not seem to warm particularly to the fellow writing that "Gawsworth has done quite a lot in poetry. He was told by the editor of Poetry Quarterly to get in touch with me. I'm afraid we have very little in common but he does know very much more about poets and poetry than I do."

As time went on Bert's opinion of Gawsworth changed. The two spent many evenings together and Bert even spent several weekends at the house in Glasgow of Gawsworth's friend Harry Isherwood where they whiled away the nights drinking and talking about poetry. By the time Gawsworth left the West Fraugh area at the end of January he and Bert had become good friends and Bert was sorry to see him go. "Gawsworth, the poetry person is to leave here shortly. I am afraid he has been most interesting company." Bert did meet Gawsworth again at least once when Gawsworth was investigating a suicide that had taken place at his camp and they kept up a regular correspondence. Once while on leave in London Bert even visited the home of Gawsworth's mother.

Although Bert and Gawsworth were not to meet again they planned several literary projects together for after the war. Gawsworth admired Bert and his poetry very much and after the war worked very hard to get a book of Bert's poems published. Sadly though, that project did not come off and seems to have ended in acrimony between Gawsworth and the Warr family, particularly Bert's mother who doesn't seem to have thought much of Gawsworth at all. The ending of this project to get Bert's poetry published in book form was especially hard on Aunty Mary who was desperate to get the project completed and see her brother's work in book form. Although very disappointed Mary did not give up. But it take another 25 years before she would see her efforts pay off and gert a book of Bert's work finally published.

Gawsworth himself was an extraordinary character. His real name was Terence Armstrong, John Gawsworth was a pen name. Gawsworth was born in London in 1912 and grew up in the Notting Hill and Holland Park regions of the city.

Amongst his accomplishments Gawsworth could list being a Freeman of London. He was awarded the Benson Medal of The Royal Society Of Literature in 1939. He was a founding editor of The English Digest poetry magazine and editor of the Literary Digest. Poet Laureate John Mansfield said of Gawsworth that " He was one of the most beautiful and promising of our writers."

Gawsworth served in the RAF in North Africa, Sicily and Italy after leaving Scotland. He started his RAF career as an

A/C 2, the lowest rank in that force and by the time he left the RAF after a stint in India he had worked his way up the ranks to being a commissioned officer.

The most extraordinary thing about this extraordinary character though was that he was the king of the tiny Caribbean Island of Redonda. This came about because Gawsworth was very good friends with the former king of the island, the writer M.P. Shiels who had been proclaimed king quite randomly by his father in the mid 1930s. The title was pretty much meaningless. This king had no powers and was king in name only. Gawsworth would hold his royal court from his home in Notting Hill every year on January 29th, his birthday. At his court each each year he would create Dukes from literary people who over the past year had help perpetuate the memory of Shiels.

He said of his reign "It is purely an intellectual aristocracy." When asked by a reporter if he ever planned on visiting his kingdom he replied "Great scot whatever for."

For Bert once Gawsworth left he found life in West Fraugh as tedious and awful as ever. Things were about to change for the better for him though because in June of 1942 Bert was promoted to Sgt and he was posted to RAF Kinloss on the north east coast of Scotland. The promotion to sergeant and new posting brought with it better quarters and much better food. Bert found Kinloss to be a beautiful place and a very welcome change from West Fraugh. "I am now a sergeant responsible and respected. One's lot improves a lot in the RAF with such a promotion."

Part of Bert's hatred of West Freugh grew out the tedium and lack of privacy of barracks life. The men were in huts witch contained twenty beds each. Privacy and quiet for writing and studying were non-existent. Both Kinloss and East Moor, and indeed all three of the bases that 158 Squadron operated out of during Bert's time on the squadron, operated a system of accommodation and aircraft hangarage known as dispersal. In this system aircraft were not parked together but instead parked separately around the airfield on hard stands with plenty of room between them. Similarly the men were quartered in huts scattered around the base or sometimes even off the base in private homes and hotels etc. Many of the administration and other buildings such as the messes and latrines etc of the base were similarly dispersed around the airfield. Spreading things out like this was done to minimize damage and death as much as possible in the event that the base was bombed.

The men would either walk or ride bikes to get around between their quarters, the mess and administration buildings such as the briefing room etc. Being billeted in these quiet quarters came as a real shot in the arm for Bert. Now that he was a sergeant he had his own private room and that alone improved his mood. "Am not working much and have many pleasant hours reading in my room, which I cherish having endured so long the barrack room existence." The room came complete with a desk where Bert could write and a fireplace to keep him warm during the cold Scottish summer nights. Coal was almost impossible to come by because of rationing but there was plenty of good wood in the woods surrounding the billet. Now that he was in more settled surroundings and after his time spent with Gawsworth Bert found that he was able to start writing again. At first though Bert's efforts at writing poetry seemed to have been very tentative and awkward. He had spent nearly a year in training and much of it was hard times for him. Often during that time he had been pushed nearly to his limits both physically and mentally. Now though he could take some time to sit back and re-evaluate his attitude and try to find himself. "Am writing a little again, although I feel like a headless hen trying to establish what was, is now and will be later, it is all very confusing."

Bert was also helping write a play, a musical that was planned to be performed for the men at the camp by "a fellow" there who had experience producing. Bert only mentions the play once in his letters so whether or not they actually performed the play or not and what role(s) Bert

119

played in getting the play put on is one of those mysteries we have to live with.

It was now late June 1942 and at about this time brother Frank had enlisted. Bert was against this of course and was loath to see his brother have to endure what he went through during training but he did write "I wish the best of luck in his new work and hope that he can endure the life, it is horrible sometimes. " I think though that Frank with the active life he had lived, was probably much more suited to the physical demands of training than Bert was.

The war news in those early days of June was a mixture of good and bad. The Japanese attack on Pearl Harbour in December of 1941 had been the brain child of Japanese admiral Isoroku Yamamoto. At the time of the attack, Yamamoto believed the attack would give the Japanese at most a six month window in which their navy would dominate the Pacific. He hoped that during that time the Japanese military would have enough time to secure the defences of the empire in the Pacific and that a negotiated peace could be worked out with the Americans. Yamamoto believed that after this initial six month period the industrial might of the Americans would start to awaken and that they would begin to get the upper hand. Yamamoto was spot on with his prediction of six months. In early June the Americans launched an attack against the Japanese carrier fleet near Midway Island some 1400 miles west of Hawaii. The Japanese carrier fleet was comprised of six carriers but only four were present at the battle. The Americans attacked the Japanese with waves of aircraft off the carriers Yorktown, Hornet and Enterprise. The American attack caught the Japanese completely by surprise and three of the four Japanese carriers were set ablaze and ultimately had to be abandoned. The Americans didn't escape the battle completely unscathed. They lost the carrier Yorktown and the destroyer Hamman. The loss of the three carriers was a devastating blow to the Japanese and destroyed the power of their Pacific fleet. After this the American navy dominated the Pacific. The only realistic hope that the

Japanese had of winning the war against the Americans now was if they could hold out with the ground forces they had in the many islands that dotted the Pacific from their home islands eastward and southward towards the Philippines and Australia.

The war news wasn't all rosy for the allies that June though because in the second week of that month Rommel's Afrika Korps took Tobruk in North Africa. This was a humiliating defeat for Britain and was a major blow to moral at home as well as being a disaster militarily. Rommel had come to Africa in January with a relatively small force of tanks and armoured cars and infantry. The Luftwaffe did dominate the skies over the area and, in combination with the Axis navies of Germany and Italy, they dominated the Med. However the British had a much larger ground force in North Africa than the Germans and they should have been able to defeat Rommel's small force. Rommel outgeneraled his British counterparts at every turn though. The British command was disorganised and not co-ordinated and they fought every battle piecemeal, getting beaten at nearly every turn. The defeat of the British and the fall of Tobruk cemented Rommel's reputation as one of the top generals of the war. Not only that but it opened the way for an all-out German assault on Egypt. The fall of Egypt would be a disaster for the allies and pave the way for the Germans to gain control of the whole of the Middle East, thus controlling not only the shipping of the area but also the all-important oil fields. The loss of Tobruk was a huge blow to moral at home. Bert in typical fashion saw this defeat in terms of the corruption and general incompetence of the ruling classes of Britain. His cynicism and contempt for the ruling class of Britain shine through in this quote from a letter he wrote home shortly after the fall of Tobruk was announced to the British public. " I compare the sportsmanlike surrender with the work of our eastern allies. They at least realise that the war is not a game at Eton and that there can be no more surrendering."
The battle of Midway and the fall of Tobruk had no impact on the day-to day life of Bert and his training his at Kinloss

continued. Kinloss was a very welcome improvement over West Fraugh. Bert was for the most part enjoying his flight training and of course he was also writing again. The general improvement of his surroundings at Kinloss added to the fact that with his promotion to sergeant he was getting better food and had better quarters led to him feeling stronger and getting healthier by the day.

This time at Kinloss was to be the last 2 months of his training. His next posting, in August, would be to the conversion unit for RAF 158 Squadron at Marston Moor. At Marston Moor newly trained crews were introduced to the heavy Halifax bomber and at that time they also usually were assigned to the crew they would fly active missions with. From Marston Moor on 24 September, Bert and his new crew were posted to 158 Squadron at RAF East Moor, just down the coast in Yorkshire from Scarborough where the year before he had begun his RAF training.

Before reporting to 158 though, Bert had ten days leave in London in early August. During this leave he doesn't seem to have relaxed and recharged, instead he seems to have spent the time rushing about here and there seeing people, watching plays and going to concerts. He stayed in his old room at Lanark mansions which he did on every leave that he took to London until the very end. I don't know whether or not Mrs Bush the landlady charged him rent or not or whether or not she kept his room empty and available to him any time that he needed it, but she always had the room ready for him when he came to London on leave.

While on leave over the August bank holiday (Long weekend) Bert went to the countryside around London, somewhere along the banks of the Thames to the west of London but Bert doesn't say where. He stayed with a writer friend whom he had taken some courses at college with and who was living in a converted bus. Bert wrote home that this friend was attempting to write a book "Which I fear will not be published as it is not good." It seems that bad book or not, Bert spent an enjoyable two days in the countryside.

At Kinloss Bert's training had been carried out in Whitworth Whitely aircraft and it was flying these aircraft that Bert was crewed for the first time with Dennis Cole, the man who was to be his pilot from that time on. Flying with Bert and Dennis were two other fellows who were to be part of the crew right up until the end, navigator Ron Stemp and wireless operator Albert Ward. Of these men we know precious little. Bert never mentions them in his letters home to the family because as we know he didn't want the family knowing he was on active combat flight duty. We do know that Dennis Cole enlisted at Euston, the same as Bert, and that he was originally from Alexandria in Egypt. Ronald Claude Stemp, the crew's navigator had enlisted at Oxford and Albert Ward, the crew's wireless operator had enlisted at Padgate in London. That Bert became close to his crew mates we know for a fact because of what he told Patricia Ledward "The members of the crew are strong and all for one another." There was a strong bond between members of all crews. They trained together, they flew together and more often than not when it was time to relax they all went to the same pubs, dances and restaurants, drinking and eating together. We don't get a sense of any of that camaraderie from any of Bert's letters home nor to Mrs Senjem. With the exceptions of John Gawsworth, Phil Pinkus and Al Sketchler, Bert never mentions the names of any of his friends, associates or other lads in any of his units.

Chapter 11 All For One Another

While Bert was enjoying his ten days of the leave, the British launched the disastrous Dieppe Raid. This raid, codenamed Operation Jubilee, was an amphibious attack on the German occupied port city of Dieppe. The plan was to attack and occupy the town for a short time, destroying as much German military infrastructure in that time as possible. The idea of the raid was to test the ability of the allies to launch an amphibious seaborne assault in preparation for the D-Day landings, which would be launched in two years. The fighting force was made up of over 6000, primarily Canadian infantry supported by a regiment of tanks, The Calgary Regiment. The Royal the navy and the RAF also supported the landings.

The attack was a disaster. The Germans had been warned by double agents that an attack in the area was likely to occur at any time and their troops in the area were on high alert. British aerial and naval support was wholly inadequate and offered little effective support to the troops on the beaches. Within ten hours of the landings, over 3,600 of the men who had been landed had been killed, wounded or captured. Furthermore, because the treads of the supporting tanks were not designed to operate on the pebble terrain that made up the beaches of the area, the tanks could not operate properly and they offered little support to the infantry.

The RAF had anticipated a Luftwaffe response of course but not on the scale that it actually occurred. The RAF lost 106 aircraft to ack-ack, fighters and accidents. Against this the Luftwaffe lost only 48 aircraft. The Royal Navy lost 33 landing craft and one destroyer.

Although loses were extremely high and the raid was wholly unsuccessful, this raid did teach the Allies valuable lessons about what to do and what not to do when attempting an amphibious landing against fortified and protected coasts. Hard lessons that would help enormously

124

in the future landings in Sicily, Italy and of course D-Day itself.

After Bert returned from his ten days leave in London he and his crew joined 158 squadron. First though they went to 165 Heavy Conversion Unit at Marston Moor in North Yorkshire. This unit was where newly trained crew were introduced to the aircraft they would be flying in at the squadron. During their initial aircrew training, aircrews trained on two engine medium bombers but now they would be flying in the much bigger heavy four engine Halifax MKII. At the conversion unit crews would make several practice flights in the new type and generally become familiar with the aircraft. Once the instructors were satisfied a crew was competent on the aircraft they would be sent along to the squadron proper and assigned to one of its flights. Each squadron usually had three flights, A, B and C and each flight usually comprised 8 aircraft, making 24 active aircraft for the entire squadron. Bert wrote that the move to East Moor was his fourth move in 10 days. The move from Kinloss to the conversion unit at Marston Moor was one move. Marston Moor was just to the west of Rufforth, which itself was just west of the city of York. Then moving from the conversion unit to the squadron proper was another move. What the other two moves were I have no idea and Bert never says. At East Moor Bert was again billeted in dispersed accommodation." We walk hundreds of miles each day as this place is widely dispersed. We have very pleasant private rooms in a wood." Bert's main complaint about East Moor, apart from all the walking was that there were swarms of flying insects plaguing the area. "There are wasps and clusters of tiny flies that get everywhere. They crawl in our ears and down our necks. The wretches are everywhere." For a lad from mosquito infested Southern Ontario this should not have been too much to handle.

Once the men were at RAF East Moor they were joined by 2 air gunners, Bill Robinson and Cliff George Dawson. Like Albert Ward both of these men had enlisted at Padgate.

Flight Engineer, Ron Gowing had enlisted at Cardington which is a suburb of Bedford to the south east of the city. Bedford itself is a few miles west of the university city of Cambridge in East Anglia. Gowing had trained at No 4 School of Technical Training in South Wales near Cardiff. The only member of Bert's crew that we have any but the most basic information about is Bill Robinson. This is thanks to Bill's daughter Patricia. Thanks to Patricia we know that Bill, the crew's Mid Upper Gunner (MUG) was born August 16 1916 in Eastham Wirral south of Liverpool. He was the youngest of 6 children, 4 boys and 2 girls. In civilian life he had been the manager of a butcher's shop. However when the war started this was a protected trade and therefore he would never be called up to join the fight. Determined to enlist and do his bit Bill quit work at the butcher's and went to work in a paper mill in Ellesemere Port. Bill was married to a girl named Violet. He had met and married Violet while he was still working as a butcher. Bill enlisted at Padgate and after his training he was posted to 158 and joined Dennis Cole's crew. Bill's daughter Patricia was born on 5th March 1943, less than a month before Bill was killed. Patricia tells us that amongst his belongings, which were returned to the family by the squadron, were several poems that he had written. I can't help but wonder if Bill had been influenced or encouraged by Bert to write poetry. From what we know about Bert I'm sure that he would have been more than happy to help out his fellow crew mate in any attempts he was making to write poetry.

And that is all that is now known about the six men who were on Bert's crew with him. Scant information to relate about the six men who, arguably were the most important people in Bert's life at this time, each relying heavily on the others to carry them through all the perils of combat operations and return safely to base after each flight. The men of a bomber crew were a close knit group. They trained together and flew together and most spent much of their off duty time socialising together. Bert's letters home make no mention of any of these fellows ever. It can be supposed

126

that this may have been because Bert was keeping from the family the fact that he was on dangerous active flight duty. Less easy to explain is that none of his letters to Nora Senjem, who was aware of Bert's flight duties, ever mention any of Bert's crew mates either. It seems that Bert made a deliberate effort to keep his military and his civilian life completely separate.

While he was in London on leave, before reporting to 158 Squadron Bert had arranged to have his photo taken by a professional photographer friend of Mrs Senjem's. His desire to keep his two worlds apart can be seen in his letters home about this photo, which relate an awful lot of effort and preparation for having this photo taken. The photo gets mentioned in several letters home and caused him a lot of worry and bother. Mindful that he was gaining some fame through publication of his poems and anxious about his reputation he wrote home "Am getting photo done, will send copy but please do not send to the St Claire collection of faces (Note: that would have been St Claire Primary School, which all the Warr children had attended and indeed which at the time my mom, then in grade six would still have been attending). I object to being included because I am being publicised as a member of the fighting forces, a roll which is still and will always remain hateful to me. I make no capital out of my uniform, it is the mark of bestiality in this age."

There are not many photos of Bert and there is only one of him in uniform, the one he himself had done professionally in London. Cameras were banned on RAF bases for all but the official forces photographers at the time that Bert was flying. Many crews ignored this rule and there are plenty of photos of men and machines from RAF bases at this time. It seems though that Bert's crew took this order seriously because I know of no photos of Bert's crew. Of course it could be that there were photos taken by other members of the crew and Bert just never bothered to get copies. There certainly would have been official photos of training and perhaps even an official flight or squadron photo taken with the full approval of the base and squadron commanders. Not surprisingly, given his attitude towards the military and how he wanted the one photo that he did have taken treated, Bert never bothered to get copies of any of these.

It may seem strange to us in this age of instant digital photos and endless and quite often somewhat pointless pics taken on phones ad nauseam but in those days not everyone even had a camera, nor was interested in getting one. Bert's one and only professionally taken photo would have been to him a very big deal. It certainly seems that way at least by the amount of space in his letters home and to Mrs Senjem that he devotes to getting the photo taken and copies sent home.

On the other hand there are plenty of photos of brother Frank in uniform, many of them taken at home with his sisters, mother and even one with Skippy the family dog. There is one glaring exception though, there are no photos of Frank and his father, nor do I know of any photos of any of the other family members taken with their father at this time. As for Bert, there are only a couple of photos of him and Frank together and none of Bert and any of other members of the family. And very unfortunately there are no photos of Bert and Frank on leave in London together the last time that the two would see each other. This may have been because neither of the brothers had a camera or because they just didn't see the need to have photos taken of their time in London together. They may have thought why bother, as after all they would probably meet up many times over the course of the war.

Bert struggled with his role in the military, especially after he had his trade changed from the passive role of navigator to the fully engaged in the fight bomb aimer. Of all of the crew of a bomber it was the bomb aimer alone who was actively involved in the destruction of the target each and every flight. All the other members of the crew were there to ensure the bomb aimer could do his job and took no part in the actual dropping of the bombs. Even the gunners didn't get involved each flight. They only fired their guns if an enemy fighter approached within their limited effective range. Bert had taken his stand and was doing his duty but the role he had ultimately been given was not one that he was proud of. The military was his life now but he struggled with this reality and fought his own internal struggle against it. He wanted his life very much to be defined by his writing and not by his role in the destruction of German cities. I don't think he would have wanted to be remembered as a war poet in spite of the number of his poems which had the war as a theme. Bert wanted his poetry to lead to social improvement for the lot of the common man. He still believed very strongly that the state leadership was corrupt and that the country was being led by a gang of criminals more interested in lining their own pockets and profiting from the war than caring for, or helping, the average working class man in the street. Bert believed the working class were carrying the huge burden of fighting the war but gaining nothing but pain, sorrow, misery and death from their struggles. He did believe that the Nazis had to be stopped but he also believed that the rulers of England should all be thrown out and the system of government and the social order completely revamped. It was still his hope that this would happen at the end of the war once Nazis and the fascists were defeated. He believed that a radical social change was needed and was coming after the war for the victors as well as the defeated, democracy or dictatorship. It was with this outlook that Bert at last began his real work in the RAF after more than a year's training.

Although Bert and his crew moved from Marston Moor to the main 158 Squadron base of East Moor in mid-September of 1942 it wasn't until 15th of October that they flew their first operation, a mission to bomb Cologne. They spent the time between moving to East moor and their first combat operation becoming more familiarised with the big Halifax bombers and flying training missions. In that month Bert and his crew flew 14 training missions before they finally saw action. That was a flight nearly every second day. After the crew's first operation, 10 more missions followed between mid October 1942 and January 1943, to places like Stuttgart, Duisberg, Lorient, Nuremberg and the dreaded Berlin. Naturally enough Bert makes no mention of these operations in his letters home, nor does he mention them in his letters to Nora Senjem. As a result we know nothing about any of these sorites apart from the entries in his flight logbook and the brief entries in the squadron ORB (Operations Record Book, which listed every single flight flown by the squadron and the outcome of that flight) and Bomber Command War Diaries. But as there are no entries of any exceptional incidents happening to Bert's crew in the squadron ORB for these ops we can assume that they were fairly routine. That is to say as routine as anything can be when you were flying into the teeth of occupied Europe with its thousands of bristling ack-ack batteries and buzzing Luftwaffe night fighters. The area of the Ruhr Valley alone had over 10,000 ack-ack batteries that bomber crews had to evade on every mission to cities there. Bomber crews had nicknamed the area "Happy Valley" because it was anything but.

The Halifax MK II bombers that Bert flew in were decent enough aircraft given their prewar design restrictions but they did have some serious flaws which made them very vulnerable to night fighter and ground attacks. They had small underpowered engines which limited the altitude the big aircraft could attain when it was fully loaded with fuel and bombs. In spite of the engineers best efforts to mask them, the exhaust flames of these engines lit up the area directly behind the aircraft like beacons calling out here I am come and kill me. Because, fully loaded the Halifax MKII had to fly lower and slower than the more powerful engined Lancaster it was an easier target for ack-ack batteries and night fighters. The loses of Halifax MK II aircraft for this part of the war were extremely high. The Halifax MK III aircraft eliminated all of these problems and more but Bert never got to fly in that aircraft. 158 squadron did fly the MK IIIs but not until late December of 1943, nearly nine months after he was killed.

Of all the targets in Nazi Germany Berlin was one of the most dreaded by aircrews because, not only did it involve a long flight deep into enemy territory, the Nazi capital was also one of the most heavily defended places on the planet. For a more detailed description and listing of all the operations that Bert flew with 158 Squadron see Appendix 2- Combat Operations Flown By Bertram War.

The time just before a mission was extremely intense for aircrew. During the long hours leading up to an operation nerves were stretched and there was a heightened anxiety as crews prepared for the operation and waited for take-off. Once they were in the air the men had to be on high alert for the whole operation until the wheels of their aircraft touched down safely back at base. Only after a safe return could the crews relax their frayed nerves for a few hours or a day or so until the whole thing started over again with preparation for the next mission.

Military flying was very different from any other branch of the service. The men of the army when in combat of course were at the front lines where they fought, ate and often slept in their fox holes far from any comforts of home. Likewise the navy man spent his time on his ship in the middle of the sea for days and sometimes weeks at a time. The airman though would live and work from his base in England leaving only to fly his missions deep into heavily defended enemy territory. This afforded the airman a unique way to recover and relax after battle that was denied to every other branch of the service while the men were in combat, the local pub. When the men were stood down they would often frequent the local pubs of the Lissett area to try to relax and let off some steam. Some of the favourite watering holes of 158 squadron crews were The Black Bull in Barnstrom, The Chestnut Horse and the Spa Ballroom in the nearby coastal resort town of Bridlington. All of which as of 2023 are still in operation in one form or another. Bridlington with the Spa Dance Hall and its promenade along the sea was a favourite destination of off duty crews from all the squadrons in the area. Bridlington at this time was a lively and jumping place almost any night of the week but especially at the weekend when there were dances at the Spa. The dances were attended by the local girls and the WAAFs (Woman's Auxiliary Air Force) of the various bases and stations in the area and many young crewmen from the RAF, RCAF, RAAF and RNZAF as well. Another very popular bar with all the aircrews was Betty's Bar in York which the crews affectionately called "The Dive." The men would spend many nights there drinking and socialising. Over the course of the war Betty's is said to have supplied over 20,000 meals and beverages to hungry and thirsty airmen. Betty's is still in operation but now it is called Betty's tea room and serves only tea and cakes, and no alcohol. Bert visited York on several occasions to see plays or go to concerts. No doubt he also found his way to Betty's for a meal and a quick beer or two or to relax with his pipe over a glass or two of whiskey. He never mentions going to Bridlington in his letters but since he was in the area from September 1942 until his death in early April 1943 it is a safe bet that he went there on occasion with his fellow crew mates as well as going to some of the other pubs in the area. In fact at least one of Bert's poems is set in a pub.

> *Like a dew worm that has swalllowe*
> *a half-crown piece*
> *he washed his hands in the heat of the fire*
> *confident as a calendar*
>
> *Someone murmured "langwidge, langwidge,*
> *ladies present mind,"*
> *and immediately on hearing this*
> *all the ladies assumed outraged expressions.*

This short fragment, all that remains of this poem now, evokes in my mind a wonderful image of a smoke filled, small, but comfortable, country pub crowded with locals and aircrew enjoying their drinks and shared conversations around the fireplace on a cold winter's night.

Of course the men would also socialise together in the Sergeants mess at the base where the rules were very relaxed so that all the members of a crew could be together, officers as well as enlisted men. We know from Nora Senjem's letters that when he was in London and he went to dinner parties and other gatherings at her flat Bert was very withdrawn. He would sit quietly smoking his pipe or a cigarette, sipping his drink and also drinking in and eagerly learning from the conversations of the writers, artists, musicians and others that were there. It is tempting to visualise Bert doing much the same thing in the RAF messes and pubs that the he went to with or without his crew. One can imagine him sitting quietly in a corner watching and listening to everything, drinking in not only his whiskey but all the local colour and conversation as well.

As time went on Bert increasingly struggled with the stress and strain of flying combat operations and the isolation from friends and colleagues that he was increasingly feeling. The poem Acknowledgement to Life ends with the very telling lines

"I am as lonely as the universe.
I am the unit whole in no association with my parts."

In spite of these internal struggles Bert continued his work flying and must have been very good at it, and even excelled at it, because he was earmarked for a leading role with the squadron. In mid-January 1943 he was sent on a Bomb Leaders course at RAF Station Mamby in Lincolnshire. Each squadron had trade leaders for each of the of crew positions. There was a Nav leader, Gunnery Leader etc. It was the Bomb Leader's job to answer to the Squadron CO (Commanding Officer) on issues regarding bomb aimers and their work and training. There was normally only one Bomb Leader per squadron. They were the coordinators of all of the bomb aimers at the squadron and, together with the other leaders they formed the working group of the CO. Sometimes these leaders were part of the CO's crew. The CO didn't often fly but when he did he would hand pick his crew so that he got to fly with the cream of the squadron. If the CO's aircraft went missing many of the squadron's best men would be lost, leaving large boots to fill for the rest. In theory being a Bomb Leader would have been a safer role for Bert than being a regular Bomb Aimer because the Squadron Bomb leader did not fly as often as regular crew. In practice though this was not the case. The bombing section leaders of 158 Squadron had a tragic record of failing to return with 5 of the 7 who held that post being reported missing on operations during the course of the war. If we add Bert to that list as having completed the training but not yet having taken up the duty, this sad record becomes 6 out of 8 Bomb Leaders lost at 158. I don't know how this figure compares with other squadrons but it does seem that 158 Bomb Leaders had particularly bad luck. Squadron Leaders were all commissioned officers, so Bert's promotion would have been imminent.

Just before beginning this course Bert went to London on leave, where he met up with his brother Frank, newly arrived from Canada with RCAF's 424 squadron and soon to be heading to North Africa. The two brothers spent an enjoyable week together. Bert showed Frank the sights of the capital and Frank told Bert all that was going on with family and friends back home in Toronto. Bert had two weeks leave but Frank only had one week and soon had to return to his base at Bournemouth. It was the last time the two brothers ever saw each other. Frank would be killed flying a mission to Italy in October just six months after his brother was killed.

Chapter 12: And That Is How The End Would Come

Glad to be able to relax away from the squadron and the constant stress that combat operations brought, nonetheless Bert felt that he was living on borrowed time. He wrote that "I shall be astonished if I live to visit London again." The stress of flying and fighting in a bomber had taken a heavy toll on Bert psychologically. This along with the fact that he deplored the role of Bomb Aimer that he found himself forced to occupy instead of his preferred job as a navigator, had sapped his spirit. He had come to the realisation and acceptance of a fate that few in Bomber Command at that time would escape. During that part of the war flying in a Halifax squadron in Bomber Command was almost like a death sentence. Casualties were extremely high. The relief the men of a crew felt arriving safely back at base after an operation was too often tinged with sadness as one or more of their fellow crews did not return. This happened on flight after flight week after week. The men knew that it was likely that it was not a matter of if it would happen to them but only when it would happen to them.

In her poem titled "The Dead" dedicated to Bert, Patricia Ledward wrote that "Back from a raid on Germany you said: You're wrong to let the physical death fill you with such dread; believe me when I say only the tragedy is large, each death is small." Len Gasparini included this poem in Bert's book and it is on the very first page of "Acknowledgement too Life."

> *The Dead*
> *(For Bertram Warr)*
> *Back from a raid on Germany you said:*
> *"You're wrong to let the physical death*
> *Fill you with such dread;*
> *Believe me when I say*
> *Only the tragedy is large, each death is small,*
> *In a bomber one is not alone,*
> *Courage is met with quietness and all*
> *The members of the crew are strong,*

135

And all for one another,
That is how the end would come."

So many go it wasn't strange to hear
You'd not returned when Essen blazed
That April night last year
Although I wished a man with Owen's feeling
And the satire of Sassoon could write
Your epitaph-how you hated war,
How kind you were with the overwrought,
The refugee, the maimed, the old,
Could tell the irony and pity in your eyes,
When German boys bombed London.
You had a bitterness I never understood,
Did not believe in afterwards
When people planned in happy mood
You kept your silence although once you said
"The dead have all the luck you see."

Patricia Ledward
From Khaki and Blue (London: Resurgam Press, 1945)

125,000 men flew in RAF Bomber Command during World War 2, of those 55,000 were killed. That is a staggering 44%. Add to that another 8,400 wounded and you get an unbelievable casualty rate of over 51%. And at the time Bert was flying Bomber Command losses were at their highest point for the entire war. It's no wonder that Bert had a fatalistic attitude. The wonder is that Bert, or any of the men carried on flying at all.

In Patrica's poem Bert continues - "In a bomber one is not alone, courage is met with quietness and all the members of the crew are strong, and all for one another, and that is how the end would come." We can imagine that that is exactly how the end came for Bert and his crew mates. Returning from their successful raid against Essen every man would have stood by his station and done his duty and his best for his crew right up until the end. Bomber crews had a deep comradeship that we can never hope to understand. They

136

supported each other and drew strength from each other and I believe that is how they found the courage and strength and the heart to carry on in the face of almost certain death night after night.

Since the beginning of the war, Bomber Command had suffered from shortages of aircraft and changes to its orders. The first problem was finally being overcome in early 1943. The new four engine heavies, the Lancaster and Halifax were coming off the assembly lines in ever increasing numbers and, for the first time, Bomber Commands numbers were increasing. Gone were the days when a new squadron would be formed only to be sent off to Coastal Command or the Middle East. New squadrons were being formed and their strength was being added to the main force. New navigation aids such as OBOE, which was a similar system to GEE but more advanced. Special marker bombs for the pathfinders were also being added to help with the fight. The second problem was still an issue and between December 1942 and early March 1943 was to plague Bomber Command and no doubt play havoc with Bert's conscience as targets were switched from tactical bombing of factories, sub pens and similar, to area bombing of whole cities and back again, time and again.

The U-Boat war in the North Atlantic was raging, the allies were desperate to turn the tide in this struggle. Bomber Command received orders to divert a major portion of its nightly effort against the ports where the U-Boats were stationed. Not only were these ports French, which meant that for the first time the men of the squadrons would be bombing the towns of an ally but the orders were to carry out area bombing and not try to hit precise targets. This meant that there would be significant damage to the cities and many, many deaths of French civilians. They were specifically ordered to focus on the French ports of Lorient, St Nazaire, Brest and La Pallice. Bert was to go on two raids in early 1943 to Lorient. We can only imagine the anguish that this must have caused him. He was already having deep moral issues with being a bomb aimer in the first place. Now add this extra torment of knowing that he was dropping his bombs not on the enemy but on the innocent French civilians who happened to have the bad luck to be living in a port city that the Germans had decided was to be a major U-Boat base.

I do not know when Bert began writing the unfinished essay which is the last work in Acknowledgement To Life. The essay is not dated and I can not find any reference to it any in any notes of Bert's that are left but it is tempting to think that it was begun around this time. This would have been one of the most difficult times for Bert mentally and from a moral standpoint he must have been very conflicted and tormented. That essay, expresses more than anything else that he wrote, the despair, and fatalism that he was feeling. In that essay Bert not only writes that he fully expects to die shortly, but that his death will be a welcome release from the moral abyss that he finds himself in because of the war and his role in it. It's a fair bet that Bert started working on that essay in late 1942 or early 1943.

Things were set to improve for Bert though. First off he went on his Bomb Leaders course in early March knowing that on his return he was due his commission and a promotion to a position which would mean less flying. There is reason to believe that Bert's mental outlook was improving with the prospect of being commissioned and being promoted within the squadron to the important position of Bomb Leader. His letters home at this time were more optimistic and he wrote repeatedly and impatiently about getting his commission. He was also very much looking forward to meeting up with Frank in London when they would both be on leave. He must have been missing his family very much. This would be the first time since he had left home over 4 years earlier that he would see any close family.

Secondly, in early March Bomber Command orders were changed yet again. They were now ordered to concentrate on bombing Germany's industrial heart land, the Ruhr Valley. Targets would still be area bombed but at least the crews could take solace in the knowledge that they were attacking the enemy, attempting to cripple his ability to supply and arm his troops by going after major industrial centres and not French civilians. Of course the Ruhr valley would not be the only target that Bomber command would go after. If it were, it would be too easy for the Germans to concentrate all their night fighters in that one area and make it very hot for the RAF bomber crews. They would of course hit other targets in Germany and Italy but the main effort for the next while was to be the Ruhr. It was an area that had a very high concentration of ack-ack batteries and extensive night fighter coverage but by flying operations to other areas as well the RAF had some hope of catching the Luftwaffe off guard at least some of the time.

At some point between arriving at 158 Squadron and his death on 03 April Bert wrote the poem from which the title of this book is taken. It is in many ways a sad poem with a forlorn almost desperate hope of survival in spite of the odds. Looked at another way though it can also be seen as a hopeful love poem. Written to the one who waits at home for the safe return of her loved one after the night's work over enemy territory had been safely carried out and the bombers had all returned safely home.

The Heart To Carry On

> *Every morning from this home*
> *I go to the aerodrome.*
> *And at evening I return*
> *Save when work is to be done.*
> *Then we share the separate night*
> *Half a continent apart.*
>
> *Many endure worse than we,*
> *Division means by years and seas.*
> *Home and lover are contained,*
> *Even cursed within their breast.*

Leaving you now with this kiss
May your sleep tonight be blest,
Shielded from the heart's alarms
Until morning I return.
Pray tomorrow I may be
Close, my love, within these arms,
And not lay dead in Germany.

Laying dead in Germany is, sadly exactly where Bert and
his crew mates ended their short lives. This poem is not
dated but it was obviously written after Bert had started
flying combat operations. That it turned out to be somewhat
prophetic is not surprising considering the casualty rates
being suffered by Bomber Command in late 1942 and early
1943. However with Bert's completion of the Bomb
Leader's course and his impending commission there was
every hope that he would indeed survive and live through
the war to pursue his dreams and work to reach the great
potential that so many saw for him.

The news from the war in general was good too at this time.
On the 02 February the beleaguered and surrounded
German 6th Army at Stalingrad surrendered. The Nazi
capture of Stalingrad turned out to be a high water mark of
Hitler's invasion of the Soviet Union. After the Soviets
recaptured Stalingrad they would push their advantage and
continue pushing the Germans out of their territory and
back eventually all the way to Berlin. In May in North
Africa, Tunis fell to the allies and the defeated German
troops Afrika Corp and their Italian allies were marched off
to prison camps. More than 200,000 Axis soldiers had been
captured. This defeat was as big a disaster for Hitler as the
loss of the sixth army at Stalingrad. The defeat of the Axis
powers in North Africa meant that the whole of the African
continent was now liberated. The Italian African Empire
was no more. Mussolini, Il Duce was now on veery thin ice
and barely clinging on to power at all. The stage was now
set for the Allies invasion of Sicily and the Italian mainland
which was planned for the summer. The Allies invaded
Sicily on 10 July 1943 and by 18 August, they controlled

the whole island. Preparing the way for an invasion of the Italian mainland. The Allies hoped that an invasion of Italy, would draw German troops away from the Soviet eastern front, and that is exactly what happened. Mussolini's grip on power in Italy was failing. Between these invasions, shortages of food, raw materials for factories and just about everything else, and coupled with the allied bombing of Italian cities the people had, had enough of Mussolini and Fascism. Italian king Victor Emmanuel sacked Mussolini on 18 July. The Allies invaded the mainland on 03 September 1943, and Italy surrendered on the 18th. As was hoped by Allied command this forced the Germans to redeploy troops from the eastern front to defend Italy for the remaining Axis powers. The Germans initially sent 25 divisions from the east to Italy. The battle for Italy would be a tough and bloody slog for the Allies. The Germans put up a determined defence, but the invasion had achieved its goal of forcing the Germans to weaken their eastern front by redeploying troops from there to Italy. Final liberation, and surrender of the last German troops in Italy was not until 02 May 1945, only five days before Germany itself surrendered ending the war in Europe.

Bert returned to flight duty as soon as he had returned to the squadron after completion of the bomb leaders course in March and flew on 4 more missions with his own crew, led by pilot Dennis Cole. Then on 29 March he flew an operation as bomb aimer to his squadron leader Wing Commander Hope. No doubt this mission was in part a chance for Wing Commander Hope to evaluate his soon to be new Bomb Leader. The mission which was to Berlin nearly ended in disaster as the aircraft was hit by flak and badly damaged. Wing Commander Hope managed to coax the wounded bird back to England and a safe landing back at base. It was a lucky escape.

For Bert and his crew mates luck would run out 5 nights later. On April 3rd 1943 on the return leg of a mission to Essen, Major Werner Streib, flying a Messerschmitt, closed in on Bert's Halifax and got it in his sights, bringing it down with deadly accurate fire for his third kill of the night. The aircraft crashed in a farmer's field near Pfalzdorf, 43 km north of Roermond from a height of 4.500 metres at 23.30 hrs with the loss of all hands. The men were less than an hour from a safe return to base. The aircraft slammed into the ground which such terrific force that pilot, Dennis Cole was thrown clear of the wreckage. Still strapped into his seat, he crashed through the roof of a nearby barn, seat and all. The aircraft had broken in to two pieces splitting apart at its mid-section. This was a trait of Halifax aircraft that had saved the life of more than one tail gunner in the past while the rest of the crew in the forward section were killed. On this night though rear gunner Leslie Watts was not so lucky and, the force of the crash was so intense that he died on impact along with the rest of his crew mates. The three men in the forward section of Bert's aircraft, namely, Bert, Wireless Operator Albert Ward and Navigator Ron Stemp could not be identified at the time and were initially interred in a communal grave together in the Stadtfreidhof, Munchen Gladbach cemetery. After the war the Commonwealth War Graves Commission (CWGC) re-interred the crew at Rheineberg War Cemetery just 40 KM west of their last target, Essen. The CWGC identified all seven of Bert's crew and now each man rests in his own grave.

As for the man who shot them down, Major Werner Strieb, he was one of the Luftwaffe's top fighter aces of the war. He claimed a total of 67 kills including the three on the night he brought down Bert's crew. On the very first day of the battle of France, May 10 1940, Strieb, flying a Messerschmitt bf 110 heavy fighter, got his first kill, shooting down an RAF Bristol Blenheim. He was awarded the Iron Cross 2nd class for that kill. Strieb was appointed *Geschwaderkommodore* (wing commander) of NJG night fighter squadron 1 on 1 July 1943 and continued to rack up kills of RAF aircraft at an impressive rate. On 23 March 1944, he was made Inspector of Night Fighters. Strieb would stay in this post as *Oberst* (colonel) until the end of the war. Strieb was awarded the Knight's Cross with Oak leaves and Swords. The Oak Leaves were presented to him by Hitler personally on 11 May 1943. Streib was often called 'Father of the *Nachtjagd'* (Night Fighters) and he was instrumental in developing the operational tactics used by the Nachtjagd during the early to mid-war years and he had a leading role in helping make the Luftwaffe's night fighters a very effective fighting force against the aircraft of RAF Bomber Command.

Werner Streib survived the war and after it ended he went in to the grocery business where he worked until 1956. Streib was then asked to join West Germany's Bundeswehr, the Federal Republic's military, where for three years he commanded Pilot School A. There he was responsible for training beginner pilots. Streib was promoted to *Brigadegeneral* and took up the post of *Inspizient Fliegende* (Inspector of Flying Forces). He retired from the miliary on 31 March 1966 and died in Munich on 31 March 1986 where he was buried with full military honours.

The dedicated men of RAF 158 Squadron continued to fly operational sorties against the enemy until the end of the war. The squadron flew its last operation of the war on April 25 1945. The mission was to knock out coastal batteries on the Frissian Island of Wangerooge. After the last of 158's aircraft touched down safely back at Lissett the squadron was stood down from Bomber Command. Shortly after the war ended the squadron was transferred to Transport Command before being disbanded entirely in December of 1945. Now the squadron exists only in the history books and memories of the crew and their families. Today the fields of the old Lissett airfield have been returned to farmland. The few wartime buildings that remain now house tractors and ploughs instead of bombers. Part of the old runway is now a wind farm. In a touching tribute to the sacrifices of the men of 158 each of the wind turbines is named after one of the Halifaxes of the Squadron. Now Friday The 13Th, Goofie's Gift, Zombie and the others help to light and warm local houses delivering power instead of bombs.

On the edge of the old airfield next to the road stands the poignant 158 Memorial to the 851 men who lost their lives flying with the squadron during the war. The memorial depicts the seven men of a Halifax Bomber crew in full flying gear as they return to base after a successful flight. Etched on both sides of the memorial is the name of each one of the fallen of the squadron. On the rear of the memorial on the far right hand side about midway down the crowded list is the name Bertram James Warr.

Chapter 13 Frank Warr

My uncle Frank Warr was born in 1916 one year before his brother Bert. Although the two were brothers they were very different from each. Frank stood 5'7 1/2 inches tall and on a good day pushed the scales at 150lbs. Frank had black hair and grey eyes and a narrow sharp nose. In many of his photos he looks like he has a sleepy, dreamy expression. Nothing could have been further from the truth. In his letters home we get a picture of an intelligent man with a sharp mind and a keen sense of humour. There is also a look of kindness in that face and in those eyes. In spite of his slight build he was very athletic and I would guess that he had an easier time in basic training than Bert, who found military life very tough going at first. Like Bert, Frank was very good academically however he did not pursue an academic career. From Bert's letters it can be guessed that Frank had leanings to the left politically just like the rest of the family. This was not surprising, the Warrs were a working class family during the depression years of the 1930s. Everyone had to chip in with whatever work they could get to keep the family household running. Socialism, with its promises of a more equitably spread wealth and a fair shake for the little guy would have been very appealing to a struggling family who were watching the rich get richer and the poor get poorer during the dirty thirties.

Frank left school at age 16 in 1932 after graduating from grade 12 at St Claire Elementary in Toronto. It seems though that he didn't find work until 1933 when he found employment at Mercer Bradford and Company. Mercer are a financial consulting firm who's offices are still located on Bay Street in the heart of Toronto's financial and banking district. Frank joined the firm as an office junior. He worked at Mercer for a year and left them to work at The National Trust Company of King Street. He worked at National Trust in the accounting department from 1934 until he enlisted in the RCAF in 1942. While working at National Trust he was taking night classes at U of T in accounting.

145

As with Bert, my primary sources for researching Frank were his letters home. But unlike Bert Frank was not a writer so there is not the additional source material of unpublished notebooks and published material to work from. Frank's surviving letters to the family naturally only begin after he left home for his overseas posting with the RCAF. This was in September 1942 when his training squadron was sent to Halifax Nova Scotia to await transport overseas to England. The unit's wait in Halifax turned out to be much longer than I would have thought and much longer than Frank and his mates wanted. They were stuck cooling their heals in Halifax from September 1942 until February of 1943, when they finally set sail for England on a troop transport. This unnamed ship would have part of one of the convoys that were escorted across the Atlantic by the navy in attempts to avoid the hunting packs of German U-boats. Frank's ship arrived safe and sound in Liverpool and he makes no mention of any encounters with German submarines along the way.

From family photos and his RCAF service record it can be guessed that Frank was a very active sportsman. There are photos of him rowing boats, skiing and golfing. His Service record lists sports that he was "extensively engaged in" as tennis, golf, skiing, baseball, skating and track, and sports that he "moderately participated in" as swimming, hockey, rugby, and riding. He was a very active person and it is easy to understand how the vigours of a military life and the thrill of flying would be attractive to him.

Not surprisingly Bert was against Frank enlisting. In a letter home written on 18 February 1940 Bert; ever mistrustful of governments wrote about the possibility of the Canadian government introducing conscription against their stated policy; he paraphrases Horace Greeley and advises Frank and all their friends "Head north young man" to avoid conscription. Of course Frank ignored this advice and volunteered for service anyway. In fact Frank seems to have been very keen to enlist and learn to fly. He joined the RCAF on March 25 1942 at No 1 M Depot Toronto. Frank

did all of his training at Malton Airport which is now
Pearson International and Toronto's main international
airport. He carried out his flight training in Anson trainers.
Frank qualified as a Navigator but also had some training in
aerial photography and bomb aiming. Navigation was his
primary trade and it was as a Navigator that he would do all
his flight training in Wellingtons in, and it was as a
navigator that he would fly his one and only combat
mission, also flown in a Wellington. Frank seems to have
taken to military life like a duck to water. He enjoyed the
comradeship of squadron life and he loved flying.

Frank's letters home are much more relaxed than Bert's.
While Bert's letters about family members are affectionate
and at times teasing they can be stiff and at times rather
impersonal. Frank's letters are much more playful especially
when it came to writing about my mom, his youngest sister
Cecelia. This is not surprising though. When Bert left home
Cecelia was only 5 and when Frank left home she was
nearly 10 but still considered the baby of the family. Frank
had those extra five years of watching his little sister grow
and being around her every day. When he got to England
whenever Frank was close to the seaside he collected a few
sea shells and saved them to send home to his little sister.
He also enjoyed teasing his other three sisters, Marjory,
Emily and Mary who he once playfully dubbed the "Warr
Glamour Girls". Frank's letters home were often very light
hearted. He often opens with something like "Dear mom,
dad and brats." Once Emily and little Babs wrote to Frank
asking if they could have his room for themselves and the
family dog Skippy. Frank's reply was typical of him, "of
course you can have my room, just don't go in it."

Frank also wrote more openly about his friends than Bert. It
seems that his best friend during training was a big lad
nicknamed General Grant. Frank and General Grant got up
to all kinds of shenanigans during their training. Once while
training in Scotland they were put in a decompression
chamber together. The pressure was slowly decreased to
simulate a rise in altitude to 30,000 feet. This was done to

find out how an airman would respond to the low oxygen levels found at that extreme altitude. Of course there was a danger of getting the bends. If a person started to experience dizziness or pain they were to signal the device operator who would stop the test and get them out of there as quickly and safely as possible. Frank had to do just that because of an acute pain in his left shoulder. The test was stopped and a battered Frank was removed from the chamber safely, having failed to reach the test altitude. It turns out though that the cause of the pain in Frank's shoulder had nothing to do with the test and was caused because during the test run Frank and General Grant were repeatedly punching each other in the shoulder as hard as they could.

Another time while training in Scotland Frank and his unit were ordered to go on a long route march as part of their training. Evidently Frank didn't feel like going for a long walk that day because he just stepped out of line and started walking along beside his unit looking for all the world like he was going somewhere important on other business. He got away with that one and no one was any the wiser. Still in Scotland, while their unit was carrying out basic infantry defence training, Frank and his squad were on their way back to quarters after finishing for the day when they spotted a newly arrived unit moving up to start their first day's training. This training had a reputation for being very tough and Frank wanted to make sure the new unit started their day with this in mind. When Frank spotted the new unit marching towards them he decided to have a little fun. He got all the lads in his unit to start limping and leaning on each other as if they could barely make it back after the gruelling day's training they had just endured. He even got them to carry one fellow back as if he had a severe leg injury. The new unit must have been wondering what they were getting into as this sorry lot limped passed.

Before all this though Frank had to undergo all the basic military and flight training that all aircrew undertook. Frank did all his basic training in Malton close to home. He got to spend a lot of his free time visiting home and was able to see family and friends right up until the time he and his unit were shipped out to go overseas. After leaving Malton in September of 1942 for Halifax Nova Scotia with his unit and finally leaving there in late January 1943 they arrived in England in early February and travelled to Bournemouth where they were to be billeted. Frank, never having been abroad before was bowled over by the beauty of the English countryside and Bournemouth. He wrote to his father that Bournemouth "most the beautiful town I have ever seen. I would like to spend the duration here."

Almost the first thing that Frank's unit did after settling into their new quarters was to go on a week's leave. This was at the time that Bert was just finishing his Bomb Leaders course and he was given two weeks leave before he had to rejoin 158 Squadron. The two brothers arranged to meet in London during their leave. Frank telephoned Bert to finalise the details of their planned visit. Frank relates that when Bert came on the phone that he didn't recognise his voice at first because Bert now had an English accent. After the two met up Frank wrote a letter home reporting to the family about his brother. Unusually Frank's letter is not very forthcoming with details. He merely says that Bert "looked well and of course a little older." It is probable that Frank, mindful of the fact that Bert had not told the family that he was flying combat missions was playing it safe by keeping his information about Bert rather general and vague so that he didn't inadvertently spill the beans revealing Bert's secret. He did make note though that Bert had left his adolescence behind, that he had grown and matured and become "a very fine chap and I suppose an intellectual." In a answer to a question asked by Mary Frank added that Bert "certainly had not become hard. A person of the sensitivity necessary to turn out such poetry could not be." I suppose that Mary asked this because she was worried that military training had changed her brother, and not for the better.

Frank's letter, while light on details about his brother does give a good report of all the things that he and Bert got up to while together in London. Bert showed Frank all the

149

main tourist sites in London and had him round to his rooms at Lanark Mansions. Frank reported to the family that they went "Sight seeing and wandering around chatting. Saw Random Harvest and two other shows, went to a couple of dances and heard London Philharmonic at The Royal Albert Hall." Bert too reported to the family about the visit. He wrote home that "Frank was very well, not delighted to be away from home but I think he is interested in his work here." That statement strikes me as odd because as we have seen Frank seemed to be completely enjoying his adventure and being away from home. I'm sure that Frank was missing family and friends but from all his letters he seemed to have loved the whole experience of Airforce life and being overseas. It seems that both brothers were playing their cards very close to the vest when it came to telling the family what was actually going on. he does make sure to tell them that he showed Frank all the sights of London and including his rooms at Lanark Mansions. Bert also thanks the family for all the parcels that they sent over for him with Frank, four in total. And that is the extent of Bert's report home on the time he and Frank spent together in London. That week was the last time the two brothers would ever see each other.

On his return from his week's leave Frank's unit was detached from the RCAF and seconded to the RAF while they carried out their ground training. This involved a move to the north east coast of Scotland where they underwent the infantry training, during which Frank pulled off the tough training prank. After Scotland, Frank's unit had postings to bases near Stratford Upon Avon and Cornwall where he regularly went swimming in the ocean. Frank was obviously made of sterner stuff than me because the times that I have been to Cornwall doing anything more than wading slowly out into the frigid waters until the water was knee deep was about all I could ever manage. In fact most people who go swimming in the sea off Cornwall wear wet suites. Frank never even mentions the cold waters at all.

150

While he missed flying, Frank was thoroughly enjoying the experience and took every opportunity to take advantage of these postings to see and experience all that rural England had to offer. He went canoeing on the Avon near Stratford and of course went to see some Shakespeare plays in Stratford itself. He also managed to buy a bicycle and learned to ride that on the country roads. Surprisingly with his sporting background he had never ridden a bicycle before but, after a shaky start and a few falls, he was soon cycling around the leafy country lanes. The picture that Frank paints in his letters home at this time is very much contrary to Bert's report that Frank was not delighted to be away from home. He seemed to be thoroughly enjoying the whole experience.

Bert and Frank had a childhood friend named Al Hymus. They both mention him numerous times in their letters. In all the letters they both just call him Hymus, never Al. Calling people by only their last names in letters seems to have been a family habit. Bert often mentions, Pinkus but seldom, if ever Phil. Carrying this further Bert often mentions people by their last name or the even less personal habit of naming them by their nationality. He often mentions 'The Hungarian Lady," in his letters, meaning Mrs Nora Senjem. It is an odd, impersonal way of referring to friends and colleagues.

It seems that Hymus joined the army around the same time that Frank joined the RCAF and he was sent overseas to England at roughly the same time as Frank was. All through the winter, spring and summer months of 1943 Frank and Hymus tried to meet. But every time that they arranged to meet up something would happen and they kept missing each other for one reason or another. The tale begins to take on a tragi-comic feel. They would arrange to meet somewhere, usually in London, but on more than one occasion in another town while both were on leave only to have one of them show up on the wrong day or the wrong time or at the wrong place. More than once one or the other had their leave cancelled at the last minute yet again spoiling their chance to get together. Finally though Bert and Hymus did meet up. Frank had two weeks leave in late August just before he was to finally ship out to North Africa. He managed to track Hymus down at his base. The two spent some together there over one weekend. When Frank arrived at Hymus' base he found his friend in the middle of a baseball game against another squad. So Frank watched that game, then the two went off to the mess together to catch up on all that had been happening since they had last seen each other and to enjoy a beer or two. The next day, Saturday the lads travelled together to London. Frank wrote that they went to Madam Tussauds's and then to the movies together. After staying the night in London they went back to Hymus' base on the Sunday. They had intended to go for a long bike ride in the countryside but someone had stolen the bike that Hymus had arranged to borrow for Frank. Instead of the bike ride they ended up taking a long bus ride out into the country where they spent the afternoon hiking. On returning to the base Frank spent the evening beating Hymus at ping-pong and winning several rounds of beer from him in the process. Frank left on Monday to go to Bristol where he would stay with relatives until Friday when he returned to base. Those three days were the last time that Frank and Hymus the two childhood friends would see each other because shortly afterwards Frank left for North Africa from where he would never return. As with Pinkus we don't know whether or not Hymus survived the war.

Chapter 14: Frank's War

Shortly after Frank's leave his training outfit was again posted to Bournemouth. It was here that Frank got the news that Bert was reported as missing. Because the family were not aware what Bert's trade was or that he was flying in combat the telegram informing them that he was missing was a shock and no doubt contributed greatly to the extreme trauma the family experienced when they learned out of the blue that he was missing. Of course Frank had known was on active duty but he kept Bert's secret.

The family, probably primarily my grandmother and Mary had wanted Frank to transfer out of an active flying role. Now, with Bert missing they put enormous pressure on him to transfer out of Bomber Command. Frank was very reluctant to request a transfer as it involved not only a demotion from Sgt to AC2 but also the stigma of being classified LMF. The initials LMF stood for Lack Of Moral Fibre and basically labelled a man as a coward. To Frank the idea of a transfer under such a dark cloud was unthinkable. Also all indications from his letters suggest that Frank was having the time of his life in the RCAF. He loved the comradery of the lads in his unit and on his crew and he loved flying. However after the news that Bert was missing he bowed to family wishes and said that if the news about Bert was found to be bad he would request a transfer, but that he would not request the transfer if the news was good and Bert was reported as being alive and safe.

Classifying a man as LMF for whatever reason was not a decision taken lightly by the RAF or the RCAF. Today such a brutal policy would never be used. Much more is understood about PTSD etc and kinder and more humane methods are used to remove a man from a role that has traumatised him. An LMF classification also carried with it a great stigma of shame and cowardice in society. In this regard the RAF used it as a blunt club held over a man's head to keep him in line, albeit it was only used as a last resort. No one wanted to be branded LMF, lack of moral fibre! Coward! There were many cases though where men, especially those in Bomber Command flying into almost certain death on a nightly basis did accept this fate. Of course in other cases the man was completely broken and the decision was inevitable. Let us not forget that all bomber aircrew were volunteers and no one entered bomber crew training who was not willing to lay down his life in this role. That some found extreme stress of the nightly trips into the hell over occupied Europe and Germany too much and were broken by the experience is not a surprise. Everyone has their breaking point. The wonder is that so many men did manage to carry on night after night and not only completed their missions but did so time and time again.

The decision to classify a man as LMF was always taken by a non flying officer, that is a desk jockey. Bomber crews themselves understood the pressures facing their unfortunate crew mate because they were right there with him every minute of every flight. Most crews would do everything they could to cover for their mate, to try to help him through this rough patch hoping his trauma was temporary and that next flight all would be well. There must have been many times when this was true. A man would lose his nerve under the extreme pressure and might bounce back next flight or the one after. However there were times when this did not happen and the crew would have no choice but to accept the man's breakdown and let him remove himself from flight duty by reporting himself to the MO as unable to carry on mentally.

For Frank the news that Bert was missing was a double blow. Not only did he have the worry that his brother was dead but he also now had to worry that he would be forced by family pressures to request a transfer out of bomber command. Frank did not want a transfer. He liked being in an active unit and being aircrew and of course he dreaded the idea of having to accept a classification as LMF. The time between Frank learning that Bert was missing and Bert being officially listed as dead on June 18 1943 must have

154

been agonising mentally for Frank. Frank, true to his word bowed to family wishes after june 18 and agreed to ask for a transfer out of Bomber Command, out of active flying duty and into a safe and boring desk job with the extra stigma and humiliation of being classified as LMF.

For Frank's mother and father and the rest of the family things looked different. They knew that Bert was in the RAF but assumed him to be reasonably safe in a non-combat role as he not said otherwise. I'm not sure why they never asked. Perhaps they did and he fobbed them off with vague replies. So when Frank announced that he was going to fly combat duty the family wanted him to transfer, thinking only of keeping both brothers safely alive for the duration of the war. However before Bert's death they seem to have been willing not to press Frank to transfer after he learned of the double whammy of demotion and classification as LMF.

The double trauma of learning at the same instant that not only had Bert been flying combat missions but that he was now missing renewed the family pressure on Frank and they again began to press Frank to do the unthinkable and request a transfer. To them, a son and brother who was alive and safe was the most important thing and Frank's parents seemed more than willing to have him take the demotion and classification as LMF that such a transfer brought with it.

Frank spent the summer months of 1943 billeted in a hotel in Bournemouth which he still considered to be the prettiest town he ever saw. When Frank learned that Bert was missing Frank was actually at an OTU (Operational Training Unit) and getting ready to start flight training on Wellingtons in preparation for finally being returned to the RCAF and joining an active squadron. It was at the OTU that Frank, bowing to family wishes and pressures put in his request for a transfer. Naturally Frank's request was taken very seriously by the brass and further extended his stay in England and away from active flight duties. After he put in

155

his request Frank was immediately pulled from flight training. Instead of flying Frank spent his time in barracks and attending the many, many interviews the brass wanted while they assessed his request.

In July Frank got more leave and he went to visit the family in Bristol. He stayed with Uncle Dick, one of his father's brothers and Dick's wife Hattie. Uncle Dick showed Frank all around Bristol and the Warr family houses where they had grown up. Uncle Dick showed Frank the little school they had attended as children, the local pub "The Black Boy", a tree they called the stumps and had used while playing cricket when they were children. He also saw the suspension bridge and all the rest of the sights in that part of Bristol. They took a trip out to Pill where Frank explored a converted brewery the family had. Frank doesn't say what the brewery was converted into but presumably it was a house. He then went into Pill with Uncle Dick, Aunt Queen and her husband Uncle Rich and their son Jim and his wife. Aunt Queen and Uncle Dick took Frank in a little pony trap out to their cottage where he met Aunt Nell, cousin Peggy and her husband and their baby. It seems strange to think of people as late as the 1940s, even in the British countryside not having cars and using buggies pulled by horses and ponies but England and indeed most of Europe was still very rural and not many people had cars. Even those who did have cars would have had trouble getting enough petrol in those war days due to rationing. They stayed at the cottage overnight. It had rained on the trip out in the pony trap and they all were soaking wet. Frank was given a pair of Uncle Richard Withers pyjamas to sleep in while his clothes dried out. I guess that Uncle Richard was not a small man and of course Frank was very slight. Frank notes in his letter home that the pyjamas he was forced to wear "are quite copious." We can imagine Frank standing in the living room in front of the fire looking very much a like a boy in his dad's pyjamas, long sleeves and trouser legs hanging down and pyjama top billowing out. He must have been quite the sight.

Joan and Tiny, by this time married, were away in the forces as we know so Frank never had the chance to meet them. The next day they rounded up the pony in the field and Uncle Richard, Aunt Nell and Frank drove back into to Pill. From there Aunt Nell and Frank took a bus into Clevedon where Frank had the chance to thoroughly explore the promenade. In the afternoon Frank went with Aunt Nell to the farm of Aunt Queen's son John, which was a nice little place close to the water. Frank got a chance to taste some forbidden fruit in those rationing years. They had some fresh Devonshire cream for tea. It was forbidden to make cream for the duration as I it takes a lot of milk to produce. One of the Jersey cows had wandered off and they had been unable to milk it in time to send the milk to the dairy. When they did find the cow and milk her they made some fresh cream, a rare treat and one that they thoroughly enjoyed. On the Saturday Uncle Dick took Frank on the train to the coastal resort town of Weston Super Mare where he saw all the sights along the waterfront and went for a swim in a saltwater pool. They returned to Bristol in the evening on the bus where Frank spent the night before finishing his leave and heading back to camp. That had been the second week of his leave. He had spent the first week in London where he had met Mrs Senjem and had spent time finding out from her all that he could about what she knew of Bert.

Back at camp Frank sat around his billet while he awaited news of his transfer request. He does mention that there were dances at a nearby WAAF camp nearly every night and that he often went to these. At about this time he also started seeing "a nice little WAAF who was educated in a convent in Belgium." Frank doesn't tell the family this girl's name in his letter nor does he give any details as to where they went together except to say that he enjoyed her company, that she was a lot of fun to be with and that he wants to see her again when he returns from duty in Africa. This letter of course must have been written after Frank's request for transfer was turned down and he was returned to active flight duty.

As we know Frank loved flying and he loved the military life and being a navigator, and he was obviously very good at what he did. During his interviews this enthusiasm may have come across to the men asking the questions and taking his statements. While they considered his fate this was no doubt a factor in their decision to deny his request and return him to active duty. They wrote that Frank was willing, in fact even keen to return to active duty. I can't be sure but I can guess that it was grandma Warr who by this time was pressing the most for Frank to carry on with his transfer request. For her part Aunt Mary, once she realised that this request would tarnish Frank's reputation and mark him out as a coward fully supported his decision to accept a return to flying. Aunt Mary wrote that "Frank was so determined to be accepted for aircrew instead of being earmarked for a safe desk job that at his own expense he underwent an operation to remove a nasal blockage that would have prevented him being selected for air crew duty. He was a brave and keen young man who would not have deserved the shame and stigma that being declared LMF would have brought him." The rest of the family seem to have accepted this decision buy the authorities to deny Frank his transfer request but grandma Warr, for one, never forgot, nor forgave the Air Force for taking her boys from her.

We can only guess at the relief that Frank must have felt when his request for transfer was denied and he was returned to active flight status with the RCAF, but it must have been immense. Frank returned to duty and resumed his flight training on Wellingtons. After several weeks of this he was assigned to 424 Squadron. 424 was operating from a base in North Africa in Tunisia on the north east coast about 50Km west of the city Kairouan. They were there in support of the Allied invasions of Scilly and Italy. The allies invaded Sicily in July 1943 and main land Italy 03 September that same year. The Allies invaded Sicily on 10 July 1943 and by 18 August, they controlled the whole island. Preparing the way for an invasion of the Italian mainland. The Allies hoped that an invasion of Italy, would draw German troops away from the Soviet eastern front, and that is exactly what happened. Mussolini's grip on power in Italy was failing. Between these invasions, shortages of food, raw materials for factories and just about everything else, coupled with the allied bombing of Italian cities the people had, had enough of Mussolini and Fascism. Italian king Victor Emmanuel sacked Mussolini on 18 July. The Allies invaded the mainland on 03 September 1943, and Italy surrendered on the 18th. As was hoped by Allied command this forced the Germans to redeploy troops from the eastern front to defend Italy for the remaining Axis powers. The Germans initially sent 25 divisions from the east to Italy. The battle for Italy would be a tough and bloody slog for the Allies. The Germans put up a determined defence, but the invasion had achieved its goals of both opening a second front and forcing the Germans to weaken their eastern front by redeploying troops from there to Italy. Final liberation, and surrender of the last German troops in Italy was not until 02 May 1945, only five days before Germany itself surrendered ending the war in Europe.

On his return to active flying duty, Frank was assigned to the crew with whom he had done his conversion training, namely, Pilot Andy Martin from Saskatchewan, J. R. Dack who was the air bomber (AB) and also from Saskatchewan, air gunner (AG) Dick Cote and Don Dodson who was the Wireless operator (WOP). Dodson was RAF. All the rest of the crew were RCAF. In his letters home Frank's enthusiasm for flying shines through. He was so excited to be returning to active flight duty that he positively gushes " We have the best crew and the best squadron." He wrote that before he had even reached the squadron who had been in Africa since June. The crew flew their Wellington to North Africa and joined the squadron on 15th September 1943. They didn't immediately go on active duty but spent a few days on leave in Morocco where Frank managed to visit Fez.

When they did join the squadron they continued to enjoy themselves "We made a lovely trip in trucks yesterday and

had a lovely swim in the Mare Nostrum. Lovely warm
water and fine golden sand" (Mare Nostrum was the Roman
name for the Mediterranean Sea). The water may have been
warm and sand golden but there were also jelly fish and
Frank got bitten by them twice. It didn't seem to bother him
though because he carried on swimming and enjoyed his
day. Of course while he was at the seaside he gathered some
seashells for his little sister Babs. It is nice to consider that
Frank and his crew mates had this one last day of fun at the
sea just days before they took off into the night skies on
their one and only combat operation and were never seen
again.

Interestingly this day trip to the seaside is mentioned in the
424 squadron ORB. ORB entries are usually confined to
relating transfers in and out of the unit and listing of crew
and aircraft and their targets and bomb loads etc on
particular ops. To make an entry about a squadron day out
to the seaside was most unusual.

In his last letter home Frank relates how glad he is to be
back in the RCAF and "in the best squadron out here."
Poignantly and perhaps tempting fate the letter continues "I
don't think you need to worry much about our safety here as
the ops are not tough and we get them over in a hurry here
which is good." And that was the last thing he ever wrote
home.

Frank and his crew took off for their first and only combat
operation on 01 Oct 1943. It was an op to bomb Formia,
which is located halfway between Rome and Naples in
southern Italy. In one of those strange quirks of fate, both
Frank and Bert took their last flights in "F" for Freddie
designated aircraft. Bomber Command aircraft all had
manufacturer's serial numbers Bert's - Halifax II DT635 and
Frank's Wellington HE795. In addition each squadron had
it's own two letter code and each aircraft in the squadron
was assigned a call letter. Bert"s Squadron number 158 had
code NP and Bert's aircraft was therefore NP-F. Franks
squadron had code QB and Frank's aircraft was therefore

QB-F. Frank's Wellington HE795 QB-F took off from base at 19:43 to bomb Formia in Italy. Nothing was ever again heard of this aircraft after take-off. It disappeared without trace.

Frank Warr Active duty Log: Frank's one and only combat mission

424 Sqn ORB entry: Lost: 01 Oct 1943. Op to bomb Formia. Wellington HE795 F.
                              T/O: 19:43. Nothing was ever heard of this aircraft after T/O
                    Crew: Pilot: Martin I A
                              Nav: Warr F
                              B/A: Dack JR
                              WOP: Dodson GD
                              A/G: Cote JR

The 424 ORB states that extensive searches failed to turn up any trace of the aircraft. The op was considered to be what was called a milk run. A milk run mission was about as safe an op as you could wish for. It was typically flown over very lightly defended areas and to an equally lightly defended target. On this occasion the enemy made no claims for having shot down any Allied aircraft. So what happened to Frank and his crew? Did they reach the target and carry out their mission and then crash on the return flight. Did they even make it to the target? It seems that they did and were then lost on the return leg of the op.

Aunt Mary persisted in trying to find out what happened to her brother Frank with a dogged determination which can only be explained by the deep love and close ties that the family shared. She managed to contact a fellow from RCAF 425 Alouette Squadron. 425 were also operating out of North Africa at the time in support of the Allied invasions. This man, named Alistair Craig, wrote back to Aunt Mary and told her what his crew had experienced and seen that night of Oct 2. He related that the weather was absolutely terrible. There were heavy thunder storms all over the area.

He said that several aircraft were even forced to abort their missions and turn back base because of the weather. However Alistair's crew carried on and bombed the target. The target, Formia was lightly defended so there was no ack-ack and there were no night fighters sent up because of the bad weather. Their bombing run went off without a hitch and Alistair's aircraft turned for home heading back out over the Med. It was over the sea that the pilot saw a flash and a huge explosion in the distance. He deduced that it could only have been caused by an aircraft being hit by lightning and then exploding. They flew to the area and made several low level passes over where they believed the aircraft must have come down but they saw nothing. They then continued back to base. The only report of any aircraft lost that night was of Frank's Wellington so the explosion Alistair's pilot witnessed must have been Frank's Wellington blowing up. Alistair continued in his letter " Francis and his crew would never have known what hit them as they would have been killed instantly in the explosion. I am sure that none of them would have been alive when the aircraft hit the water."

The loss of Frank's aircraft to a lightning strike on an operation which otherwise was a safe as any could ever hope to be was a strange and cruel quirk of fate. There are a good many unanswered questions about the op. Why did Frank's crew even attempt the mission? After all the weather was so bad that many more experienced crews didn't even take off or turned back before even reaching the target. Was it the determination of the new boys to prove themselves in combat or was it perhaps a lack of experience that a more seasoned crew would have had? What are the odds of a lightning strike so violent hitting the aircraft that it was completely destroyed? They must be very long. Looking through squadron ORBs I didn't find accounts of any other aircraft being lost in this fashion. I'm sure that a thorough examination of ORBs of all the squadrons operating over the Med would turn up accounts of aircraft being hit by lightning but very few would have been brought down by the strike, let alone have been completely destroyed by it.

The loss of Frank's aircraft in this way was a very unlucky, one in a million shot.

Chapter 15: Bert's Legacy

The news that Bert was missing in action and then finally
that he had been killed rocked the family. I don't think that
my grandparents ever fully got over Bert's death, followed a
scarce six months later by Frank's. The shock and the
trauma caused by the loss of "the boys" left deep wounds
that never fully healed. As we know Bert's family were only
vaguely aware what his trade in the Airforce had been and
they did not know that he was flying in combat. He didn't
want them to worry about him so he didn't tell them that he
was flying combat missions. They didn't seem to want to
press the issue and were more than happy to carry on
assuming that Bert's job in the RAF was in a non-combat
roll.

After they received of the telegram informing them that
Bert was missing the family held their collective breaths
waiting for official news one way or another. No one more
so than Frank, whose future stood to be affected the most by
whether or not Bert was alive or not. His promise to the
family that if the news was the worst that he would indeed
ask for a transfer from active flying duty weighed heavily
on him. They all figuratively held their breaths as the days
passed and they waited for official confirmation of Bert's
fate. There was every hope that Bert and his crew mates
survived the crash and had been taken as prisoners or else
had evaded capture and were hiding out with hopes of
trying to make their way back to England. Those days of
uncertainty must have been an agony for the family. Every
time there was a knock at the door they must have been
dreading that it would be the telegram informing them of
the worst.

Bert's aircraft was shot down on the night of April 3rd 1943
and it was on 18 April that he was officially declared to
have been killed in action. A Telegram from Air Ministry to
Frank and another one to the family informing them that
Bert was officially listed as having been killed was sent on
18 April 1943. In the usual terse style of telegrams and cold

official language of military messages the telegram sent to Frank reads as follows:

"Immediate from Air Ministry deeply regret to advise that that according to information received through the international Red Cross Committee your brother Sgt Bertram James Warr is believed to have lost his life as a result of air operations on 03 April 1943. stop. The Air Council express their profound sympathy. His mother is being informed Under Secretary of State. stop."

The telegram sent to the family would have been very similar, written in just as a cold and terse a manner. The British had gotten confirmation of Bert and his crew's death from the International Red Cross who had been informed by the German authorities that none of the crew had survived the crash.

On 05 May Frank true to his word put in a transfer request. I'm sure he did so very reluctantly and with fingers crossed that he would be turned down. A future blighted by a classification as LMF was not something anyone would want, let alone a man of Frank's quality and bravery. He wanted to keep flying and didn't want to be chained to a desk in a non flying role. In the short term he was immediately pulled from training and put into a sort of official limbo while his request was considered by the brass. This left him cooling his heels in his billet. With nothing to do but wait for whatever fate the powers that be deemed was in store for him.

Frank took some of that downtime to write a letter home in an attempt to ease the pain of his family. He wrote of his impression of Bert when they met up on leave in London that March "Bert had grown into a very fine chap and his life in recent years had been interesting and eventful. In giving it up we can hope it was not in vain. Flying is not sordid warfare, clean and interesting. The dangers are not terrifying but exhilarating. His main regret would have been the pain and sorrow caused to you folks at home."

165

As well as causing chaos in Frank's life and devastating the family, the news of Bert's death resulted in a flurry of sympathetic letters to Bert's parents from family and friends. John Gawsworth wrote Bert's obituary in The Times Literary Supplement and in a letter to Bert's sister Mary dated Nov 29 1943 he introduced himself to her and sent the family his condolences. At this time he requested that they let him have Bert's manuscripts for editing and publishing in book form in England and Canada after the war. Of course in letters home Bert had often written of Gawsworth so they were at least familiar with him from those and knew that he was a friend they could trust. Bert had become close friends with Gawsworth. The pair had been planning on collaborating on a book after the war. Now Gawsworth wanted to carry on with his own project to keep Bert's memory alive.

John Gawsworth's obituary of Bert in the Times Literary Supplement August 7th 1943 ran as follows:

I have been informed through a member of his family that the loss of Bertram Warr, at the age of twenty five, on air operations, has been confirmed. It was my good fortune to be stationed for several months with this young but intellectually mature Canadian poet, the while he qualified as an air observer. Frail in appearance a very "parfait gentile" serious young man, it was difficult to imagine the self chosen vicissitudes he had endured: hitch-hiking across Canada, stowing away one Christmas Eve and landing in Liverpool with but ten shillings in his pocket, to starve at times, wash dishes and clerk at Billingsgate, solely because he desired to add to the literature of the mother country. His modesty would have it that it was but a mite that he had to offer. Alas that we will never know the full sum! Nevertheless he has his place and it is right and fitting that he should have found it under English imprints. A broadsheet of some dozen poems in the Favil Press Series of Resurgam Younger Poets (with a prose preface that clearly states his poetic principle), a few uncollected poems in Mr

166

*Wrey Gardiner's Poetry Quarterly, and representation in
"Poems of The Forces" and Miss Patricia Ledward's
Cambridge University Press anthology of wartime verse:
such are his published beginnings. After the war I sincerely
hope it may be possible to issue a volume concurrently in
England and Canada, selected from the above and from his
assembled manuscripts.*

Gawsworth thought a great deal of Bert and admired his
talent and potential so much so that not only did he want to
publish a book of Bert's poems but he also dedicated one of
his own poems to Bert. The poem is titled "Permanence."

*Permanence
(For Bertram Warr)*

*The bomb obliterates.
The dream remains.
No thing may mankind utterly destroy.
Within the ether unity obtains.
A great loss often is a cause for joy.*

*Anarchy's triumph is a moments spell;
Culture's long travail augers longer life.
A poem slays more spirits than a shell.
An essay comforts longer than a wife.*

*How short our living we seldom know;
What seems beginnings like as not are ends.
Beneath life's current runs an underflow
That drags us down from fancies and from friends.*

*Who knows that laughter is
(When all else fails and falls)
The quintessence of bliss,
Though echoed under broken walls,*

Sees symbols of a better day,
Achieves crustacean hardihood.
No heart insensible to clay
Creates for public good.

Gawsworth wanted to get all of Bert's manuscripts and
papers that were in the care of Mrs Senjem and Patricia
Ledward. The family agreed to this and Bert's sister Mary
wrote letters to both these ladies asking that they send any
papers of Bert's that they had to Gawsworth. The family and
Mary especially, were very keen to have a book of Bert's
poems published. Mary worked tirelessly to help
Gawsworth with this project. And Gawsworth, true to his
word worked long and hard himself on the project after the
war when he had returned to civilian life. Sadly,
Gawsworth's effort were ultimately fruitless and he was
unable to see the project through. He never did publish a
book of Bert's work.

Patricia Ledward also expressed interest in publishing a
book of Bert's material. In her letter of condolence to Mary
she offered to contact Mrs Senjem whom she knew had
many of Bert's papers. This project of Patricia's came to
nothing because Mary and her parents had already
committed to Gawsworth's planned project. Bert must have
had some contact with Patricia over the last months of his
life. He had written home in July of 1941 that he had not
seen nor heard from Patricia Ledward in over 6 months but
at some point they must have seen each other because in her
poem dedicated to Bert, Patricia relates words Bert had said
to her about his expected death. In fact that poem reads as if
they were having a conversation and not something taken
from a letter. So it would seem likely that they had met up
at some point after Bert had started flying combat
operations with 158 Squadron.

At some point after the war Patricia seems to have had a
change of heart about the papers and letters of Bert's that
she had. When Aunt Mary, having decided that Gawsworth

168

was the fellow to get a book of Bert's work published wrote to Patricia requesting that she send them any and all material of Bert's that she had, Patricia wrote back that she had destroyed everything, published and unpublished that she had held of Bert's. We can only speculate as to why she did this. Perhaps the pain of Bert's loss was too much for her. Perhaps she now found herself in a new relationship and either destroyed Bert's letters and papers at the request of her new fella or she wanted to cut ties with that part of her past. Obviously the decision to destroy any letters that Bert had sent her was her right and likewise destroying any of Bert's published work that she had was her right. Where I think Patricia crossed the line is in destroying all Bert's unpublished work and notes that she had. She should have sent these to the family. Whether or not any of this material was any good or not is beside the point. Legally all this material belonged to Bert's mother who held copyright on all his material. Sadly whatever, if any, unpublished papers of Bert's that Patricia Ledward held are now lost to us, likely all because of the whims of a broken heart.

Many others had comforting words of condolence for the family. Frank was in contact with Aunt Queen after Bert's death and from her he learned that Bert had told Joan Withers "I shall just about learn to fly then, one bomb and I shall be gone." Frank wrote that Aunt Queen also thought Bert "very loveable."

It is from Nora Senjem that we get the best idea of Bert's mental state in the months leading up to his death. Of course we know from his essay about dying that ends Acknowledge To Life that Bert was resigned to death. He was even to an extent ready and wanting to die because of the strains of flying combat. It is from Nora Senjem that we get an idea of how much this affected his thoughts and actions. Frank went to London and met Nora Senjem after Bert's death and afterwards wrote to the family what she had related to him about Bert. Nora Senjem herself also wrote to Aunt Mary several times. Frank wrote that Nora Senjem had known Bert since the first days of his arrival in

169

London from Canada. As I have related elsewhere Bert seems to have considered her to be a sort of surrogate mother or perhaps a very close aunt. That feeling was mutual and Nora Senjem cared a great deal about Bert. She related that Bert was always very careless with all his things. Throwing away and giving away his money and possessions to any needy person. Then he would end up having to borrow money for his own needs. Consequently he was always broke and in debt. Bert was not only careless with his money but with pretty much everything else as well, lending his typewriter to one of his girlfriends. One time while in his cups in Scotland Bert had bought quite a few records from a local shop. He seems to have just left the whole lot of them somewhere in Kinloss or West Fraugh. Mrs Senjem convinced Bert to open a bank account but he only managed to save £5 in it. After he enlisted his friends had quite a time keeping track of him. He would arrive in London on leave suddenly and just as suddenly leave again without the slightest warning. He was never now on time for appointments if he kept them at all. It would seem that military life was taking a toll on him right from the day he enlisted.

In one of her letters to Mary, Nora Senjem wrote that she wanted to collect all the details that she had concerning Bert and pass them along to the family. She adds though that these amount to very little real information and that their mutual friends knew even less about Bert. As one would expect in letters to his family after his death all comments are very kind and positive and paint Bert's character in the best light. Nora continues, writing that everybody without exception liked him and appreciated him for his very decent and sweet nature. He was always very quiet in society. At parties and dinners he spoke very little but tried to help everybody, usually beyond his means. This description tallies with what Bert himself wrote in his letters home the few times that he did mention dinner parties or other gatherings at Mrs Senjem's house. It seems he was more than content to sit in a quiet corner with his glass of whiskey, perhaps puffing on a favourite pipe and enjoy the

170

conversation and other entertainment around him making very little effort to join in. But no doubt listening intently to the writers, deep thinkers and other artists who attended these gatherings at Mrs Senjem's house. Many of these people were refugee intellectuals and others that were high on the list of people that the Nazis wanted to persecute. They seem to have been primarily from Austria and Nora Senjem's native Hungary.

After the war, John Gawsworth Alan Crawley and Canadian poet Earl Birney published several of Bert's poems in their respective poetry magazines and in 1949 Birney read Bert's poem "The Heart Carry On" on his CBC radio show about poets of World War 2.

Once Gawsworth had made his way back to England from India after the war he proceeded to carry out his plans for publishing Bert's work in book form. He worked diligently, gathering manuscripts of as much of Bert's work, published and unpublished that he could find. He was in close contact with the family, specifically Aunt Mary. Although it was Grandma Warr who now owned the copyright to all of Bert's work it was Aunt Mary who looked after all the administration and correspondence etc. Gawsworth got permission from the family to carry on with his book project and they sent him all the papers of Bert's that they had. He also contacted Patricia Ledward and Nora Senjem and got all of Bert's papers that they had. How much material he got from Patricia Ledward is unknown because as we have seen she destroyed Bert's papers that were in her care. At this point unfortunately, Gawsworth's efforts stalled. He became ill and also was very much involved with other projects that were more urgent than getting Bert's book published and he put the project on a back burner. Even so there was great hope that Gawsworth's book would be published. Canadian poet Earle Birney was impressed with the selection of poems that Gawsworth was planning to include in the book. Writing to Aunt Mary he said "here is some fine work. The record of an original, honest and thoughtful mind of a young man who was already inwardly a developed poet, with a subtle yet easy way with him, imaginative but with his feet on the ground. I am eager to see it all published."

As Gawsworth's project languished and stalled Birney became more concerned as did Aunt Mary. On 22 September 1949 Aunt Mary wrote to Birney voicing her concerns which Birney seems to have shared. They were both worried about Gawsworth's choice of publisher and the excessive amount of time that he was taking to get the project to press. Aunt Mary wrote "I can't tell him that I don't want his edition, I do - sight unseen, but I owe it to Bert to ensure the finest publication."

In the summer of 1948 grandma Warr and my mom went to England on holiday. My mom would have been 16 at this time. At or near the top of their to do list was a meeting with Gawsworth. They had lunch with him and grandam Warr came away singularly unimpressed by this fellow. As Aunt Mary wrote to Birney "My mother considered that he was greatly concerned with his own affairs, new wife, sovereignty of his island, etc and placed little confidence that he would look after the work." Mary however didn't share this view as she adds "That it seems was unjust." It seems that Mary's assessment was right because Gawsworth's project did finally reach the stage when contracts were ready for signature and it seemed that publication was set to proceed. He sent a contract ready for signatures to the family but it had no cover letter and that of course raised major concerns. There must have been other things at play and other concerns about Gawsworth's project within the family but it seems that the fallout from the contract letter was the straw that broke this projects back. The family decided to cancel Gawsworth's project outright and Aunt Mary wrote to him requesting the return of all of Bert's papers. Gawsworth duly sent everything that he had of Bert's to Mary with nary a word surviving as to the why's and wherefores and that is the last we hear of John Gawsworth.

But this was not yet the end of Bert's legacy. Earle Birney in particular was very impressed with Bert's work and often included one or more of Bert's poems in his publications. Earle Birney was born in Calgary on 13 May 1903 and died of a heart attack at the age of 92 in Toronto. He grew up in Erickson B.C. and as a young man worked variously as a farm hand, a bank clerk and a park ranger. Entering university his plan was to get a degree in chemical engineering but after time at UBC, U of T, UC Berkley and the University of London he graduated with a degree in English. During the war he served overseas as a personnel officer. In 1946 Birney began his teaching career at the University of British Columbia where he founded the universities first creative writing program. Drawing on his wartime experiences Birney wrote the book Turvey which was a best seller in Canada and won him the Stephen Leacock Medal for Humour. Today it is for his poetry that Birney is mainly remembered. He twice won the Governor General's Award, Canada's top literary award and in 1970 he was made an Officer Of The Order Of Canada for his poetry.

At the end of the war in 1949 Birney broadcast a live radio program on CBC directly from Canada to England. During the program he read Bert's poem "The Heart Carry On" as part of the show. Birney tried on several occasions to get a book of Bert's work published and supported Gawsworth's efforts as well. In the end though none of that came to fruition and the prospect of getting a book of Bert's poems published seemed as remote as ever.

In July 1965 Bert's poem "Working Class was read out live on the CBC television program "Camera Canada" and that it seems was the last anyone would ever hear of Bertram Warr. By the 1960s even Aunt Mary must have thought that the chances of any book of Bert's poems being published were highly unlikely. Enter Len Gasparini. Len Gasparini was a Canadian poet, editor and publisher born in Windsor Ontario in 1941. Just how Gasparini became interested in Bertram Warr's poetry is not known, but he did and in

173

spades. Gasparini was so impressed with Bert's work that he
believed a book should finally be published and that he was
the fellow to make it happen. Sometime in 1968 he
contacted the family and together with Aunt Mary worked
diligently over the next two years to get a book of Bert's
work published. Even so the publishing of Bert's book
"Acknowledgement To Life" very nearly didn't happen.
There were problems with the publisher and some ruffled
feathers between Earle Birney and Gasparini. Mary still
wanted to have Birney involved in the project and Birney
for his part was more than happy to have a part in the
publishing of a book of Bert's work. Birney was enlisted to
write the preface to the book. The problem was that Birney
had very little faith that Gasparini was up to the job of
carrying the project off properly. He was very unhappy with
the selection of some of the poems that Gasparini wanted to
include. Birney felt that some of the poems were not good
enough or not sufficiently developed, being works in
progress. He did not think these should be included. Birney
was also very unhappy with Gasparini's initial introduction
written for the book so much so that he threatened to
withdraw his support for the project completely if Gasparini
was allowed to stay involved. This set off alarm bells with
the publishers, The Ryerson Press. They contacted Mary
and informed her that if Birney pulled out there was a real
danger that the project would be cancelled altogether. Mary
however persevered and was determined to at last see a
book of her brother's work published. Mary managed to get
Gasparini to rewrite his introduction, addressing Birney's
concerns and the selection of poems to be included was also
worked out to everyone's satisfaction. With Mary in the role
of peace maker things were patched up between Gasparini
and Birney and eventually Birney agreed to contribute his
preface to the book. By this time it was late 1969 and yet
another hurdle had arisen. The Ryerson Press was about to
be sold to McGraw Hill Publishing Company and there was
a danger that if the book was not published before this sale
that the project would be scuppered by the new publishers.
Finally though all the T's were crossed and the I's were
dotted and in 1970 "Acknowledgement to Life" was sent to

the presses and it was one of the last books published under the Ryerson Press banner. Mary's dedication and perseverance had paid off and Bert's legacy lives on. In his preface to the book Earl Birney wrote that - "Had Bert lived I think this book is evidence he could have been a leading poet of his generation."

Epilogue

Bert's life, like the lives of so many who are caught up in the struggles great and small of their times was cut brutally short by the cruel randomness of war. His is a story of remarkable accomplishments and even more so of potential unrealised. Bert's skill as a poet is recognised and greatly admired by all who read his work but much of it is just a glimpse of what might have been had he lived to hone his skills and master his art. Bert Warr only lived a short 25 years but he has left us a rich body of work. Much of Bert's writing stands on its own, complete and fully developed but also much of it is a glimpse of what he may have become. There are many of his poems which lack those finishing touches that a more experienced writer would have added. His legacy is as much about what he has left us as it is about what heights he may have attained had he lived and continued to master his art. As full and rich as his 25 years were his story is above all a story of vast potential unrealised, a life barely begun. Bert firmly believed that it was the duty of the modern poet to point the way to a better life for everyone and he tried to live his life by his beliefs not only through his poetry but through his every day actions. Through his work with The People's Convention, the various refugee organisations that he was involved in and his day to day dealings with people Bert practiced what he preached. The best of Bert's poems challenge us to take up the fight where he left off, to try to make ourselves higher and finer and to help people. But above all Bert challenges us to live like he himself did, keeping a warm heart and an open mind no matter how large the task before us is or how the odds are stacked against us to have the heart to carry on.

Appendix I

List Of Bertram Warr's Published Poems

Yet A Little Onwards

Introduction
War Widow
I Sit With Nothing In My Hands
Death Of An Elephant
Winter Stalks
Working Class
Discord
The Murder
Rejuvenation
From Atheism
The Deviator
Immaculate Conception
The End Of The World
To A Passionate Socialist
On A Child With A Wooden Leg

Acknowledgment To Life: The Collected Poems Of Bertram Warr
The Dead (For Bertram Warr) Patricia Ledward

Part 1 Yet A Little Onwards

Working Class
War Widow
The Deviator
On A Child With A Wooden Leg
Death Of An Elephant
The Murder
Winter Stalks
To A Passionate Socialist
Rejuvenation
I Sit With Nothing In My Hands

177

Acknowledgement To Life

The Outcasts Of Society
An Unfinished Essay

Poems Of This War by Younger Poets

War Widow
Children In The Dusk
Poets In Time Of War (For Wilfred Owen)
Working Class

Poetry Quarterly Spring 1941

Tears Who Are Distant As Another's Reality

Contemporary Verse: A Canadian Quarterly October 1945

Winter Stalks
Death Of An Elephant
The Heart To Carry On
Stepney 1941

Appendix II

Bertram Warr Military Service

Service No. 1391138

Royal Air Force Volunteer Reserve

Background

Enlisted at Euston

Pre War Address: 84 Cloverlawn Avenue, Toronto, Ontario

Canadian

Training

No. 158 Squadron Conversion Flight

Service

Posted to No. 158 Squadron 4 Group Bomber Command at East Moor 24/9/42

Flew as Air Bomber to F/Lt. J.D. Cole on Operations to

15/10/42 – Cologne: 289 aircraft: 289 aircraft -109 Wellingtons, 74 Halifaxes, 62 Lancasters, 44 Stirlings. 18 aircraft lost - 6 Wellingtons, 5 Halifaxes, 5 Lancasters, 2 Stirlings. 6.2% of the force. This was not a successful raid. Winds made establishing their position and the marking of the target by the Pathfinders difficult. Also the Germans lit a large decoy fire away from the target which attracted most of the main force and received most of the bombing.

Aircraft: Halifax II W1157 NP-A
      Crew: Pilot: Pilot Officer (PO) J.D. Cole
            Nav:Sgt R.C. Stemp
            A/B: Sgt B.J. Warr
            WOP: Sgt A. Ward
            MUG: Sgt P. Harrison
            RG: Sgt L. G. H. Watts
            FE: Sgt R. Gowing

7/11/42 – Genoa: 175 aircraft - 85 Lancasters, 45 Halifaxes, 39 Stirlings, 6 Wellingtons. 6 aircraft lost - 4 Halifaxes, 1 Lancaster, 1 Wellngton. 3.4% of the force. Returning crews claimed a very successful and concentrated raid and this was confirmed by photographs.
    Aircraft: Halifax II BB209 NP-G
    Crew: Pilot: PO J.D. Cole
            Nav: Sgt R.C. Stemp
            A/B: Sgt B.J. Warr
            WOP: Sgt A. Ward
            MUG: Sgt W. A. Robinson
            RG: Sgt W. J. Hanks
            FE: Sgt R. Gowing

26/11/42 – Mining Operation: 30 aircraft minelaying off Lorient and St-Nazaire and in the Frisians Kattegat. No aircraft lost.
    Aircraft: Halifax II DT505 NP-H
    Crew: Pilot: PO J.D. Cole
            Nav: Sgt R.C. Stemp,
            A/B: Sgt B.J. Warr
            WOP: Sgt A. Ward
            MUG: Sgt W. A. Robinson
            RG: Sgt W. J. Hanks
            FE: Sgt R. Gowing

3/12/42 – Frankfurt: 112 aircraft - 48 Halifaxes, 27
Lancasters, 22 Stirlings, 15 Wellingtons, 6 aircraft lost - 3
Halifaxes, 1 each of the other types. 5.4% of the force.
Thick haze prevented the Pathfinders finding Frankfurt.
Most bombs fell in the country areas south-west of the city
    Aircraft: Halifax II DT505 NP-H
    Crew: Pilot: PO J.D. Cole
          Nav: Sgt R.C. Stemp
          A/B: Sgt B.J. Warr
          WOP: Sgt A. Ward
          MUG: Sgt W. A. Robinson
          RG: Sgt L.G.H. Wattss
          FE: Sgt R. Gowing

6/12/42 – Mannheim: 272 aircraft - 101 Lancasters, 65
Halifaxes, 57 Wellingtons, 49 Stirlings. 10 aircraft lost - 5
Wellingtons, 3 Halifaxes, 1 Lancaster, 1 Stirling. 3.7% of
the force. Target completely cloud covered and many crews
bombed on dead reckoning. Mannheim reported only 500 or
so incendiary bombs and some leaflets
    Aircraft: Halifax II W1217 NP-S
    Crew: Pilot: PO J.D. Cole
          Nav: Sgt R.C. Stemp
          A/B: Sgt B.J. Warr,
          WOP: Sgt A. Ward
          MUG: Sgt W. A. Robinson
          RG: Sgt C. G. Dawson
          FE: Sgt G Reynolds

8/12/42 – Mining Operation: 80 aircraft of 1, 3 and 4
Groups to the German and Danish coasts. 5 aircraft lost. 3
Stirlings, 1 Halifax, 1 Lancaster. 6% of the force.
    Aircraft: Halifax II W1257 NP-S
    Crew: Pilot: PO J.D. Cole
          Nav: Sgt R.C. Stemp
          A/B: Sgt B.J. Warr,
          WOP: Sgt A. Ward
          MUG: Sgt W. A. Robinson
          RG: Sgt C. G. Dawson
          FE: Sgt E. Heweston

11/12/42 – Turin: 82 aircraft of 1, 4 and 5 Groups and the Pathfinders. 48 Halifaxes, 20 Lancasters, 8 Stirlings 6 Wellingtons. 4 aircraft lost - 3 Halifaxes, 1 Stirling, 4.8% of the force. More than half the force turned back before crossing the Alps due to severe icing conditions. 28 crews claimed to have bombed Turin but the city reported only 3 high explosive bombs and a few incendiaries.

     Aircraft: Halifax II DT585 NP-L
     Crew: Pilot: PO J.D. Cole
            Nav: Sgt R.C. Stemp
            A/B: Sgt B.J. Warr,
            WOP: Sgt A. Ward
            MUG: Sgt W. A. Robinson
            RG: Sgt C.G. Dawson
            FE: Sgt R. Gowing

20/12/42 – Duisburg: 232 aircraft - 111 Lancasters, 56 Halifaxes, 39 Wellingtons, 26 Stirlings. 12 aircraft lost - 6 Lancasters, 4 Wellingtons, 2 Halifaxes, 5.2% of the force.Target area was clear and bombing force claimed much damage.

     Aircraft: Halifax II W1221 NP-M
     Crew: Pilot: PO J.D. Cole
            Nav: Sgt R.C. Stemp
            A/B: Sgt B.J. Warr
            WOP: Sgt A. Ward
            MUG: Sgt W. A. Robinson
            RG: Sgt C.G. Dawson
            FE: Sgt R. Gowing

14/1/43 – Lorient: 122 aircraft - 63 Halifaxes, 33 Wellingtons, 20 Stirling, 8 aircraft lost - 6 Lancasters. 2 Wellingtons lost, 4% of the force. This was the first of 8 raids carried out against this French port being used as a U-Boat base. The Pathfinder marking was accurate but later bombing by the main force was described as "wild."

Aircraft: Halifax II DT559 NP- D
        Crew: Pilot: PO J.D. Cole
                Nav: Sgt R.C. Stemp
                A/B: Sgt B.J. Warr,
                WOP: Sgt A. Ward
                MUG: Sgt W. A. Robinson
                RG: Sgt C.G. Dawson
                FE: Sgt R. Gowing

Detached to No. 1 AAS Manby for No. 59 Bombing
Leaders Course 17/1/43

Ceased detachment 1/2/43

7/2/43 – Lorient: 323 aircraft - 100 Wellingtons, 81
Halifaxes, 80 Lancasters, 62 Stirlings. 7 aircraft lost - 3
Lancasters, 2 Halifaxes, 2 Wellingtons. 2% of the force. The
Pathfinder marking plan worked well and two Main Force
waves produced a devastating attack.
        Aircraft: Halifax II DT635 NP-F
        Crew: Pilot: PO J.D. Cole
                Nav: Sgt R.C. Stemp
                A/B: Sgt B.J. Warr
                WOP: Sgt A. Ward
                MUG: Sgt W. A. Robinson
                RG: Sgt C.G. Dawson
                FE: Sgt R. Gowing

8/3/43 – Nuremberg: 335 aircraft -170 Lancasters, 103
Halifaxes, 62 Stirlings. 8 aircraft lost - 4 Stirlings, 2
Halifaxes, 2 Lancasters. 2.3% of the force. This distant
target was out of range of the target marking aid known as
OBOE
and would prove typical of raids to such distant targets.
There was no cloud
over the target but it was hazy and the Pathfinders had great
difficulty in

marking the target. The marking and bombing spread over 10 miles along the
line of the attack with more than half the bombs falling outside the city.
However Nuremberg reported that much damage was caused in the city.

      Aircraft: Halifax II DT635 NP-F
      Crew: Pilot: PO J.D. Cole
             Nav: Sgt R.C. Stemp
             A/B: Sgt B.J. Warr
             WOP: Sgt A. Ward
             MUG: Sgt W. A. Robinson
             RG: Sgt C.G. Dawson
             FE: Sgt R. Gowing

11/3/43 – Stuttgart: 314 aircraft - 152 Lancasters, 109 Halifaxes, 53 Stirlings. 11 aircraft lost - 6 Halifaxes, 3 Stirlings, 2 Lancasters. 3.5% of the force. This was not a successful raid. The Pathfinders reported accurate target marking but the Main Force was late arriving over the target. Also there was the reported use by the Germans of dummy target markers. Most of the bombing fell in open country but the suburbs of Vaihengen and Kaltental were hit.

      Aircraft: Halifax II DT635 NP-F
      Crew: Pilot: PO J.D. Cole
             Nav: Sgt R.C. Stemp
             A/B: Sgt B.J. Warr
             WOP: Sgt A. Ward
             MUG: Sgt W. A. Robinson
             RG: Sgt C.G. Dawson
             FE: Sgt R. Gowing

27/3/43 – Duisburg: 455 aircraft - 173 Wellingtons, 157 Lancasters, 114 Halifaxes, 9 Mosquitoes, 2 Stirlings. 6 aircraft lost - 3 Wellingtons, 1 Lancaster, 1 Halifax, 1 Mosquito. 1.3% of the force. This raid was a failure. It was a cloudy night and OBOE sky marking was lacking because 5 OBOE Mosquitos were forced to return early due to damaged aircraft, resulting in a widely scattered raid.

Aircraft: Halifax II DT635 NP-F
Crew: Pilot: PO J.D. Cole
      Nav: Sgt R.C. Stemp
      A/B: Sgt B.J. Warr
      WOP: Sgt A.Ward
      MUG: Sgt W. A. Robinson
      RG: Sgt C.G. Dawson,
      FE: Sgt R. Gowing

Flew as Air Bomber to W/Cdr T.R. Hope DFC on Operation to

29/03/43 - Berlin: 329 aircraft - 162 Lancasters, 103 Halifaxes, 64 stirlings. 21 aircraft lost - 11 Lancasters, 7 Halifaxes, 3 Stirlings. 6.4% of the force.
Wing Commander Hope's aircraft was damaged by flack and was forced to return to base early not having bombed the target.

Aircraft: Halifax II HR715 NP-A
Crew: Pilot: W/Cdr Hope
      Nav: Sgt R.C. Stemp
      A/B: Sgt B.J. Warr
      WOP: Sgt K. G. Cottrell
      MUG: Sgt W. J. Hanks
      RG: Sgt C. H. Garner
      FE: F/Lt V.G. Hope.

3/4/43 – Essen: 348 aircraft - 225 Lancasters, 113 Halifaxes, 10 Moquitoes. 21maircraft lost - 12 Halifaxes, 9 Lancasters. 6% of the force. Due to predicted poor weather conditions the Pathfinders planned a combination of sky marking and ground marking. However the weather over the target was clear and crews found the use of two types of marking confusing. The resultant bombing, however was accurate and a higher proportion of aircraft produced good bombing photographs than on an any previous successful raid on Essen.

Aircraft: Halifax II DT635 NP-F
        Crew: Pilot: PO J.D. Cole
                    Nav: Sgt R.C. Stemp
                    A/B: Sgt B.J. Warr,
                    WOP: Sgt A. Ward
                    MUG: Sgt W. A. Robinson
                    RG: Sgt C.G. Dawson,
                    FE: Sgt R. Gowing

The aircraft was shot down near Pfalzdorf, north of Goch.
There were no survivors.
The crew are buried in Reinberg War Cemetary.

Decorations

None

Promotions

Sgt.

Appendix III

A Brief History of RAF 158 Squadron

No. 158 Squadron Royal Air Force was formed on 4 September 1918 at Upper Heyford in the county of Oxfordshire. The Squadron was scheduled to receive Sopwith Salamander aircraft but may not have received any. The squadron did not see any action before the First World War came to an end and was disbanded in November 1918. World war two began on September 01 1939 and the RAF began bomber operations on 03 September with an operation to bomb German naval vessels moored at Wilhelmshaven Naval Base. As the war progressed RAF bombing intensified and new squadrons, as well new bigger and better aircraft, entered service. A major construction campaign was being carried out to build many more and bigger airfields across the UK to support the fighter and bomber squadrons. One such squadron was 104 which was flying the Wellington two engine bomber affectionately known as the "Wimpy" named after the hamburger eating character from the Popeye cartoon. In October of 1940 a detachment from 104 Squadron was sent to Malta in October of 1941. the remaining home contingent of 104 Squadron based at RAF Driffield in the East Riding of Yorkshire was renumbered and 158 squadron was reborn.

158 was attached to No 4 Bomber Group (RAF) and was initially equipped with Vickers Wellington Mk. II aircraft. The squadron flew its first operation of the war on 14 February 1942. On that date 7, 158 squadron Wellingtons along with 60 aircraft from other squadrons raided Mannheim. On 01 June 1942 the squadron flew its last operation with Wellingtons when 6, 158 Wellingtons joined with hundreds of aircraft from other squadrons for a raid on

188

Essen. This was the second of the so called "thousand bomber raids" of the war.

In early June the squadron converted to the Handley Page Halifax Mk. II and was rebased at RAF East Moor in Yorkshire. 158 flew its first operation in Halifax aircraft on 25 June 1942 when 11 squadron Halifax aircraft joined in another thousand bomber raid, this time to Bremen. In November of 1942 the squadron was again moved, this time to RAF Rufforth. The squadron would call Rufforth home for a scant three months, In 1941, a suitable site for a bomber airfield was identified near the village of Lissett in East Yorkshire and construction of the infrastructure and runways was completed and ready for use in late 1942. Of all the Yorkshire airfields, Lissett was the closest to Germany and only two miles from the coast. Lissett was a typical wartime station with three intersecting runways with the main one running almost East/West. Accommodation for air and ground crews was in 'dispersed' buildings to the north and east. The first occupants at Lissett were Blenheims and Beufighters from RAF Catfoss. In February 1943, 158 Squadron arrived at RAF Station Lissett and was to remain there until the end the war. The first operation from Lissett was mounted on March 12, 1943, against Stuttgart, with the loss of one aircraft and all of the crew. Successive raids on Berlin later in the month cost the squadron two more aircraft and the lives of nine airmen. This was the beginning of a terrible spring and summer for the men of 158 Squadron. Many of the aircraft fell victim to flak or German night fighters, and a few struggled back to England before crashing short of an available runway.

In December of 1943 the squadron converted to the much improved Halifax MK III. 158 would fly the MK III for the rest of the war. Halifax Mk.VI. aircraft were brought on to the squadron in April 1945 and flew alongside the

189

squadrons MK III aircraft on the last two operations that the squadron and the whole of No 4 Bomber group would fly during the war. After the cessation of hostilities in Europe, the Squadron was transferred to RAF Transport Command and rebased at RAF Stradishall in Suffolk. Here the squadron flew the Short Stirling in the air trooping role.

The end of the war against Japan led to the downsizing of the Royal Air Force and No.158 Squadron was disbanded on 1 January 1946.

158 squadron, like most other RAF Bomber Command squadrons was composed of three flights, A, B and C of 8 aircraft each. The squadron was commanded by a Wing Commander and each flight was commanded by a Squadron Leader. Crews were posted to one of the three flights, A, B or C and usually spent their entire time with the squadron in the same flight.

On the 7th of January 1944 the men and aircraft (Halifax IIIs) of 'C' flight were detached from the squadron and used to form the nucleus of a new squadron, number 640 based at RAF Leconfield in East Yorkshire.

Although the majority of 158 crew were British there were men from many other nations who served with the squadron. Canadian and Australian crewmen were by far the most numerous of non-British personnel in the squadron numbering 384 (380 RCAF, 4 RAF) and 163 men respectively, many more came from New Zealand and there were also men from the U.S.A, Rhodesia, South Africa, Ceylon, The West Indies, Jamaica and Poland in the squadron.

Appendix IV

Introduction to The Halifax Bomber

The Halifax was a four engine, long range heavy bomber developed by the Handley Page Aircraft Company. The Halifax first took to the skies on 25 October 1939 and the aircraft entered service with the RAF in November of 1940. By the end of 1943 every squadron of Number 4 Bomber Group, including 158 squadron, had been equipped with Halifax bombers. Halifax aircraft were also flown by Number 6 RCAF Group. A total of 6,116 Halifax bombers were built during the war. The type proved to be so versatile that it was used in a variety of roles besides that of bomber throughout the war. Halifax aircraft were used in mine laying, anti-submarine, reconnaissance and metrological roles operations as well as being used to carry cargo throughout the war. Halifaxes were also used to drop paratroops and special agents behind enemy lines for the SOE. Halifaxes were used to tow gliders and in fact the Halifax was the only aircraft the RAF had that was capable of towing the large Hamilcar gliders used in Operation Overload during the D-Day invasion.

The list of duties that the Halifax was capable of filling is impressive but its primary role was that of bomber, it was in this roll that 158 Squadron flew its Halifaxes. Although entering World War II flying Wellingtons and ending its existence flying Short Stirlings for transport command in 1946, RAF 158 Squadron will always be remembered as a Halifax squadron. The squadron flew all but its first 35 operations of the war in Halifax aircraft. Between 25 June 1942, when the first Halifax operation was flown by the squadron and 25 April when 158 flew its last operation of

191

the war, Halifax aircraft flew an incredible 4,175 individual sorties with 158 squadron to some of the most heavily protected targets in Germany and occupied Europe.

Based in Yorkshire in the heart of what was to become known as Halifax country, 158 Squadron flew three variants of the Halifax, Mark II, Mark III and Mark VI during the war. Mark II and Mark III three aircraft flew the bulk of operations for the squadron. The Mark VI did not come on to the squadron until April 1945 and these aircraft were only used on the last two operations the squadron flew during the war.

All marks of the Halifax used by 158 carried a crew of seven, pilot, navigator, bomb aimer, wireless operator, flight engineer and two gunners, mid upper and rear. These men trained and worked together many long hours ensuring they could operate in all conditions and under all situations as a closely knit team.

The Halifax MK II flew its first operation with 158 in June of 1942. MK II Halifaxes had a long range, were able to carry a heavy bomb load and could fly at a higher altitude than the Short Stirling which was the RAFs only other 4 engine bomber at this time. Halifax MK II aircraft carried a very heavy work load for the RAF during the early years of the war.

Mark II Halifaxes were very sturdy and strong aircraft able to sustain a considerable amount of damage and still maintain controlled flight. However the MK II's did have flaws, several of them serious. Fitted with 4 Rolls Royce Merlin engines the aircraft was under powered and this, coupled with trouble caused by its pointed Delta shaped twin rudders, led to the MK II gaining a reputation as a difficult aircraft to fly.

Perhaps the most serious flaw of the MK II Halifax was the pointed delta shaped twin rudder. This design made it difficult to keep the aircraft straight on take-off. It could also lead to the aircraft overbalancing at low speeds or when a prop was feathered and during tight turns. This last was especially true during the corkscrew manoeuvre the crews used to try to evade enemy fighter aircraft. This rudder overbalancing led to the aircraft entering a deadly spin from which it was nearly impossible to recover. These flaws were a major contributor to the high aircraft loss and casualty rates Halifax squadrons suffered during this part of the war.

Appendix V

Bert's Unpublished Essays About his conscientious objector Stance: Exact dates written unknown but the first essay must have been written sometime after June 1940 and the second sometime afterwards but before March 1942.

Essay One: Untitled

Until now I have had no conscious association with this war. I have gone on with my life, aware certainly of the war, subject to the restrictions and sacrifices of the new life we lead, but not accepting the struggle as mine, and hence conscious driven to lunge into it with that wholehearted fanaticism of complete giving which is my way.

In each of the crisis that have so far arisen, I have experienced periods of doubt and indecision. In September when Poland was invaded, when the Russians entered Finland, when Norway and Denmark fell to the Nazis, each of these examples of injustices almost drove me from my position of rationality by the feelings of horror, at the monstrous inhumanity of the Nazis and of an emotion stirred duty that was mine, to avenge these innocent victims and to throw all of me into the struggle to wipe out the evil of their suffering. The influence of the newspapers was strong and their work upon my imagination made difficult the maintenance of rational attitudes against the unreasoning emotional impulses to rush out as a crusader for the right. I do not condemn my emotions. Their case is strong enough, for Nazism is evil and its final abolition, for ethical reasons, is justifiable cause for war. I say ethical reasons, but in our decision we are guided by no ethics. Conquer or perish is the cry. It is a struggle for power between the intolerant old champion and the challenger, feeling his strength and ready at last to pit himself in the battle field, for the material prize. Germany is envious of England's position, and provoked war, so that our power may pass to her by conquest. But to assume that, because we have been led into evil, by a force whose aspirations irk

194

him into a challenge of our superior position, that justice and the right are on our side, is falsehood. The position of the altruist, is therefore difficult. Conscious bidden, he goes out to defend the right, but in order to carry out his task he forced to ally himself with, and become the exploited instrument of, a power whose motives he must as a lover of justice abhor.

His position, together with that of his fellows in the army, is simply that of a misguided fool. And is this not one of the damndest (sp), blackest tragedies of the war. The army itself embodies the spirit of Nazism. Have we not the same blind surrender of the personality to the cause, the total absence of freedom of will, the the will disciplined to the dictates of the Books of Regulations. we may argue reasonably, that since such a system is proved of most efficiency in our own country in the fighting forces, a unit where the utmost cohesion is essential, then the same system, extended to the nation, should produce a similar efficiency in operation, and increased potentiality of each individual as part of the nation, united under a common discipline.

Thus then it must be considered that in the Totalitarian State we do see evidence of the workings of evolution. A sobering thought indeed.

Why does the British Government seek seek friendship with Russia. As champions of Self-Determination and Freedom, we are at war with Germany. She has killed, we say, innocent people, robbed them and expelled them from their homes into misery and horrible privation. Our fight is to restore to these hundreds of thousands of innocents, their rightful place in society; and to carry our fight until we have made for evermore impossible a recurrence of all the late years of hideousness.
And to Russia, the partner in the crime of Poland, we extend now the hand of friendship. Even after Poland, there came the murder of Finland and still he have no cause for friction with Russia. Our hands stretch forth to Russia in friendship

and in Russia, much more so even than in the Germany of Hitler, the blood purge has been employed to mould the nation into a unit. It is a fact that more people have been killed in Russia since the Third International assumed power, than have been killed in Germany since the coming of Hitler.

Second Essay: Why I Object

All life is a battle and we come into the world variously equipped for our fight. We are tough and cunning and selfish enough, most of us, to stand up boldly against the world. How eagerly we rush forward, in victory, to claim our bit of plunder, never forgetting though -- wise old campaigners that we are -- to keep a shrewd eye on our flank lest the fore rush in in our unguarded moment, to wrest from us those things which by conquest have become our rights. There are two kinds of men, each few in number, who fare badly in the battle - the virtuous man and the coward. The virtuous man is defeated by his principles; they lie heavily on his smiting arm and rot his armour; he is a dull fighter and easily succumbs to the alert enemy.

As for the coward, poor blessed shrinking creature, the blow that toughens us, that sends us roaring for vengeance, that rouses our anger, flattens him in his shivering defencelessness. Back he crawls, naked and beaten. His whole whole life is a retreat and we must tread upon him and try to forget him.

If it is such a fierce useless world, why cling to it so tenaciously? Is it worthwhile? Yes, the fight is sweet, and we want not to leave the field of battle. Against these impulses to duty. I have two weapons. One of them is fear. Of it I need say nothing. I have thought simply of suffering and horror and probable death, and its influence has been strong. The other, the dominant one, is reason. In periods of calm, I can look dispassionately at the lying presses, listen to the smoothing oil and large hypocrisies of the old men who rule, and consolidate my position with regard to what

196

they represent. I hate them for their insincerity and greed, and acknowledge with awe the immense inhumanity of their dealings with the people. I see then the division between the nation and its leader. The decent idealism of the mass, geared to sacrifice and effort for good, exhorted and whipped into new energies, contrasts itself with the desires of those men who seek only for selfish gain through those energies.

Appendix VI

Warr is Visited: From the March edition of Free Expression magazine

Warr is Visited - by himself

Warr was informed one evening by the lady of the house that an unusually courteous young man had that day called to see him and seemed disappointed to find him not at home. As no one ever visits Warr, and certainly none of his acquaintances either treat him with courtesy or experience disappoint through his absence from their company, the most courteous young man aroused his curiosity. Perhaps it was a worshipper who, having paid his shilling and read Warr's literary effort, was come to meet the flesh to express appreciation to the flesh and even to invite it to tea. But perhaps it was a hypocrite coming wreathed in smiles to steal Warr's typewriter for which the monthly instalments had ceased to be met quite half a year ago.

The young man telephoned the following day and requested that Warr remain at home that afternoon for an hour in order that he might have the privilege of an interview. Warr is indulgent, and sometimes the queerest people bob up. The young man came, courteously remarked "How cosy your room is. May I sit by the fire? I'll just remove my coat" , was solicitous about the cat on which he had walked, and began to chat about books - Nanking Road, The Rains Came, and what he thought about D H Lawrence, a volume of whose works he noticed in his rapid scrutiny of Warr's bookshelf. He was quite tall, quite slim, quite bald at the top front, an unimposing brow with shrewd vertical wrinkles between the brows, a beaky sort of nose with blackheads that ascended to, or descended from - it doesn't really matter - a pair of hard, hard, hard service grey eyes. After he had gone Warr was unable to remember whether or not the moustache existed. Certainly he would remember that Warr hadn't one. There he sat in Warr's more more comfortable chair (Il n'y en a que deaux) with his legs crossed, smiling and chatting and staring all the time very hard at Warr who dared to wonder who the devil was his visitor.

Your English plainclothes men are well disguised. In America one simply looks at the feet of a suspect to learn whether or not he is of the law. This young man would pass anywhere for a gentleman. His feet were medium and probably moved well to music. Hence it was a surprise to Warr when he displayed, with an apologetic smile, the little black C.I.D. folder with a quite recognisable photograph of himself inside it. Yes he had a moustache in the photograph, although not an ostentatious one. One concentrates more on photographs; they don't speak and distract the visual sense.

The young man had lost interest in D H Lawrence. Warr sat opposite him. trying to see the fire at least and waiting to learn why and what the young man though he had done. Of course he knew the police existed, and had tried many times without success to make policemen give way to him on the pavement by walking rapidly with a stern expression on his face. But they never do. Sometimes he used to sigh and wish for a teazle (Note a teazle is a tall, wild plant with leaves, flowers, and seed heads that are prickly, presumably Bert wanted to whack the constables with it.)

The representative sat for a minute, not speaking, looking at a sheet of paper that had come from his pocket. He handed this to Warr and said pleasantly: "I suppose you are curious about my visit. This will explain it. do you remember those words?" On the paper was typed a single line, 'I am a communist. Heil the revolution.' Warr thought at once of, 'A spectre is haunting Europe, the spectre of communism.' Equally majestically silly.

"Yerss" he answered because he did remember those words. Rather he remembered some of them, 'Heil the revolution'. This was a literal quotation from a letter he had written to America some time ago, in December he thought. 'I am a communist', however, was not his statement. It looked like something from a police report, standing up alone without the support of an adjective; not in the least as he himself would have worded such a declaration. He would have shouted, 'Hosannah, I'm a throbbing red" or something something just a little more becoming to an exhibitionist. But there it was, on Scotland Yard's own paper, factual and unelate (sp), 'ich bin communist'. But what stupidity it was not typed in German. It was English, 'I am communist.' It appeared to Warr that this statement was was the result of an attempt to paraphrase a sentence in his letter which was roughly this: 'I have joined the ranks of the dialectical materialists having read some of Karl Marx.'(Note: dialectical materialism is an approach for explaining the transition from capitalism to socialism. Derived from the writings of Karl Marx and Friedrich Engels.) Then followed the correctly quoted, 'Heil the revolution.'

Warr is unmalicious and tolerant, not by nature, twas grown in him. His mind dwelt on the vision of a weary civil servant, wife and little ones waiting at home with hot dinner of sprouts and carrots and oatmeal, scurrying to finish the last of work near end of day, and faced with a long quotation which must be typed into an official form. Could Warr find it in his heart to rebuke said civil servant for shortening his statement. Indeed it pleased Warr to feel that by cutting it down while preserving the kernel of sense, the creature was able to dash out of the office several moments before the rest of the army. But dreams about civil service are futile. Warr forgave on the instant, and only pointed out the paraphrasical 'inexactitude', to employ half the term attributed to some hack journalist. The young man looked surprised by Warr's denial of authorship, and wrote some words in his notebook. Then he began: "You know of course how careful we must be these days in tracking down and dealing with what are known as subversive influences in this country." His voice smiled charmingly, but his metallic eyes looked at Warr as though he were the personification of the subversive influences itself. He continued: "Your letter was read by the censor, and because of that statement was passed along to us. It is my job to visit the people who make such statements to learn something about them as well as to ask them to explain. Now, would you care to tell me what you meant by it."

Warr tried only to explain the word 'revolution'. He said that he that he held the Marxism conception of history, and that the revolution which he had heiled in his letter was already kin progress and its result would be a better world. The young man seemed to consider this harmless enough. "After all" he said, "that is what we are fighting this war for, a better world. But I have read Marx - part of my job of course to learn about these people and their theories". (part of his job indeed). "But I can't say that IR agree with the Russian method of changing the world. Do you mean a revolution stirred up by foreign agitators, a bloody revolution?" The eyes looked at Warr again. Evidently the young man placed much importance in the answer to this question. Revolution that said please and was without blood he tolerated; revolution with a mess on the pavement, nicht gut, "'ere wat's awl this abaht?" Warr attempted circumspection and mumbled about means and ends and justice. Then the young man, after writing again in his note book, went on:
A\"Are you a member of the Communist Party of Great Britain, or of any other organisation financed by a foreign power?" Warr was not. "Do you read the Daily Worker?" Warr replied "Not anymore", and the eyes were active. "Have you read any of the others, besides Marx, I mean the big bugs like Harry Pollitt and Pritt?" He appeared not to notice Warr's 'no' to this question, but suddenly remarked in a tone of animation: "By the way Churchill was excellent in the House today. I have it here in the Evening News." He reached for his overcoat which lay on Warr's bed, and continued, "He is replying to a question by Gallacher, do you know of him? He is the Communist MP in the House." He read some wittily worded innuendo attributed to the man, and watched Warr closely in order to gauge the extent of his appreciation. "He's magnificent, don't you agree?" Warr said "Really a master rhetorician." This was apparently satisfactory.

201

Then particulars were taken. Identity card and military service registration what-is-called-a-certificate but is, in reality a cheap little buff card, were inspected and written about the the note book. How long had Warr been in England? Where had he lived, worked? The inevitable "What do you think of England?" with its inevitable reply. Had he any friends who visited him, and lastly, "To whom was this letter addressed?" Warr replied that it was written to a woman in New York. "Friend?" "Yes, a friend." "Is she an English girl?" Warr replied that the girl was an Austrian refugee, and was disturbed when the young man said, "Yes, I know she is. I've been looking through her record. There seems to be nothing wrong, although one never knows." Later in the evening Warr learned that Die Schwarz, a soul who inhabits his flat, had met the young man on his previous visit, and described him as "a very nice young man. I felt that I could tell him anything.' Apparently she had told him about the Austrian girl.

Then it was half-past six and the young man rose to go. "I have a chess game booked at seven-thirty" he said, "mustn't be late. Thank you so much Mr Warr, for your help. I hope I haven't inconvenienced you by asking you by asking you to remain at home for this interview. But I am sure you understand now the difficulties created by statements such as yours in that letter. So if, in the future you could confine yourself to - what shall I say - less provocative expression, why you would help us tremendously."

Still he smiled, held out his hand courteously, and threatened with his eyes. Then he put on his coat, and left Warr's room, this time not walking in the cat.

"I must pay my respects to the lady of the house," he said, "She seemed a charming person." Which he did, and then went away.

Bibliography

Altmark, German Supply ship,
https://en.wikipedia.org/wiki/German_tanker_Altmark, 10
Nov 2023, at 05:30

Battle Of The Atlantic,
https://en.wikipedia.org/wiki/Battle_of_the_Atlantic, 30
November at 06:00

Betty's Café Tea Rooms, York,
https://www.bettys.co.uk/timeline-1940s, 01 NOV 2023 at
07:03

Bigwin Inn, Historic Bigwin Island residences,
https://www.bigwinmcc1.ca/Bigwin-Island/Bigwin-
History.aspx#:~:text=Bigwin%20Inn%20opened%20its
%20doors,fireplaces%20and%20large%20open
%20verandas. 21 September 2023 at 05:12 (UTC)

Birney, Earle, https://en.wikipedia.org/wiki/Earle_Birney,
01 Nov 2023 at 06:00

Chorley W. R, In Brave Company, Salisbury 1990

Culture 360, https://culture360.asef.org/resources/czech-
pen-club/, 15 October 2023, at 05:54

Dieppe Raid, https://en.wikipedia.org/wiki/Dieppe_Raid, 23
January, at 06:00

Fraser, C.S., Canada's War Poet: The Writings Of Bertram
Warr, The Poetry review, London Nov/Dec 1950

Gawsworth J, Bertram Warr Obituary, Times Literary
Supplement, London, 07 August 1943

Gawsworth, John, Wikipedia,
www.ea.wikipedia.org/wiki/John Gawsworth, 23 March
2023, at 04:02 (UTC)

Graf Spee, German Pocket Battleship, https://en.wikipedia.org/wiki/ German_cruiser_Admiral_Graf_Spee, 10 Nov 2023 at 05:30

Hess, Rudolf https://en.wikipedia.org/wiki/Rudolf_Hess 27 November at 05:30

Lang, David, unpublished notes and letters

Middlebrook, M. and Everett, C., The Bomber Command War Diaries: An Operational Reference Book 1939- 1945, Leicester 1996

Owen, Wilfred, https://www.poetryfoundation.org/poets/wilfred-owen#:~:text=Owen%20wrote%20vivid%20and %20terrifying,poetry%20into%20the%20Modernist%20era. 26 November 2023 at 07:00

RAF Bomber Command Aircrew of WW II, https://en.wikipedia.org/wiki/RAF_Bomber_Command_airc rew_of_World_War_II, 20 Oct 2023, at 15:00 (UTC)

Rationing, Imperial War Museum, https://www.iwm.org.uk/history/what-you-need-to-know-about-rationing-in-the-second-world-war, 30 November 2023 06:00

Raynor, Patricia, unpublished notes and letters

S-Plan, Wikipedia, https://en.wikipedia.org/wiki/S-Plan, 01 Oct 2023 at 07:01

Streib, Werner, Wikipedia, https://en.wikipedia.org/wiki/Werner_Streib, 28 July 2023, at 13:22 (UTC).

Warr, Bertram., Acknowledgement To Life: The Collected Poems Of Bertram Warr, Editor: Gasparini, L., Toronto/Winnipeg/Vancouver 1970

Warr, Bertram., Unpublished letters, notes and essays

Warr, Francis., Unpublished letters

Windsor Star, https://windsorstar.remembering.ca/obituary/len-gasparini-1086441860, Gasparini L, obituary, accessed 24 October 2023 at 05:000 UTC

About The Author

Neither his BSc from The Open University, U.K., nor his 30 years as a licenced aircraft engineer prepared Tony Frost to write a historical biography. But his lifelong passion as an amateur historian, long-term membership in the RAF 158 Squadron Association, and his service as an archivist and webmaster for Burt's RAF 158 Squadron made him uniquely qualified to tell the life story of the uncle he never met - Bertram Warr.

Tony Frost was born in Toronto Canada and moved to the U.K in 1988 after an 8-year stint in the Canadian Airforce. He has lived in the UK ever since. He worked in civil aviation, mostly at London's Heathrow Airport, until his retirement in 2016. He has recently moved from London to the quiet countryside of Suffolk to be near his two lovely daughters, Rhiannah and Esmeralda.

Printed in Great Britain
by Amazon